The Gift

A Year in the Prayer Jesus Taught His People How to Pray

COPYRIGHT PAGE

Scripture quotations are taken from the King James Version (KJV) of the Bible. Public domain.

Printed in the United States of America

ISBNs:

Paperback: 979-8-9940899-0-3

Hardcover: 979-8-9940899-1-0

eBook: 979-8-9940899-2-7

Publisher:

The Lord's Prayer Across America Ministries

Permissions & Inquiries:

thelordsprayeracrossamerica@gmail.com

Dedication

To God - who entrusted me with this calling and gave me the prayer that changed my life. To my family - who stood with me, encouraged me, and made room for this assignment. To the community who prayed with me across America - thank you for believing in the power of humble, unified prayer. And to you, the reader - may these pages draw you deeper into the presence of the Father who hears you, loves you, and walks with you every single day.

TABLE OF CONTENTS

Introduction

The Gift - From His Hands to Yours: How This Book Came to Be

My connection to The Lord's Prayer began long before I understood how powerful it was. The very first time I ever heard it - or prayed it - was on a high school football field. Our freshman team said it together before games, and every time those words rolled through the room in unison, something happened in me. Chills. Weight. A sense of unity I couldn't explain.

Even scenes like the one in *Rudy*, where the team prays The Lord's Prayer before the game, captured that same feeling. There's something powerful about many voices saying the exact same words with one heart and one purpose. Jesus told us why:

"For where two or three are gathered together in My name, there am I in the midst of them."

- Matthew 18:20 (KJV)

That same prayer has been important to me when I'm alone or in silence as well, though.   When I can't sleep, I begin saying The Lord's Prayer and it turns my anxiety to calm, and restlessness to sleep.   I often don't finish the prayer one time before I'm fast asleep and not realizing until morning that I had not completed the prayer.

The calling that was given to me to create this book came during one of the darkest and most uncertain moments I had ever lived through. The world had shut down. Our routines collapsed. Our churches closed their doors. People were afraid, angry, isolated, and confused. In the middle of that storm, God spoke to me through the simplest and most familiar Scripture of all - the Lord's Prayer.

During that COVID season, I had an experience that's hard to fully describe - part dream, part vision, yet clearer than anything I'd ever felt. It came quietly, not with fear or urgency, but with peace. In it, I remember a Being larger than the mountains, and perfect in every way – smile, hair - presenting me with a purple glowing globe. When I woke, that image stayed with me. It didn't feel like a message in words, but a conviction - a steady, settled knowing. I found myself drawn again and again to Matthew 6:9–13, the very prayer Jesus taught His disciples. And for the first time in my life, it didn't feel like a recitation. It felt like a roadmap. A lifeline. A weapon. A call to gather people to pray God's Word with boldness and unity.

Around that same time, another Scripture began gripping me - 2 Chronicles 7:14:

"If My people, who are called by My name, will humble themselves, and pray, and seek My face, and turn from their wicked ways; then will I hear from heaven, and will forgive their sin, and will heal their land."

In a season when our land was hurting, divided, fearful, and uncertain, that verse felt like a direct assignment. A reminder that healing begins with God's people praying - not casually, not occasionally, but humbly, consistently, and together. I felt the Lord nudging me: Don't just pray privately - call people to pray publicly. Call them to seek My face. Call them to return to the foundation Jesus Himself gave you: The Lord's Prayer.

It was as if God aligned these Scriptures together - the call to pray (Matthew 6), the call to gather (2 Chronicles 7:14), and the call to speak His Word aloud so faith can rise (**Romans 10:17**).

That's when I felt compelled to stop just thinking about prayer and start leading prayer - out loud, publicly, and consistently. Before I fully understood what I was doing, I created a Facebook group called *The Lord's Prayer Across America*. I invited friends, family, coworkers, and complete strangers. People joined. People shared. People prayed. Hundreds became thousands. People from Germany, India, the Philippines, and across the United States joined in. We were separated by distance but united in prayer. We weren't physically together, but when two or more gathered (online) in His name, He was there.

I learned firsthand that praying God's Word builds faith:

"So then faith cometh by hearing, and hearing by the word of God."
- *Romans 10:17 (KJV)*

Faith builds boldness. Boldness builds expectation. And expectation positions us for God to move.

This book was born from that movement - not to replace it, but to strengthen it. To help people pray Scripture every day, with The Lord's Prayer as the foundation. To give families, individuals, and entire communities a simple, powerful way to grow closer to God by praying as Jesus taught.

Prayer changes things. Prayer changes people. **And when God's people pray the same prayer across a nation - humbly, consistently, and together - there is no limit to what God can do.**

Chapter One

Why the Lord's Prayer?

Jesus gave everything, but when it comes to prayer, He was specific. Not specific in the sense that The Lord's prayer is a script to memorize, but as a pattern - a framework for a healthy, powerful, Scripture-based prayer life.

The Lord's Prayer is simple enough for a child to memorize, yet deep enough for theologians to study forever. It is complete. It covers worship, surrender, provision, forgiveness, spiritual warfare, and the sovereignty of God. Every need of the human heart - emotional, spiritual, relational, physical - fits within this prayer.

Here is what Jesus taught us:

"Our Father in heaven,
Hallowed be Your name.
Your kingdom come,
Your will be done,
On earth as it is in heaven.
Give us this day our daily bread.
And forgive us our debts,
As we forgive our debtors.
And lead us not into temptation,
But deliver us from evil.
For Yours is the kingdom,
And the power,
And the glory forever. Amen."

Every line is intentional:

- **"Our Father"** reminds us of identity - we pray as His children, not beggars.
- **"Hallowed be Your name"** sets our posture - worship first.
- **"Your kingdom come"** aligns us with His priorities, not ours.
- **"Your will be done"** removes self and invites obedience.
- **"On earth as it is in heaven"** without resistance.
- **"Give us today our daily bread"** teaches daily dependence.
- **"Forgive us"** heals the heart.
- **"As we forgive others"** breaks bitterness.
- **"Lead us not into temptation"** shapes holiness.
- **"Deliver us from evil"** acknowledges the spiritual battle.

- **"Yours is the kingdom…"** reminds us who reigns / praise Him again.
- **"Amen"** – let it be done.

This prayer is not a ritual. It is a reset button - a way to align every part of our heart with the heart of God.

Praying the Lord's Prayer transforms us because it puts us exactly where we belong:

under God's authority, in God's presence, with God's Word in our mouths.

Chapter Two

How to Use This Book

This book is structured to guide you into a daily rhythm of prayer, Scripture, reflection, and action. Each of the 365 daily prayers follows a simple, powerful flow:

Prayer

Every prayer is rooted in Scripture, shaped around the structure of the Lord's Prayer, and written from the identity of a child approaching a loving Father. Speak the prayers out loud. Let the Word enter your ears, because faith comes by hearing it.

Reflection

This is where the prayer becomes personal. Reflection questions help you slow down and consider what God is doing in your heart. Spiritual growth rarely happens fast - reflection invites transformation.

Action

Faith grows through movement. Each action prompt is a small but meaningful step of obedience, forgiveness, thoughtfulness, or worship. These actions reinforce the prayer and make the truth practical.

Notes Section

One of the most important parts of this book is not the printed prayers - it is the words you will write. Your reflections, your thoughts, your confessions, and your prayers become spiritual markers. Written prayers live beyond the moment. They outlive fear, frustration, and even the seasons you walk through. They become a record of God's faithfulness that can last generations if the pages are preserved. What you write in this book matters - not just for today, but for your family, your legacy, and for anyone who will one day read the testimony of your walk with God. Every day includes space for you to write what God is speaking. Written prayers live beyond the moment.

This book is not meant to be rushed. It is meant to be lived.

Scripture Study

Every daily prayer includes **full, un-truncated Bible verses from the King James Version**. These verses are not an afterthought - they are the backbone of the prayer. They serve as a built-in, day-by-day Bible study woven into the rhythm of your prayer life.

Here's how to use them:

Read Them Slowly

Don't skim the verses. Read them slowly, out loud if possible. Let the Word speak to you before you speak back to God. Slow reading builds understanding. Slow reading builds faith.

See How Scripture Shapes the Prayer

Every line of the prayer aligns with a verse printed below it. This is intentional. When you pray Scripture, you are praying God's will with God's words. You are training your heart to think, feel, and respond the way He teaches in His Word.

Use the Verses for Personal Study

These passages are more than supporting references - they are invitations. If a verse stands out, circle it. Underline it. Go read the full chapter. Study the context. Ask:

- *What does this reveal about God?*
- *What does this reveal about me?*
- *What is God asking me to believe, surrender, or obey through this Scripture?*

This book becomes a year-long guided Bible study if you allow the Scriptures to lead you deeper.

MONTH 1 THEME: RENEWAL & REORIENTATION

Month 1 invites you to begin again - to return to the foundation, the center, and the truth of who God is and who you are in Him. This is the month where everything slows down just enough for you to breathe, reset, and reorient your heart toward the One who already knows the road ahead. Renewal is not merely about starting over; it's about rediscovering what matters most and building your life upon the presence of God. This month teaches you to let go of what has weighed you down, to release the thoughts that have clouded your mind, and to return to the simplicity of being God's beloved child. As you step into this year of prayer, Month 1 becomes the gentle doorway - the place where God clears the fog, restores clarity, and aligns your heart with His steady rhythm.

This month will help you:

- Slow down and listen for God's voice again
- Lay aside distractions and rediscover spiritual focus
- Release what has been draining your energy or joy
- Turn your attention back to God's presence
- Rebuild your spiritual foundation with intention
- Allow God to reorder your priorities
- Welcome peace where there has been pressure
- Start the year rooted, grounded, and centered

Let the Lord's Prayer guide your renewal and reorientation this month:

- **"Our Father in Heaven"** - Your renewal begins with remembering whose child you are.
- **"Hallowed be Your name"** - Worship clears what the world has cluttered and restores your perspective.
- **"Your kingdom come"** - Let God realign your heart and reorder what you've allowed to drift.
- **"Your will be done"** - Release control and trust His direction more than your plans.
- **"Give us this day..."** - Anchor yourself in the grace and provision of *today*, not the weight of *tomorrow*.
- **"Forgive us..."** - Let mercy wash over you and free you from regret, shame, or disappointment.

- **"Lead us not…"** - Ask God to protect your renewed heart from old patterns of distraction.
- **"Yours is the kingdom…"** - Remember who reigns over your year, your days, and your destiny.

As you begin this journey, take a deep breath. Slow down. Let God meet you right where you are. This month is your reset - your invitation to step forward with a clear mind, a grounded spirit, and a heart fully reoriented toward Him. Renewal begins here.

DAY 1 – Returning to God's Presence

Prayer:
Mighty God, I come as Your beloved child, hungry for Your nearness and longing for Your presence to steady my soul (Psalm 73:28). Hallowed be Your name; be the desire of my heart and the joy of my mornings. Let Your kingdom come and breathe new strength into everything weary within me (Isaiah 40:31). Let Your will be done as I release every anxious thought into Your hands (1 Peter 5:7). Give me today my daily bread-quiet peace, deep rest, and the sweetness of Your presence. Forgive me for seeking comfort in places that could never satisfy, and I forgive those who left me feeling unseen or unheard. Lead me not into the temptation of self-reliance, but deliver me into Your tenderness, where my soul finds rest. Yours is the kingdom, the power, and the glory forever. Amen.

Reflection:
Where do you sense God gently drawing you closer today?

_____

_____

_____

Action:
Slow your breathing for 3 minutes today and whisper, "Lord, I am here."

_____

_____

_____

Scriptures Referenced Today:
Psalm 73:28 (KJV) - "But it is good for me to draw near to God: I have put my trust in the Lord God, that I may declare all thy works."
Isaiah 40:31 (KJV) - "But they that wait upon the Lord shall renew their strength; they shall mount up with wings as eagles; they shall run, and not be weary; and they shall walk, and not faint."
1 Peter 5:7 (KJV) - "Casting all your care upon him; for he careth for you."

DAY 2 – Returning to God's Word

Prayer:
Lord, I come with a longing to hear Your voice again through Your Word (Matthew 4:4). Hallowed be Your name; speak life to me. Let Your kingdom come and awaken my desire to read and meditate on Scripture (Psalm 119:105). Let Your will be done as Your Word shapes my steps today (Joshua 1:8). Give me today my daily bread of revelation and truth. Forgive me for neglecting Your Word, and I forgive those who discouraged my pursuit of it. Lead me not into the temptation of spiritual laziness, but deliver me into hunger for Your truth. Yours is the kingdom, the power, and the glory forever. Amen.

Reflection:
What Scripture do you feel drawn to revisit today?

_____

_____

_____

Action:
Read one chapter of Scripture slowly and prayerfully.

_____

_____

_____

Scriptures Referenced Today:
Matthew 4:4 (KJV) - "But he answered and said, It is written, Man shall not live by bread alone, but by every word that proceedeth out of the mouth of God."
Psalm 119:105 (KJV) - "Thy word is a lamp unto my feet, and a light unto my path."
Joshua 1:8 (KJV) - "This book of the law shall not depart out of thy mouth; but thou shalt meditate therein day and night, that thou mayest observe to do according to all that is written therein: for then thou shalt make thy way prosperous, and then thou shalt have good success."

DAY 3 – Rest for the Weary Soul

Prayer:
Shepherd of my soul, I quiet myself before You, longing for the rest my heart has needed (Psalm 131:2). Hallowed be Your name; calm every storm within me. Let Your kingdom come and cover me with stillness where chaos once lived (Psalm 46:10). Let Your will be done as I lay down every burden I was never meant to carry (Matthew 11:28). Give me today my daily bread-rest, renewal, and the peace that settles deep. Forgive me for holding tightly to worries that belong in Your hands, and I forgive those who added weight to my weary shoulders. Lead me not into the temptation of anxious striving, but deliver me into Your gentle rest. Yours is the kingdom, the power, and the glory forever. Amen.

Reflection:
What burden is God inviting you to finally lay down?

Action:
Sit in silence for one full minute with open hands, offering God every worry.

Scriptures Referenced Today:
Psalm 131:2 (KJV) - "Surely I have behaved and quieted myself, as a child that is weaned of his mother: my soul is even as a weaned child."
Psalm 46:10 (KJV) - "Be still, and know that I am God: I will be exalted among the heathen, I will be exalted in the earth."
Matthew 11:28 (KJV) - "Come unto me, all ye that labour and are heavy laden, and I will give you rest."

DAY 4 – Peace for the Restless Heart

Prayer:
Everlasting Father, draw me into the peace that only Your presence can give (Isaiah 26:3). Hallowed be Your name; steady my racing thoughts and quiet my heart. Let Your kingdom come and bring holy calm to the anxious places within me (Psalm 62:5). Let Your will be done as I lean on Your wisdom rather than my own understanding (Proverbs 3:5–6). Give me today my daily bread-stillness, clarity, and a mind anchored in truth. Forgive me for rushing ahead of Your pace, and I forgive those who have pushed me when I needed rest. Lead me not into the temptation of inner turmoil, but deliver me into Your perfect peace. Yours is the kingdom, the power, and the glory forever. Amen.

Reflection:
What anxious thought needs God's peace today?

_____
_____
_____

Action:
Take a slow, phone-free walk today and talk to God as you walk.

_____
_____
_____

Scriptures Referenced Today:
Isaiah 26:3 (KJV) - "Thou wilt keep him in perfect peace, whose mind is stayed on thee: because he trusteth in thee."
Psalm 62:5 (KJV) - "My soul, wait thou only upon God; for my expectation is from him."
Proverbs 3:5–6 (KJV) - "Trust in the Lord with all thine heart; and lean not unto thine own understanding. In all thy ways acknowledge him, and he shall direct thy paths."

DAY 5 – A Renewed Mind in God's Truth

Prayer:
Holy Lord, renew my mind today and reshape the thoughts that drift from You (Romans 12:2). Hallowed be Your name; let Your truth wash over every anxious or wandering place within me (Philippians 4:8). Let Your kingdom come and break the patterns that keep me from Your peace (Isaiah 26:3). Let Your will be done as I bring every thought under the authority of Christ (2 Corinthians 10:5). Give me today my daily bread-clarity, focus, and a mind strengthened by truth. Forgive me for entertaining thoughts that do not honor You, and I forgive those who have spoken fear into my life. Lead me not into the temptation of negativity, but deliver me into renewed thinking. Yours is the kingdom, the power, and the glory forever. Amen.

Reflection:
Which recurring thought needs to be surrendered to God today?

_____

_____

_____

Action:
Replace one negative or fearful thought with a scripture from today.

_____

_____

_____

Scriptures Referenced Today:
Romans 12:2 (KJV) - "And be not conformed to this world: but be ye transformed by the renewing of your mind, that ye may prove what is that good, and acceptable, and perfect, will of God."

Philippians 4:8 (KJV) - "Finally, brethren, whatsoever things are true, whatsoever things are honest, whatsoever things are just, whatsoever things are pure, whatsoever things are lovely, whatsoever things are of good report; if there be any virtue, and if there be any praise, think on these things."

2 Corinthians 10:5 (KJV) - "Casting down imaginations, and every high thing that exalteth itself against the knowledge of God, and bringing into captivity every thought to the obedience of Christ."

DAY 6 – Renewing Your Focus

Prayer:
Lord, I come needing clarity and focus today (Proverbs 4:25). Hallowed be Your name; steady my attention. Let Your kingdom come and remove distractions that pull me away from You (Hebrews 12:1–2). Let Your will be done as You align my focus with what matters most (Colossians 3:2). Give me today my daily bread of clarity. Forgive me for wandering thoughts, and I forgive those who distracted me. Lead me not into the temptation of scattered living, but deliver me into centered focus in You. Yours is the kingdom, the power, and the glory forever. Amen.

Reflection:
What distraction is God asking you to set aside today?

_____

_____

_____

Action:
Choose one distraction to remove from your day.

_____

_____

_____

Scriptures Referenced Today:
Proverbs 4:25 (KJV) - "Let thine eyes look right on, and let thine eyelids look straight before thee."
Hebrews 12:1–2 (KJV) - "Wherefore seeing we also are compassed about with so great a cloud of witnesses, let us lay aside every weight, and the sin which doth so easily beset us, and let us run with patience the race that is set before us, Looking unto Jesus the author and finisher of our faith; who for the joy that was set before him endured the cross, despising the shame, and is set down at the right hand of the throne of God."
Colossians 3:2 (KJV) - "Set your affection on things above, not on things on the earth."

DAY 7 – Trusting God Completely

Prayer:
Father, I come before You as Your beloved child, choosing to trust You with all my heart. Hallowed be Your name; steady my spirit and direct my steps (Proverbs 3:5–6). Let Your kingdom come and quiet every anxious thought within me. Let Your will be done as I surrender the outcomes I cannot control. Give me today my daily bread of confidence in Your faithfulness. Forgive me for doubting Your goodness, and I forgive those who have caused me to fear. Lead me not into the temptation of self-reliance, but deliver me from every worry that rises against Your peace (Psalm 56:3–4). Yours is the kingdom, the power, and the glory forever. Amen.

Reflection:
Where is God asking you to trust Him more fully today?

_____

_____

_____

Action:
Write down one fear you are releasing to God today.

_____

_____

_____

Scriptures Referenced Today:
Proverbs 3:5–6 (KJV) - "Trust in the LORD with all thine heart; and lean not unto thine own understanding. In all thy ways acknowledge him, and he shall direct thy paths."
Psalm 56:3–4 (KJV) - "What time I am afraid, I will trust in thee. In God I will praise his word, in God I have put my trust; I will not fear what flesh can do unto me."

DAY 8 – Seeking God First

Prayer:
Father, I come to You with a heart that longs to place You above all things. Hallowed be Your name; center my desires on Your kingdom (Matthew 6:33). Let Your kingdom come and reorder my priorities according to Your wisdom. Let Your will be done as You draw my eyes away from distractions. Give me today my daily bread of clarity and spiritual focus. Forgive me for chasing what does not satisfy, and I forgive those whose influence has pulled me off course. Lead me not into the temptation of putting other things before You, but deliver me into single-minded devotion (Psalm 27:4). Yours is the kingdom, the power, and the glory forever. Amen.

Reflection:
What area of life do you need to bring back under God's priority?

Action:
Surrender one misplaced priority to God today.

Scriptures Referenced Today:
Matthew 6:33 (KJV) - "But seek ye first the kingdom of God, and his righteousness; and all these things shall be added unto you."
Psalm 27:4 (KJV) - "One thing have I desired of the LORD, that will I seek after; that I may dwell in the house of the LORD all the days of my life, to behold the beauty of the LORD, and to enquire in his temple."

DAY 9 – Overcoming Fear Through God's Presence

Prayer:
Father, I come as Your child, grateful that fear has no authority in Your presence. Hallowed be Your name; fill my heart with the power, love, and sound mind that You freely give (2 Timothy 1:7). Let Your kingdom come and drive out every anxious thought. Let Your will be done as You strengthen me with courage grounded in Your nearness. Give me today my daily bread of bold faith. Forgive me for letting fear shape my decisions, and I forgive those whose words or actions planted worry in me. Lead me not into the temptation of dwelling on what could go wrong, but deliver me from all fear, for You are with me (Isaiah 41:10). Yours is the kingdom, the power, and the glory forever. Amen.

Reflection:
Name one fear God is calling you to surrender today.

Action:
Write down a truth from God's Word that replaces that fear.

Scriptures Referenced Today:
2 Timothy 1:7 (KJV) - "For God hath not given us the spirit of fear; but of power, and of love, and of a sound mind."
Isaiah 41:10 (KJV) - "Fear thou not; for I am with thee: be not dismayed; for I am thy God: I will strengthen thee; yea, I will help thee; yea, I will uphold thee with the right hand of my righteousness."

DAY 10 – Renewed Strength in the Lord

Prayer:
Father, I come weary at times, yet grateful that You are the strength of my heart. Hallowed be Your name; renew me through Your presence (Isaiah 40:31). Let Your kingdom come and overwhelm my weakness with Your power. Let Your will be done as I depend on You instead of myself. Give me today my daily bread of endurance and spiritual vitality. Forgive me for striving without You, and I forgive those who have drained or discouraged me. Lead me not into the temptation of self-reliance, but deliver me from everything that weighs my spirit down. Yours is the kingdom, the power, and the glory forever. Amen.

Reflection:
Where do you need God's strength the most today?

Action:
Give that area to God and ask Him to renew your strength.

Scriptures Referenced Today:
Philippians 4:13 (KJV) - "I can do all things through Christ which strengtheneth me."
Isaiah 40:31 (KJV) - "But they that wait upon the LORD shall renew their strength; they shall mount up with wings as eagles; they shall run, and not be weary; and they shall walk, and not faint."

DAY 11 – God's Peace Guarding Your Heart

Prayer:
Father, I come before You seeking the peace that only You can give. Hallowed be Your name; let Your peace settle over my mind and guard my heart (Philippians 4:7). Let Your kingdom come and silence every anxious voice. Let Your will be done as I rest in Your presence instead of my worries. Give me today my daily bread of calm and stillness. Forgive me for letting fear control my thoughts, and I forgive those who have contributed to my unrest. Lead me not into the temptation of overthinking, but deliver me into the peace that passes all understanding (John 14:27). Yours is the kingdom, the power, and the glory forever. Amen.

Reflection:
Where do you need God's peace to guard your heart today?

_____

_____

_____

Action:
Take one anxious thought and surrender it to God in prayer.

_____

_____

_____

Scriptures Referenced Today:
Philippians 4:7 (KJV) - "And the peace of God, which passeth all understanding, shall keep your hearts and minds through Christ Jesus."
John 14:27 (KJV) - "Peace I leave with you, my peace I give unto you: not as the world giveth, give I unto you. Let not your heart be troubled, neither let it be afraid."

DAY 12 – God as Your Refuge

Prayer:
Father, I come to You as my refuge and strength. Hallowed be Your name; be my shelter in every storm (Psalm 46:1). Let Your kingdom come and steady my heart in the midst of uncertainty. Let Your will be done as I rest under the shadow of Your wings. Give me today my daily bread of safety, assurance, and confidence in Your protection. Forgive me for running to other things for comfort, and I forgive those who have left me feeling exposed or unprotected. Lead me not into the temptation of fear-driven choices, but deliver me from all harm, for You are with me (Psalm 91:2). Yours is the kingdom, the power, and the glory forever. Amen.

Reflection:
How is God inviting you to rest in Him as your refuge today?

_____

_____

_____

Action:
Write down one way you will intentionally seek God's refuge today.

_____

_____

_____

Scriptures Referenced Today:
Psalm 46:1 (KJV) - "God is our refuge and strength, a very present help in trouble."
Psalm 91:2 (KJV) - "I will say of the LORD, He is my refuge and my fortress: my God; in him will I trust."

DAY 13 – God's Guidance in Every Step

Prayer:
Father, I come trusting that You will guide my steps. Hallowed be Your name; shine Your light on the path before me (Psalm 119:105). Let Your kingdom come and lead me in wisdom, not confusion. Let Your will be done as You order my steps according to Your purpose. Give me today my daily bread of direction and clarity. Forgive me for moving ahead without seeking You, and I forgive those who have influenced me toward wrong paths. Lead me not into the temptation of relying on my own understanding, but deliver me into Your perfect guidance (Isaiah 30:21). Yours is the kingdom, the power, and the glory forever. Amen.

Reflection:
Where do you need God's guidance most right now?

_____

_____

_____

Action:
Ask God a specific question today and wait for His direction.

_____

_____

_____

Scriptures Referenced Today:
Psalm 119:105 (KJV) - "Thy word is a lamp unto my feet, and a light unto my path."
Isaiah 30:21 (KJV) - "And thine ears shall hear a word behind thee, saying, This is the way, walk ye in it, when ye turn to the right hand, and when ye turn to the left."

DAY 14 – Resting in God's Faithfulness

Prayer:
Father, I come resting in Your unwavering faithfulness. Hallowed be
Your name; remind me that Your mercies are new every morning
(Lamentations 3:22–23). Let Your kingdom come and lift the weight
from my shoulders. Let Your will be done as I rest in the truth that You
are steady when I am not. Give me today my daily bread of renewal and
hope. Forgive me for forgetting Your past faithfulness, and I forgive
those who have disappointed me. Lead me not into the temptation of
discouragement, but deliver me into the confidence of Your steadfast love
(Psalm 36:5). Yours is the kingdom, the power, and the glory forever.
Amen.

Reflection:
What part of God's faithfulness do you need to remember today?

_____

_____

_____

Action:
Write down one way God has been faithful to you in the past.

_____

_____

_____

Scriptures Referenced Today:
Lamentations 3:22–23 (KJV) - "It is of the LORD'S mercies that we are
not consumed, because his compassions fail not. They are new every
morning: great is thy faithfulness."
Psalm 36:5 (KJV) - "Thy mercy, O LORD, is in the heavens; and thy
faithfulness reacheth unto the clouds."

DAY 15 – Finding Strength in Weakness

Prayer:
Father, I come acknowledging my weakness and embracing Your strength. Hallowed be Your name; let Your power rest upon me where I am weak (2 Corinthians 12:9). Let Your kingdom come and transform my insufficiency into Your sufficiency. Let Your will be done as I depend wholly on You. Give me today my daily bread of resilience and endurance. Forgive me for pretending to be strong on my own, and I forgive those who have expected more of me than I could give. Lead me not into the temptation of hiding my weakness, but deliver me into the freedom of relying on You (Psalm 73:26). Yours is the kingdom, the power, and the glory forever. Amen.

Reflection:
Where do you feel weak today-and how might God show His strength there?

_____

_____

_____

Action:
Invite God into the place where you feel the weakest.

_____

_____

Scriptures Referenced Today:
2 Corinthians 12:9 (KJV) - "And he said unto me, My grace is sufficient for thee: for my strength is made perfect in weakness. Most gladly therefore will I rather glory in my infirmities, that the power of Christ may rest upon me."
Psalm 73:26 (KJV) - "My flesh and my heart faileth: but God is the strength of my heart, and my portion for ever."

DAY 16 – God's Wisdom for Every Decision

Prayer:
Father, I come seeking Your wisdom above my own. Hallowed be Your name; fill my heart with the understanding that comes from You alone (James 1:5). Let Your kingdom come and guide my decisions with clarity and truth. Let Your will be done as I choose the path that honors You. Give me today my daily bread of discernment. Forgive me for relying on my own opinions, and I forgive those who pressured me toward unwise choices. Lead me not into the temptation of impulsive decisions, but deliver me into the wisdom that comes from above (Proverbs 2:6). Yours is the kingdom, the power, and the glory forever. Amen.

Reflection:
What decision today requires God's wisdom?

Action:
Ask God for wisdom in one specific area of your life.

Scriptures Referenced Today:

James 1:5 (KJV) - "If any of you lack wisdom, let him ask of God, that giveth to all men liberally, and upbraideth not; and it shall be given him."

Proverbs 2:6 (KJV) - "For the LORD giveth wisdom: out of his mouth cometh knowledge and understanding."

DAY 17 – God's Presence in Your Pain

Prayer:
Father, I come with the aches and burdens that weigh on my heart.
Hallowed be Your name; be near to me in every place that hurts (Psalm
34:18). Let Your kingdom come and bring comfort where I feel broken.
Let Your will be done as You heal the wounds I cannot fix myself. Give
me today my daily bread of peace and hope. Forgive me for hiding my
pain from You, and I forgive those who have caused or deepened it.
Lead me not into the temptation of bitterness, but deliver me into Your
healing presence (Psalm 147:3). Yours is the kingdom, the power, and the
glory forever. Amen.

Reflection:
Where are you hurting today-and how might God meet you there?

_____

_____

_____

Action:
Write down what you need God to heal in your heart.

_____

_____

_____

Scriptures Referenced Today:

Psalm 34:18 (KJV) - "The LORD is nigh unto them that are of a broken
heart; and saveth such as be of a contrite spirit."

Psalm 147:3 (KJV) - "He healeth the broken in heart, and bindeth up
their wounds."

DAY 18 – God's Strength in Temptation

Prayer:
Father, I come acknowledging my weakness and seeking Your power to stand firm. Hallowed be Your name; strengthen me where I am tempted (1 Corinthians 10:13). Let Your kingdom come and fortify my heart with righteousness. Let Your will be done as You lead me in purity and obedience. Give me today my daily bread of spiritual strength. Forgive me for the moments I have given in, and I forgive those who have influenced me toward sin. Lead me not into temptation, but deliver me from the enemy's schemes (Psalm 119:11). Yours is the kingdom, the power, and the glory forever. Amen.

Reflection:
What temptation do you need God's strength to resist today?

_____

_____

_____

Action:
Write a scripture that will help you stand firm against temptation.

_____

_____

_____

Scriptures Referenced Today:

1 Corinthians 10:13 (KJV) - "There hath no temptation taken you but such as is common to man: but God is faithful, who will not suffer you to be tempted above that ye are able; but will with the temptation also make a way to escape, that ye may be able to bear it."

Psalm 119:11 (KJV) - "Thy word have I hid in mine heart, that I might not sin against thee."

DAY 19 – God's Provision for Your Needs

Prayer:
Father, I come trusting that You know every need I carry. Hallowed be Your name; be my provider in all things (Philippians 4:19). Let Your kingdom come and replace my worry with confidence in Your faithfulness. Let Your will be done as I depend on You for what I cannot supply myself. Give me today my daily bread and remind me that You are enough. Forgive me for doubting Your care, and I forgive those who have failed to provide what I hoped for. Lead me not into the temptation of fear-driven striving, but deliver me into restful trust (Matthew 6:26). Yours is the kingdom, the power, and the glory forever. Amen.

Reflection:
What need can you trust God to provide for today?

_____

_____

_____

Action:
Release one specific worry about provision to God.

_____

_____

_____

Scriptures Referenced Today:

Philippians 4:19 (KJV) - "But my God shall supply all your need according to his riches in glory by Christ Jesus."

Matthew 6:26 (KJV) - "Behold the fowls of the air: for they sow not, neither do they reap, nor gather into barns; yet your heavenly Father feedeth them. Are ye not much better than they?"

DAY 20 – God's Comfort in Your Weariness

Prayer:

Father, I come weary and in need of Your rest. Hallowed be Your name; give rest to my soul as only You can (Matthew 11:28). Let Your kingdom come and renew what has been depleted. Let Your will be done as You lead me beside still waters and restore my strength. Give me today my daily bread of rest, refreshment, and renewed hope. Forgive me for pushing beyond what You've asked, and I forgive those who have demanded more of me than I could carry. Lead me not into the temptation of burnout, but deliver me into Your peace and restoration (Psalm 23:2–3). Yours is the kingdom, the power, and the glory forever. Amen.

Reflection:

Where are you feeling weary-and how is God inviting you to rest?

_____

_____

_____

Action:

Choose one way to intentionally rest in God today.

_____

_____

_____

Scriptures Referenced Today:

Matthew 11:28 (KJV) - "Come unto me, all ye that labour and are heavy laden, and I will give you rest."

Psalm 23:2–3 (KJV) - "He maketh me to lie down in green pastures: he leadeth me beside the still waters. He restoreth my soul: he leadeth me in the paths of righteousness for his name's sake."

DAY 21 – Returning to God With Your Whole Heart

Prayer:
Father, I come returning to You with my whole heart. Hallowed be Your name; draw me nearer as I seek You with sincerity and truth (Jeremiah 29:13). Let Your kingdom come and restore every place where I have drifted. Let Your will be done as You cleanse my heart and renew my devotion to You. Give me today my daily bread of closeness and clarity. Forgive me for wandering, and I forgive those who have pulled my attention away from You. Lead me not into the temptation of lukewarmness, but deliver me back into wholehearted pursuit of Your presence (Joel 2:12). For Thine is the kingdom, and the power, and the glory forever and ever. Amen.

Reflection:
Where has your heart drifted from God, and how is He calling you back?

_____

_____

_____

Action:
Write one step you can take today to return to God in a deeper way.

_____

_____

_____

Scriptures Referenced Today:

Jeremiah 29:13 (KJV) - "And ye shall seek me, and find me, when ye shall search for me with all your heart."

Joel 2:12 (KJV) - "Therefore also now, saith the LORD, turn ye even to me with all your heart, and with fasting, and with weeping, and with mourning."

DAY 22 – Rekindling Your First Love

Prayer:
Father, I come longing to return to my first love for You. Hallowed be
Your name; revive the flame of devotion that once burned bright within
me (Revelation 2:4–5). Let Your kingdom come and awaken my heart to
desire You above all else. Let Your will be done as You draw me back to
the joy of loving You with all my heart, soul, mind, and strength (Mark
12:30). Give me today my daily bread of renewed passion for Your
presence. Forgive me for letting my love grow cold, and I forgive those
who have distracted or discouraged me. Lead me not into the temptation
of spiritual complacency, but deliver me into a rekindled, wholehearted
love for You (Psalm 73:25). Yours is the kingdom, the power, and the
glory forever. Amen.

Reflection:
What part of your love for God needs to be rekindled today?

_____

_____

_____

Action:
Return to one practice that once stirred your love for God-worship,
prayer, scripture, or quiet reflection.

_____

_____

_____

Scriptures Referenced Today:
Revelation 2:4–5 (KJV) -"Nevertheless I have somewhat against thee,
because thou hast left thy first love. Remember therefore from whence
thou art fallen, and repent, and do the first works; or else I will come unto
thee quickly, and will remove thy candlestick out of his place, except thou
repent."
Mark 12:30 (KJV) - "And thou shalt love the Lord thy God with all thy
heart, and with all thy soul, and with all thy mind, and with all thy
strength: this is the first commandment."
Psalm 73:25 (KJV) -
"Whom have I in heaven but thee? And there is none upon earth that I
desire beside thee."

DAY 23 – Restoring Your Joy in God

Prayer:
Father, I come asking You to restore the joy of my salvation. Hallowed be Your name; fill my heart with gladness rooted in Your presence (Psalm 51:12). Let Your kingdom come and lift away the heaviness that has dimmed my joy. Let Your will be done as You renew a willing spirit within me. Give me today my daily bread of joy that cannot be taken away. Forgive me for allowing discouragement to settle in my heart, and I forgive those who have contributed to my sorrow. Lead me not into the temptation of despair, but deliver me into the joy that comes from abiding in You (Psalm 16:11). All glory be to You, forever and ever. Amen.

Reflection:
What has been weighing down your joy, and how can God restore it?

_____

_____

_____

Action:
Write one thing God has done for you that brings you joy when you remember it.

_____

_____

_____

Scriptures Referenced Today:

Psalm 51:12 (KJV) - "Restore unto me the joy of thy salvation; and uphold me with thy free spirit."

Psalm 16:11 (KJV) - "Thou wilt shew me the path of life: in thy presence is fulness of joy; at thy right hand there are pleasures for evermore."

DAY 24 – Quieting Your Soul Before God

Prayer:

Father, I come to quiet my soul before You. Hallowed be Your name; still the noise within me and surround me with Your peace (Psalm 131:2). Let Your kingdom come and calm the storms of my thoughts. Let Your will be done as You teach me to rest like a child in Your arms. Give me today my daily bread of stillness and surrender. Forgive me for letting my mind run in anxious circles, and I forgive those who have added pressure or unrest. Lead me not into the temptation of constant striving, but deliver me into holy rest in Your presence (Isaiah 30:15). For Yours alone is the kingdom, the power, and the glory. Amen.

Reflection:
What thoughts or pressures do you need God to quiet today?

_____

_____

_____

Action:
Take three minutes today to sit in silence before God, breathing deeply in His presence.

_____

_____

_____

Scriptures Referenced Today:

Psalm 131:2 (KJV) - "Surely I have behaved and quieted myself, as a child that is weaned of his mother: my soul is even as a weaned child."

Isaiah 30:15 (KJV) - "For thus saith the Lord GOD, the Holy One of Israel; In returning and rest shall ye be saved; in quietness and in confidence shall be your strength: and ye would not."

DAY 25 – Drawing Near to God Daily

Prayer:
Father, I come drawing near to You again today with a willing heart. Hallowed be Your name; meet me as I seek Your face (James 4:8). Let

Your kingdom come and deepen the habit of daily nearness. Let Your will be done as I make room for You in my thoughts, time, and priorities. Give me today my daily bread of consistency and hunger for Your presence. Forgive me for neglecting time with You, and I forgive those who have crowded my life with demands. Lead me not into the temptation of spiritual neglect, but deliver me into daily communion with You (Psalm 42:1–2). To You be the glory, now and forever. Amen.

Reflection:

How can you make space to draw near to God every day?

_____

_____

_____

Action:

Write down one daily commitment that will keep you close to God.

_____

_____

_____

Scriptures Referenced Today:

James 4:8 (KJV) - "Draw nigh to God, and he will draw nigh to you. Cleanse your hands, ye sinners; and purify your hearts, ye double minded."

Psalm 42:1–2 (KJV) - "As the hart panteth after the water brooks, so panteth my soul after thee, O God. My soul thirsteth for God, for the living God: when shall I come and appear before God?"

DAY 26 – Renewing Your Hunger for God

Prayer:

Father, I come longing for a deeper hunger for You. Hallowed be Your name; stir my soul to crave Your presence above all things (Matthew 5:6). Let Your kingdom come and awaken a fresh desire to seek You daily. Let Your will be done as You satisfy me with the richness of Your Word and the sweetness of Your presence (Psalm 63:1). Give me today my daily bread of spiritual appetite and renewal. Forgive me for feeding on things that do not satisfy, and I forgive those who have distracted my heart. Lead me not into the temptation of spiritual dullness, but deliver me into a renewed hunger for You (Psalm 119:40). For Thine is the kingdom, and the power, and the glory forever and ever. Amen.

Reflection:

Where is God awakening fresh spiritual hunger in you?

Choose one way today to intentionally seek God-through Scripture, prayer, worship, or silence.

Scriptures Referenced Today:

Matthew 5:6 (KJV) - "Blessed are they which do hunger and thirst after righteousness: for they shall be filled."

Psalm 63:1 (KJV) - "O God, thou art my God; early will I seek thee: my soul thirsteth for thee, my flesh longeth for thee in a dry and thirsty land, where no water is."

Psalm 119:40 (KJV) - "Behold, I have longed after thy precepts: quicken me in thy righteousness."

DAY 27 – Returning to God's Word

Prayer:
Father, I return to the truth and strength of Your Word. Hallowed be Your name; open my eyes to behold wondrous things from Your law (Psalm 119:18). Let Your kingdom come and shape my thoughts as I meditate on Your truth. Let Your will be done as Your Word steadies my heart and directs my steps (Psalm 19:7). Give me today my daily bread of wisdom and understanding. Forgive me for neglecting the Scriptures, and I forgive those who distracted me from Your truth. Lead me not into empty things, but deliver me into the life and clarity found in Your Word (Hebrews 4:12). Yours is the kingdom, the power, and the glory forever. Amen.

Reflection:
How is God calling you back to His Word today?

_____

_____

_____

Action:
Read one passage of Scripture slowly-listening for what God highlights to your heart.

_____

_____

Scriptures Referenced Today:
Psalm 119:18 (KJV) - "Open thou mine eyes, that I may behold wondrous things out of thy law."
Psalm 19:7 (KJV) - "The law of the LORD is perfect, converting the soul: the testimony of the LORD is sure, making wise the simple."
Hebrews 4:12 (KJV) - "For the word of God is quick, and powerful, and sharper than any two-edged sword, piercing even to the dividing asunder of soul and spirit, and of the joints and marrow, and is a discerner of the thoughts and intents of the heart."

DAY 28 – Letting God Search Your Heart

Prayer:
Father, I come inviting You to search my heart and reveal what needs to change. Hallowed be Your name; shine Your light within me and expose anything that hinders intimacy with You (Psalm 139:23–24). Let Your kingdom come and purify my motives. Let Your will be done as You lead me in the everlasting way. Give me today my daily bread of honesty, humility, and openness before You. Forgive me for hiding the parts of my heart that need healing, and I forgive those who have wounded or shaped me in ways that led me astray. Lead me not into the temptation of self-deception, but deliver me into truth and freedom (Psalm 51:6). All glory be to You, forever and ever. Amen.

Reflection:
What area of your heart is God gently bringing into the light today?

_____

_____

_____

Action:
Write down one area you want God to heal, cleanse, or strengthen.

_____

_____

_____

Scriptures Referenced Today:

Psalm 139:23–24 (KJV) - "Search me, O God, and know my heart: try me, and know my thoughts: And see if there be any wicked way in me, and lead me in the way everlasting."

Psalm 51:6 (KJV) - "Behold, thou desirest truth in the inward parts: and in the hidden part thou shalt make me to know wisdom."

DAY 29 – Restoring Your Faith in God's Promises

Prayer:
Father, renew my faith in Your promises. Hallowed be Your name;
strengthen my belief where doubt has crept in (Mark 9:24). Let Your
kingdom come and revive trust in every word You have spoken. Let Your
will be done as I hold tightly to all You have promised (Joshua 23:14).
Give me today my daily bread of confident faith. Forgive me for doubting
Your goodness, and I forgive those whose words weakened my trust.
Lead me not into unbelief, but deliver me into unshakable confidence in
what You have spoken (2 Corinthians 1:20). Yours is the kingdom, the
power, and the glory. Amen.

Reflection:
Which promise of God do you need to hold onto today?

_____

_____

Action:
Choose one promise from Scripture and write it here-keep it before you
today.

_____

_____

Scriptures Referenced Today:
Mark 9:24 (KJV) - "And straightway the father of the child cried out, and
said with tears, Lord, I believe; help thou mine unbelief."
Joshua 23:14 (KJV) - "And, behold, this day I am going the way of all the
earth: and ye know in all your hearts and in all your souls, that not one
thing hath failed of all the good things which the LORD your God spake
concerning you; all are come to pass unto you, and not one thing hath
failed thereof."
2 Corinthians 1:20 (KJV) - "For all the promises of God in him are yea,
and in him Amen, unto the glory of God by us."

DAY 30 – Returning to Daily Surrender

Prayer:
Father, I come surrendering myself to You once again. Hallowed be Your name; take my life and let it be wholly Yours (Romans 12:1). Let Your kingdom come and align every part of me with Your heart. Let Your will be done as I yield my desires, plans, and fears to You. Give me today my daily bread of strength to surrender moment by moment. Forgive me for resisting Your leading, and I forgive those who have pushed me toward self-dependence. Lead me not into the temptation of taking control back into my hands, but deliver me into joyful surrender (Luke 9:23). To You be the glory, now and forever. Amen.

Reflection:
What is God inviting you to surrender to Him today?

_____

_____

_____

Action:
Write down one area you are choosing to surrender fully to God.

_____

_____

_____

Scriptures Referenced Today:

Romans 12:1 (KJV) - "I beseech you therefore, brethren, by the mercies of God, that ye present your bodies a living sacrifice, holy, acceptable unto God, which is your reasonable service."

Luke 9:23 (KJV) - "And he said to them all, If any man will come after me, let him deny himself, and take up his cross daily, and follow me."

MONTH 1 CLOSING REFLECTION - RENEWAL & REORIENTATION

Month 1 has brought you back to center - back to the place where God stills the noise, clears the fog, and restores your footing. This month wasn't about dramatic change; it was about sacred recalibration. God invited you to breathe again, to slow down, and to rediscover what it means to walk closely with Him.

Throughout these days, the Lord gently reordered your heart. He revealed what was draining you, what was distracting you, and what was distorting your perspective. Renewal came not through striving, but through returning - returning to His presence, His truth, His voice, and His peace.

This month, God helped you:

- Release old burdens and mental clutter

- Rebuild spiritual focus

- Rediscover rest in His presence

- Realign priorities with His wisdom

- Quiet the inner noise

- Open your heart again to His leading

- Step away from what was stealing peace

- Anchor your identity in Him

Month 1 reminded you of something essential:

**Renewal begins with remembering who your Father is.
Reorientation begins with remembering who you are to Him.**

As you look back, consider:

- What clarity did God restore?

- What weight did He lift?

- What habits or thoughts did He begin reshaping?

- Where did peace replace pressure?

- What did you hear when you finally slowed down enough to listen?

This month has prepared you for the journey ahead.
You now step forward with a clearer mind, a steadier spirit, and a heart more aligned with the Father who walks with you into every day of this year.

Renewal was the beginning. Reorientation was the foundation. And the God who met you in Month 1 will lead you faithfully into Month 2 - where deeper healing awaits.

MONTH 2 THEME: TRUST, HEALING, & SURRENDER

Month 2 invites you into the deeper places - the tender places - where God desires to bring healing, trust, and restoration. Healing happens when we stop carrying everything alone and allow the Lord to tend to what hurts. This month is not about revisiting pain for the sake of pain; it is about letting God bring comfort, clarity, and courage where you once felt overwhelmed.

This is the month where God begins to loosen the grip of fear, anxiety, or discouragement. Where He gently reveals what needs healing and shows you how to trust Him in the process. This isn't quick healing - it's deep healing. Restoration that lasts.

This month will help you:

- Allow God into areas you've tried to manage alone
- Release emotional burdens and hidden fears
- Invite God to heal wounds you've carried for too long
- Trust God with outcomes you cannot control
- Lay down old patterns of self-protection
- Replace inner turmoil with inner peace
- Surrender expectations, disappointments, and uncertainties
- Walk in the freedom that comes through honesty and dependence

Let the Lord's Prayer guide your healing and surrender this month:

- **"Our Father in Heaven"** - Your healing begins with belonging. You aren't alone.
- **"Hallowed be Your name"** - Worship softens wounded places and restores hope.
- **"Your kingdom come"** - Invite God to reign where pain has ruled.
- **"Your will be done"** - Surrender the outcomes and allow God to heal as *He* knows best.
- **"Give us this day…"** - Ask Him for emotional manna: courage, comfort, peace, release.
- **"Forgive us…"** - Healing flows through repentance - and through forgiving others.

- **"Lead us not…"** - Ask God to protect your healing heart from bitterness, fear, or despair.
- **"Yours is the kingdom…"** - Your story is safe in His hands.

As you walk through this month, let God's gentleness meet your vulnerability. Healing isn't weakness. It's strength being restored. God is not exposing you; He is rebuilding you. Surrender becomes easier when you realize nothing surrendered to God is ever lost - only redeemed.

DAY 31 – Surrendering Control to God

Prayer:

Father, I release every part of my life into Your hands. Hallowed be Your name; teach me to trust You with what I cannot control (Psalm 37:5). Let Your kingdom come and quiet the urge to manage outcomes myself. Let Your will be done as You shape my desires and decisions with Your wisdom. Give me today my daily bread of surrender and peace. Forgive me for holding too tightly to my plans, and I forgive those whose expectations pressured me to carry more than I should. Lead me not into self-reliance, but deliver me into freedom as I trust everything to You (Proverbs 3:5–6). For Thine is the kingdom, the power, and the glory forever. Amen.

Reflection:

What are you trying to control that God is asking you to release?

_____

_____

_____

Action:

Write one thing today that you will consciously place back into God's hands.

_____

_____

_____

Scriptures Referenced Today:

Psalm 37:5 (KJV) - "Commit thy way unto the LORD; trust also in him; and he shall bring it to pass."

Proverbs 3:5–6 (KJV) - "Trust in the LORD with all thine heart; and lean not unto thine own understanding. In all thy ways acknowledge him, and he shall direct thy paths."

DAY 32 – Trusting God's Timing

Prayer:
Father, I come learning to trust Your perfect timing. Hallowed be Your name; remind me that every season of my life is safely held in Your hands (Ecclesiastes 3:11). Let Your kingdom come and align my expectations with Your plan. Let Your will be done as I wait with hope instead of frustration. Give me today my daily bread of patience and faith. Forgive me for rushing ahead of You, and I forgive those who have pushed me to move before I was ready. Lead me not into the temptation of impatience, but deliver me into the peace of trusting Your timing (Psalm 27:14). Yours is the kingdom, the power, and the glory forever. Amen.

Reflection:
In what area of life do you struggle to wait on God's timing?

_____

_____

_____

Action:
Write one prayer of surrender regarding the timing of something important to you.

_____

_____

_____

Scriptures Referenced Today:
Ecclesiastes 3:11 (KJV) - "He hath made every thing beautiful in his time: also he hath set the world in their heart, so that no man can find out the work that God maketh from the beginning to the end."

Psalm 27:14 (KJV) - "Wait on the LORD: be of good courage, and he shall strengthen thine heart: wait, I say, on the LORD."

DAY 33 – Casting Your Anxiety on God

Prayer:

Father, I come laying every worry and anxious thought before You. Hallowed be Your name; remind me that You care for every detail of my life (1 Peter 5:7). Let Your kingdom come and break the grip of fear in my mind. Let Your will be done as You teach me to trust You with what overwhelms me. Give me today my daily bread of calm assurance. Forgive me for carrying what You never asked me to bear, and I forgive those who contributed to my anxiety. Lead me not into the temptation of dwelling on worst-case scenarios, but deliver me into Your perfect peace (Philippians 4:6–7). All glory be to You, forever and ever. Amen.

Reflection:

What anxiety do you need to place into God's hands today?

_____

_____

_____

Action:

Write a prayer releasing that specific fear to God.

_____

_____

_____

Scriptures Referenced Today:

1 Peter 5:7 (KJV) - "Casting all your care upon him; for he careth for you."

Philippians 4:6–7 (KJV) - "Be careful for nothing; but in every thing by prayer and supplication with thanksgiving let your requests be made known unto God. And the peace of God, which passeth all understanding, shall keep your hearts and minds through Christ Jesus."

DAY 34 – Trusting God in Uncertainty

Prayer:
Father, I come trusting You even when the path is unclear. Hallowed be Your name; be my light when I cannot see the next step (Psalm 56:3). Let Your kingdom come and steady my heart when the unknown feels overwhelming. Let Your will be done as You teach me to walk by faith and not by sight (2 Corinthians 5:7). Give me today my daily bread of courage and confidence in You alone. Forgive me for fearing what I do not understand, and I forgive those whose words have increased my uncertainty. Lead me not into the temptation of doubting Your leadership, but deliver me into bold trust in You. For Yours alone is the kingdom, the power, and the glory. Amen.

Reflection:
Where do you feel uncertain-and how can you trust God there?

Action:
Identify one unknown that you will intentionally trust God with today.

Scriptures Referenced Today:

Psalm 56:3 (KJV) - "What time I am afraid, I will trust in thee."

2 Corinthians 5:7 (KJV) - "For we walk by faith, not by sight."

DAY 35 – Depending on God Daily

Prayer:
Father, I come choosing to depend fully on You today. Hallowed be Your name; teach me to lean on Your strength instead of my own (Psalm 73:26). Let Your kingdom come and reorder my heart so that I rely on You moment by moment. Let Your will be done as You lead me into deeper trust and dependence. Give me today my daily bread of grace, guidance, and strength. Forgive me for trying to carry life alone, and I forgive those who expected me to be stronger than I could be. Lead me not into the temptation of independence from You, but deliver me into joyful dependence on Your presence (John 15:5). To You be the glory, now and forever. Amen.

Reflection:
What area of your life requires deeper dependence on God today?

_____

_____

_____

Action:
Write one way you will intentionally rely on God instead of yourself today.

_____

_____

_____

Scriptures Referenced Today:

Psalm 73:26 (KJV) - "My flesh and my heart faileth: but God is the strength of my heart, and my portion for ever."

John 15:5 (KJV) - "I am the vine, ye are the branches: He that abideth in me, and I in him, the same bringeth forth much fruit: for without me ye can do nothing."

DAY 36 – Letting God Heal Your Burdens

Prayer:
Father, I come laying every burden at Your feet. Hallowed be Your name; heal the places in me that have carried weight for too long (Psalm 147:3). Let Your kingdom come and bring restoration to the hidden wounds of my heart. Let Your will be done as You teach me to trust You with the pain I've tried to manage myself. Give me today my daily bread of comfort, healing, and renewed strength. Forgive me for holding onto hurts instead of giving them to You, and I forgive those who contributed to my pain. Lead me not into the temptation of carrying burdens alone, but deliver me into Your rest and healing (Matthew 11:28). For Thine is the kingdom, and the power, and the glory forever and ever. Amen.

Reflection:
Which burden is God inviting you to place into His healing hands today?

_____

_____

Action:
Write down one hurt you will intentionally surrender to God.

_____

_____

Scriptures Referenced Today:
Psalm 147:3 (KJV) - "He healeth the broken in heart, and bindeth up their wounds."
Matthew 11:28 (KJV) - "Come unto me, all ye that labour and are heavy laden, and I will give you rest."

DAY 37 – Trusting God With Your Past

Prayer:
Father, I come trusting You with every part of my past. Hallowed be Your name; redeem what was broken and heal what still lingers in my heart (Isaiah 43:18–19). Let Your kingdom come and bring newness where old wounds once lived. Let Your will be done as I surrender the memories, regrets, and pain I cannot change. Give me today my daily bread of courage to move forward with You. Forgive me for holding onto the past, and I forgive those who shaped my wounds. Lead me not into the temptation of looking back, but deliver me into the freedom of Your new beginning (2 Corinthians 5:17). Yours is the kingdom, the power, and the glory forever. Amen.

Reflection:
What part of your past do you need God to redeem and heal?

_____

_____

_____

Action:
Write one old wound or regret you will surrender to God today.

_____

_____

_____

Scriptures Referenced Today:
Isaiah 43:18–19 (KJV) - "Remember ye not the former things, neither consider the things of old. Behold, I will do a new thing; now it shall spring forth; shall ye not know it? I will even make a way in the wilderness, and rivers in the desert."
2 Corinthians 5:17 (KJV) - "Therefore if any man be in Christ, he is a new creature: old things are passed away; behold, all things are become new."

DAY 38 – Allowing God to Restore Your Soul

Prayer:
Father, I come asking You to restore my soul. Hallowed be Your name; renew the weary places within me and make me whole again (Psalm 23:3). Let Your kingdom come and refresh my spirit with Your presence. Let Your will be done as You lead me out of emotional exhaustion and into quiet waters. Give me today my daily bread of rest, healing, and spiritual renewal. Forgive me for pushing myself beyond what You desired, and I forgive those who drained or wounded me. Lead me not into the temptation of pretending I'm fine, but deliver me into honest healing before You (Psalm 34:17–18). All glory be to You, forever and ever. Amen.

Reflection:
What part of your soul feels tired or wounded right now?

_____

_____

_____

Action:
Write one way you will allow God to restore you today.

_____

_____

_____

Scriptures Referenced Today:
Psalm 23:3 (KJV) - "He restoreth my soul: he leadeth me in the paths of righteousness for his name's sake."
Psalm 34:17–18 (KJV) - "The righteous cry, and the LORD heareth, and delivereth them out of all their troubles. The LORD is nigh unto them that are of a broken heart; and saveth such as be of a contrite spirit."

DAY 39 – Trusting God Through Emotional Healing

Prayer:
Father, I come trusting You with the emotional wounds I still carry. Hallowed be Your name; bring healing to the deep places that only You can reach (Psalm 30:2). Let Your kingdom come and replace sorrow with Your joy. Let Your will be done as You heal the pain that has shaped my reactions and fears. Give me today my daily bread of comfort and renewal. Forgive me for trying to heal myself, and I forgive those who caused my hurt. Lead me not into the temptation of hiding my pain, but deliver me into Your healing presence (Jeremiah 17:14). For Yours alone is the kingdom, the power, and the glory. Amen.

Reflection:
What emotion or wound do you need God to touch today?

_____

_____

_____

Action:
Write one emotion you are surrendering to God for healing.

_____

_____

_____

Scriptures Referenced Today:
Psalm 30:2 (KJV) - "O LORD my God, I cried unto thee, and thou hast healed me."
Jeremiah 17:14 (KJV) - "Heal me, O LORD, and I shall be healed; save me, and I shall be saved: for thou art my praise."

DAY 40 – Finding Peace in God's Presence

Prayer:
Father, I come resting in the peace that only You can give. Hallowed be
Your name; calm the storms within me and heal the anxieties that trouble
my heart (John 14:27). Let Your kingdom come and bring quietness to
my spirit. Let Your will be done as You teach me to surrender every fear
into Your hands. Give me today my daily bread of stillness, comfort, and
faith. Forgive me for letting anxiety control me, and I forgive those who
contributed to my unrest. Lead me not into the temptation of fear-based
living, but deliver me into Your perfect peace (Isaiah 26:3). To You be
the glory, now and forever. Amen.

Reflection:
What fear or anxiety do you want God to replace with His peace?

_____

_____

Action:
Write down a fear you are choosing to surrender to God today.

_____

_____

Scriptures Referenced Today:
John 14:27 (KJV) - "Peace I leave with you, my peace I give unto you:
not as the world giveth, give I unto you. Let not your heart be troubled,
neither let it be afraid."
Isaiah 26:3 (KJV) - "Thou wilt keep him in perfect peace, whose mind is
stayed on thee: because he trusteth in thee."

DAY 41 – Trusting God With Your Future

Prayer:
Father, I come placing my future entirely in Your hands. Hallowed be
Your name; order my steps and calm every fear about what lies ahead
(Psalm 37:23). Let Your kingdom come and guide me into the path You
have prepared for me. Let Your will be done as I surrender every
unknown, every possibility, and every concern. Give me today my daily
bread of trust and confidence in Your leading. Forgive me for trying to
control what I cannot see, and I forgive those who have spoken fear into
my future. Lead me not into the temptation of worry, but deliver me into
Your peace and assurance (Jeremiah 29:11). For Thine is the kingdom,
and the power, and the glory forever and ever. Amen.

Reflection:
What part of your future do you need to trust God with today?

_____

_____

_____

Action:
Write one concern about your future that you are giving to God.

_____

_____

_____

Scriptures Referenced Today:
Psalm 37:23 (KJV) - "The steps of a good man are ordered by the
LORD: and he delighteth in his way."
Jeremiah 29:11 (KJV) - "For I know the thoughts that I think toward
you, saith the LORD, thoughts of peace, and not of evil, to give you an
expected end."

DAY 42 – Healing From Hidden Wounds

Prayer:
Father, I come asking You to heal the wounds I rarely speak of.
Hallowed be Your name; shine Your gentle light into the places I have
kept hidden (Psalm 139:1). Let Your kingdom come and bring healing to
the memories, disappointments, and hurts that linger beneath the surface.
Let Your will be done as You restore peace where pain once lived. Give
me today my daily bread of inner renewal and emotional wholeness.
Forgive me for burying wounds instead of bringing them to You, and I
forgive those who caused the hurt. Lead me not into the temptation of
hiding my pain, but deliver me into Your freedom and healing (Psalm
147:3). Yours is the kingdom, the power, and the glory forever. Amen.

Reflection:
What hidden wound is God inviting you to bring into His healing light?

Action:
Write one area of hidden hurt you will open before God today.

Scriptures Referenced Today:
Psalm 139:1 (KJV) - "O LORD, thou hast searched me, and known me."
Psalm 147:3 (KJV) - "He healeth the broken in heart, and bindeth up
their wounds."

DAY 43 – Surrendering Your Plans to God

Prayer:
Father, I come surrendering every plan, dream, and desire to You. Hallowed be Your name; align my heart with Your perfect purpose (Proverbs 16:3). Let Your kingdom come and reshape every plan that isn't from You. Let Your will be done as You lead me in the direction that honors You most. Give me today my daily bread of trust, flexibility, and surrender. Forgive me for holding too tightly to my own ideas, and I forgive those who pressured me to follow paths You didn't intend. Lead me not into the temptation of insisting on my own way, but deliver me into joyful submission to Your plan (Psalm 37:4–5). All glory be to You, forever and ever. Amen.

Reflection:
Which plan or dream is God asking you to surrender or hold loosely?

_____

_____

_____

Action:
Write one plan you will commit to God's direction and timing.

_____

_____

_____

Scriptures Referenced Today:
Proverbs 16:3 (KJV) - "Commit thy works unto the LORD, and thy thoughts shall be established."
Psalm 37:4–5 (KJV) - "Delight thyself also in the LORD: and he shall give thee the desires of thine heart. Commit thy way unto the LORD; trust also in him; and he shall bring it to pass."

DAY 44 – Trusting God With Emotional Brokenness

Prayer:
Father, I come bringing You the places in my heart that feel fragile and broken. Hallowed be Your name; meet me in my weakness and strengthen me with Your love (Psalm 34:18). Let Your kingdom come and mend what has been damaged by hurt, fear, or disappointment. Let Your will be done as You restore my emotional strength from the inside out. Give me today my daily bread of comfort and renewal. Forgive me for shutting down emotionally, and I forgive those who caused my hurt. Lead me not into the temptation of withdrawing or numbing myself, but deliver me into healing through Your presence (Psalm 147:3). For Yours alone is the kingdom, the power, and the glory. Amen.

Reflection:
What part of your emotional life needs the healing touch of God?

_____

_____

_____

Action:
Write a short prayer inviting God into your emotional brokenness.

_____

_____

_____

Scriptures Referenced Today:
Psalm 34:18 (KJV) - "The LORD is nigh unto them that are of a broken heart; and saveth such as be of a contrite spirit."
Psalm 147:3 (KJV) - "He healeth the broken in heart, and bindeth up their wounds."

DAY 45 – Surrendering Your Fears to God

Prayer:
Father, I come bringing my fears into Your presence. Hallowed be Your name; replace every fear with Your perfect love (1 John 4:18). Let Your kingdom come and calm the anxieties that have taken root in my heart. Let Your will be done as You teach me to trust You in every circumstance. Give me today my daily bread of courage, peace, and surrender. Forgive me for letting fear lead my decisions, and I forgive those who contributed to my fear. Lead me not into the temptation of fear-driven thinking, but deliver me into the freedom of trusting You completely (Isaiah 41:10). To You be the glory, now and forever. Amen.

Reflection:
What fear do you need to surrender to God right now?

_____

_____

_____

Action:
Write down a specific fear and declare it surrendered to God.

_____

_____

_____

Scriptures Referenced Today:
1 John 4:18 (KJV) - "There is no fear in love; but perfect love casteth out fear: because fear hath torment. He that feareth is not made perfect in love."

Isaiah 41:10 (KJV) - "Fear thou not; for I am with thee: be not dismayed; for I am thy God: I will strengthen thee; yea, I will help thee; yea, I will uphold thee with the right hand of my righteousness."

DAY 46 – Trusting God When You Feel Weak

Prayer:
Father, I come acknowledging my weakness and trusting You to be my strength. Hallowed be Your name; meet me in my limitations and empower me with Your grace (2 Corinthians 12:9). Let Your kingdom come and replace my striving with Your sufficiency. Let Your will be done as You strengthen me where I feel incapable or overwhelmed. Give me today my daily bread of courage, perseverance, and hope. Forgive me for despising my weakness, and I forgive those who expected more of me than I could give. Lead me not into the temptation of relying on myself, but deliver me into the freedom of trusting Your strength (Isaiah 40:29). For Thine is the kingdom, and the power, and the glory forever and ever. Amen.

Reflection:
Where do you feel weak today-and how can you trust God there?

_____

_____

_____

Action:
Write down one weakness you will surrender to God instead of striving on your own.

_____

_____

_____

Scriptures Referenced Today:
2 Corinthians 12:9 (KJV) - "And he said unto me, My grace is sufficient for thee: for my strength is made perfect in weakness. Most gladly therefore will I rather glory in my infirmities, that the power of Christ may rest upon me."
Isaiah 40:29 (KJV) - "He giveth power to the faint; and to them that have no might he increaseth strength."

DAY 47 – Letting God Heal Your Identity

Prayer:
Father, I come asking You to heal the places in my identity that have been wounded or distorted. Hallowed be Your name; speak truth over every false belief I have carried about myself (Psalm 139:14). Let Your kingdom come and restore the identity You created within me. Let Your will be done as You replace shame with confidence, and fear with belonging. Give me today my daily bread of security in who I am in You. Forgive me for agreeing with lies instead of Your truth, and I forgive those who spoke words that damaged my sense of worth. Lead me not into the temptation of defining myself by past hurt, but deliver me into the healing of knowing who I am in Christ (Ephesians 2:10). Yours is the kingdom, the power, and the glory forever. Amen.

Reflection:
What lie about yourself do you need God's healing truth to replace?

Action:
Write a truth from God's Word about your identity to replace that lie.

Scriptures Referenced Today:
Psalm 139:14 (KJV) - "I will praise thee; for I am fearfully and wonderfully made: marvelous are thy works; and that my soul knoweth right well."
Ephesians 2:10 (KJV) - "For we are his workmanship, created in Christ Jesus unto good works, which God hath before ordained that we should walk in them."

DAY 48 – Surrendering What You Cannot Change

Prayer:
Father, I come surrendering what is beyond my ability to change. Hallowed be Your name; remind me that You are sovereign over every detail of my life (Psalm 103:19). Let Your kingdom come and bring peace to the places where I feel powerless. Let Your will be done as I release my grip on outcomes, people, and circumstances. Give me today my daily bread of acceptance and trust. Forgive me for trying to force what only You can transform, and I forgive those who contributed to my frustration. Lead me not into the temptation of control, but deliver me into restful surrender (Philippians 4:11). All glory be to You, forever and ever. Amen.

Reflection:
What situation do you need to surrender because you cannot change it?

_____

_____

_____

Action:
Write one thing you will stop trying to control and release fully to God.

_____

_____

_____

Scriptures Referenced Today:
Psalm 103:19 (KJV) - "The LORD hath prepared his throne in the heavens; and his kingdom ruleth over all."
Philippians 4:11 (KJV) - "Not that I speak in respect of want: for I have learned, in whatsoever state I am, therewith to be content."

DAY 49 – Trusting God to Heal the Heart

Prayer:
Father, I come asking You to heal the deep places of my heart. Hallowed be Your name; restore what has been broken, bruised, or worn down (Psalm 147:3). Let Your kingdom come and breathe new life into my emotions, my hopes, and my spirit. Let Your will be done as You mend the hurts that have shaped my reactions and guarded my heart. Give me today my daily bread of comfort, renewal, and restoration. Forgive me for resisting Your healing touch, and I forgive those who contributed to my brokenness. Lead me not into the temptation of shutting down emotionally, but deliver me into the wholeness that comes through Your love (Psalm 34:17–18). For Yours alone is the kingdom, the power, and the glory. Amen.

Reflection:
What part of your heart needs God's healing today?

_____

_____

_____

Action:
Write one prayer asking God to heal a specific emotional wound.

_____

_____

_____

Scriptures Referenced Today:
Psalm 147:3 (KJV) - "He healeth the broken in heart, and bindeth up their wounds."
Psalm 34:17–18 (KJV) - "The righteous cry, and the LORD heareth, and delivereth them out of all their troubles. The LORD is nigh unto them that are of a broken heart; and saveth such as be of a contrite spirit."

DAY 50 – Trusting God When You Don't Understand

Prayer:

Father, I come trusting You even when I cannot understand what You are doing. Hallowed be Your name; remind me that Your ways are higher than mine (Isaiah 55:8–9). Let Your kingdom come and bring clarity where I am confused and peace where I am unsettled. Let Your will be done as I surrender the need to have answers and embrace faith instead. Give me today my daily bread of patience, perspective, and trust. Forgive me for demanding explanations, and I forgive those who have added confusion to my life. Lead me not into the temptation of leaning on my own understanding, but deliver me into the security of trusting You fully (Proverbs 3:5–6). To You be the glory, now and forever. Amen.

Reflection:

What situation in your life do you not understand but must trust God with?

_____

_____

_____

Action:

Write one unanswered question you are surrendering to God today.

_____

_____

_____

Scriptures Referenced Today:

Isaiah 55:8–9 (KJV) - "For my thoughts are not your thoughts, neither are your ways my ways, saith the LORD. For as the heavens are higher than the earth, so are my ways higher than your ways, and my thoughts than your thoughts."

Proverbs 3:5–6 (KJV) - "Trust in the LORD with all thine heart; and lean not unto thine own understanding. In all thy ways acknowledge him, and he shall direct thy paths."

DAY 51 – Trusting God With Your Disappointments

Prayer:
Father, I come bringing my disappointments before You. Hallowed be
Your name; heal the places where hope has been shaken and expectations
have fallen short (Proverbs 13:12). Let Your kingdom come and breathe
life into the dreams that felt lost or delayed. Let Your will be done as You
reshape my desires according to Your perfect plan. Give me today my
daily bread of renewed hope and trust. Forgive me for letting
disappointment harden my heart, and I forgive those who contributed to
my pain. Lead me not into the temptation of bitterness, but deliver me
into Your healing and restoration (Psalm 34:19). For Thine is the
kingdom, and the power, and the glory forever and ever. Amen.

Reflection:
Which disappointment are you inviting God to heal today?

_____

_____

_____

Action:
Write one area where you will choose hope again through God's strength.

_____

_____

_____

Scriptures Referenced Today:
Proverbs 13:12 (KJV) - "Hope deferred maketh the heart sick: but when
the desire cometh, it is a tree of life."
Psalm 34:19 (KJV) - "Many are the afflictions of the righteous: but the
LORD delivereth him out of them all."

DAY 52 – Healing From Fear of Failure

Prayer:
Father, I come surrendering the fear of failing. Hallowed be Your name; remind me that You uphold me even when I stumble (Psalm 145:14). Let Your kingdom come and fill me with courage where fear once held me back. Let Your will be done as You teach me to trust Your strength more than my own ability. Give me today my daily bread of boldness and assurance. Forgive me for letting fear dictate my choices, and I forgive those who spoke words that fed my insecurity. Lead me not into the temptation of shrinking back, but deliver me into confidence rooted in You (Joshua 1:9). Yours is the kingdom, the power, and the glory forever. Amen.

Reflection:
Where has fear of failure been holding you back?

_____

_____

_____

Action:
Write an area where you will step forward in faith instead of fear.

_____

_____

_____

Scriptures Referenced Today:
Psalm 145:14 (KJV) - "The LORD upholdeth all that fall, and raiseth up all those that be bowed down."
Joshua 1:9 (KJV) - "Have not I commanded thee? Be strong and of a good courage; be not afraid, neither be thou dismayed: for the LORD thy God is with thee whithersoever thou goest."

DAY 53 – Trusting God Through Emotional Fatigue

Prayer:
Father, I come tired and emotionally drained. Hallowed be Your name; renew my strength and refresh my heart (Isaiah 40:31). Let Your kingdom come and lift the heaviness that has settled within me. Let Your will be done as You restore joy where exhaustion has taken hold. Give me today my daily bread of rest, renewal, and healing. Forgive me for pushing myself too hard, and I forgive those who placed expectations on me that I could not carry. Lead me not into the temptation of burnout, but deliver me into Your sustaining peace (Psalm 73:26). All glory be to You, forever and ever. Amen.

Reflection:
What part of your heart feels most emotionally drained today?

_____

_____

_____

Action:
Write one way you will slow down and let God renew you today.

_____

_____

_____

Scriptures Referenced Today:
Isaiah 40:31 (KJV) - "But they that wait upon the LORD shall renew their strength; they shall mount up with wings as eagles; they shall run, and not be weary; and they shall walk, and not faint."
Psalm 73:26 (KJV) - "My flesh and my heart faileth: but God is the strength of my heart, and my portion for ever."

DAY 54 – Surrendering People You Cannot Carry

Prayer:
Father, I come releasing the people I've been trying to carry in my own strength. Hallowed be Your name; remind me that You are their Savior, not me (Psalm 55:22). Let Your kingdom come and lift the weight of responsibility I was never meant to hold. Let Your will be done in their lives as You work in ways I cannot. Give me today my daily bread of freedom from unnecessary burdens. Forgive me for trying to fix others in my own strength, and I forgive those who placed emotional weight on me they should not have. Lead me not into the temptation of carrying others' loads, but deliver me into trusting You with their lives (Matthew 11:28–30). For Yours alone is the kingdom, the power, and the glory. Amen.

Reflection:
Who have you been trying to "fix" or carry that you need to entrust to God?

_____

_____

_____

Action:
Write down one person you are releasing to God's care.

_____

_____

_____

Scriptures Referenced Today:
Psalm 55:22 (KJV) - "Cast thy burden upon the LORD, and he shall sustain thee: he shall never suffer the righteous to be moved."
Matthew 11:28–30 (KJV) - "Come unto me, all ye that labour and are heavy laden, and I will give you rest. Take my yoke upon you, and learn of me; for I am meek and lowly in heart: and ye shall find rest unto your souls. For my yoke is easy, and my burden is light."

DAY 55 – Trusting God to Turn Pain Into Purpose

Prayer:
Father, I come believing that You can turn every pain into purpose.
Hallowed be Your name; work through every hardship for my good and
for Your glory (Romans 8:28). Let Your kingdom come and reshape the
painful parts of my story into testimonies of Your faithfulness. Let Your
will be done as You use what hurt me to strengthen me and help others.
Give me today my daily bread of hope, meaning, and trust. Forgive me
for doubting that good could come from my struggles, and I forgive those
who caused the pain. Lead me not into the temptation of resentment, but
deliver me into the healing of Your redemptive purpose (Genesis 50:20).
To You be the glory, now and forever. Amen.

Reflection:
What pain from your life do you want God to use for purpose?

_____

_____

_____

Action:
Write how God might use one of your struggles to strengthen someone
else.

_____

_____

_____

Scriptures Referenced Today:
Romans 8:28 (KJV) - "And we know that all things work together for
good to them that love God, to them who are the called according to his
purpose."
Genesis 50:20 (KJV) - "But as for you, ye thought evil against me; but
God meant it unto good, to bring to pass, as it is this day, to save much
people alive."

DAY 56 – Healing From What You Cannot Forget

Prayer:
Father, I come asking You to heal the memories that still hurt. Hallowed be Your name; touch the places in my mind where pain still echoes (Psalm 147:3). Let Your kingdom come and replace lingering sorrow with Your peace. Let Your will be done as You give me strength to release what I cannot forget. Give me today my daily bread of emotional clarity and comfort. Forgive me for replaying old wounds, and I forgive those who made the memories painful. Lead me not into the temptation of dwelling on the past, but deliver me into the freedom of healing in Your presence (Philippians 3:13–14). For Thine is the kingdom, and the power, and the glory forever and ever. Amen.

Reflection:
Which painful memory is God inviting you to release into His healing?

_____

_____

_____

Action:
Write down one memory you are giving to God for healing today.

_____

_____

_____

Scriptures Referenced Today:
Psalm 147:3 (KJV) - "He healeth the broken in heart, and bindeth up their wounds."
Philippians 3:13–14 (KJV) - "Brethren, I count not myself to have apprehended: but this one thing I do, forgetting those things which are behind, and reaching forth unto those things which are before, I press toward the mark for the prize of the high calling of God in Christ Jesus."

DAY 57 – Trusting God When Your Heart Feels Fragile

Prayer:
Father, I come with a heart that feels fragile and vulnerable. Hallowed be Your name; hold me close and strengthen me where I feel weak (Psalm 61:2). Let Your kingdom come and surround me with Your protection. Let Your will be done as You steady my emotions and speak peace to my soul. Give me today my daily bread of courage, quietness, and rest. Forgive me for withdrawing when I am overwhelmed, and I forgive those who contributed to my fragility. Lead me not into the temptation of shutting down, but deliver me into the safety of trusting You fully (Psalm 73:26). Yours is the kingdom, the power, and the glory forever. Amen.

Reflection:
Where does your heart feel fragile-and how can you trust God there?

_____

_____

_____

Action:
Write one emotion you will invite God to strengthen today.

_____

_____

_____

Scriptures Referenced Today:
Psalm 61:2 (KJV) - "From the end of the earth will I cry unto thee, when my heart is overwhelmed: lead me to the rock that is higher than I."
Psalm 73:26 (KJV) - "My flesh and my heart faileth: but God is the strength of my heart, and my portion for ever."

DAY 58 – Surrendering the Need to Be Strong

Prayer:
Father, I come surrendering the pressure to be strong all the time.
Hallowed be Your name; remind me that Your power is made perfect in
my weakness (2 Corinthians 12:9). Let Your kingdom come and lift the
burden of pretending I have everything together. Let Your will be done
as You free me from unrealistic expectations. Give me today my daily
bread of rest, honesty, and grace. Forgive me for masking my struggles,
and I forgive those who expected more from me than I could give. Lead
me not into the temptation of self-reliance, but deliver me into the
freedom of depending on You (Psalm 46:1). All glory be to You, forever
and ever. Amen.

Reflection:
Where have you been trying to appear strong instead of relying on God?

Action:
Write one area where you will allow yourself to be honest and open
before God.

Scriptures Referenced Today:
2 Corinthians 12:9 (KJV) - "And he said unto me, My grace is sufficient
for thee: for my strength is made perfect in weakness. Most gladly
therefore will I rather glory in my infirmities, that the power of Christ may
rest upon me."
Psalm 46:1 (KJV) - "God is our refuge and strength, a very present help
in trouble."

DAY 59 – Trusting God While You Heal

Prayer:
Father, I come trusting You in the slow and sacred work of healing. Hallowed be Your name; remind me that healing is a process You walk through with me (Psalm 30:2). Let Your kingdom come and bring restoration one layer at a time. Let Your will be done as You teach me to trust Your pace, not mine. Give me today my daily bread of patience, gentleness, and hope. Forgive me for growing discouraged in the process, and I forgive those who expect me to "be fine" too quickly. Lead me not into the temptation of rushing healing, but deliver me into the peace of resting in Your timing (Isaiah 58:11). To You be the glory, now and forever. Amen.

Reflection:
What area of healing do you need to trust God's timing with?

_____

_____

_____

Action:
Write down how God has already begun healing you, even if in small ways.

_____

_____

_____

Scriptures Referenced Today:
Psalm 30:2 (KJV) - "O LORD my God, I cried unto thee, and thou hast healed me."
Isaiah 58:11 (KJV) - "And the LORD shall guide thee continually, and satisfy thy soul in drought, and make fat thy bones: and thou shalt be like a watered garden, and like a spring of water, whose waters fail not."

DAY 60 – Surrendering Your Whole Heart to God

Prayer:
Father, I come giving You not just pieces of my heart, but all of it. Hallowed be Your name; heal what is broken, strengthen what is weak, and cleanse what is wounded (Psalm 51:10). Let Your kingdom come and reign fully within my heart. Let Your will be done as You shape me into someone who trusts You completely. Give me today my daily bread of surrender, devotion, and healing. Forgive me for holding back parts of myself, and I forgive those who influenced my hesitancy. Lead me not into the temptation of partial surrender, but deliver me into wholehearted devotion to You (Deuteronomy 6:5). For Thine is the kingdom, and the power, and the glory forever and ever. Amen.

Reflection:
What part of your heart have you not fully surrendered to God?

_____

_____

_____

Action:
Write one area of your heart or life that you are fully surrendering today.

_____

_____

_____

Scriptures Referenced Today:
Psalm 51:10 (KJV) - "Create in me a clean heart, O God; and renew a right spirit within me."
Deuteronomy 6:5 (KJV) - "And thou shalt love the LORD thy God with all thine heart, and with all thy soul, and with all thy might."

MONTH 2 CLOSING REFLECTION - TRUST, HEALING, & SURRENDER

Month 2 has been a month of holy healing - the kind that reaches deeper than surface emotion and touches the places you've carried quietly for far too long. This was the month where God asked you to trust Him not just with your future, but with your wounds. Not just with your hopes, but with your history.

This month, God gently pulled back the layers - not to shame you, but to free you. He revealed where fear was hiding, where disappointment had settled, and where pain had shaped your decisions. And with every prayer, He met you in those places with tenderness, strength, and compassion.

This month, God invited you to:

- Let Him into the rooms you rarely open
- Release control and surrender outcomes
- Trust Him in uncertain places
- Allow grace to soften long-held tension
- Lay down fear, anxiety, and self-protection
- Replace old narratives with His truth
- Forgive where your heart resisted
- Receive healing where your heart hurt

Month 2 taught you something life-changing:

Healing is not a moment. Healing is a partnership. And God is faithful in every step of it.

As you close this month, pause and ask:

- Where did God touch a hidden wound?
- What fear began to lose its power?
- What burden felt lighter than before?
- What truth replaced an old lie?
- What outcome did you finally release into His hands?

This month has softened your heart, strengthened your trust, and prepared you for the courage that Month 3 will call you into. God has begun a deep work within you - and He is far from finished.

What He healed, He will strengthen.

What He restored, He will grow.

What He revealed, He will redeem.

You leave Month 2 not wounded - but healing. Not overwhelmed - but surrendered. Not fearful - but trusting.

And now, you step into Month 3 with a heart that is lighter, a spirit that is stronger, and a deeper confidence in the God who carries you forward.

MONTH 3 THEME: FAITH, BOLDNESS, & COURAGE

Month 3 calls you to rise - to step out of hesitation and into holy confidence. This is the month where God strengthens your spirit, awakens courage within you, and teaches you to stand firm in truth even when fear whispers otherwise. Faith isn't built in comfort; it's strengthened in the moments when you choose God over fear.

This month marks a turning point in your spiritual journey. You've been renewed. You've been healed. Now God invites you to live boldly - to trust Him on deeper levels and walk with the courage that comes from His presence, not your own strength.

This month will help you:

- Break agreement with fear, doubt, and insecurity
- Pray bold prayers instead of timid ones
- Step forward in obedience even when the path is unclear
- Stand firm on God's promises
- Replace hesitation with confidence
- Recognize and reject spiritual intimidation
- Walk with renewed spiritual authority
- Strengthen your resilience in the face of adversity

Let the Lord's Prayer guide your courage this month:

- **"Our Father in Heaven"** - Boldness begins with sonship and daughterhood.
- **"Hallowed be Your name"** - Worship strengthens courage; it magnifies God over fear.
- **"Your kingdom come"** - Courage grows when you embrace God's purpose for you.
- **"Your will be done"** - Faith deepens when you obey even before you understand.
- **"Give us this day…"** - God gives daily courage, not lifetime courage - one step at a time.
- **"Forgive us…"** - Fear loses its grip when shame and guilt are removed.
- **"Lead us not…"** - Ask God to protect you from the temptation to shrink back.

- **"Yours is the kingdom…"** - Courage is rooted in who reigns - not what you face.

As you enter Month 3, step forward with lifted head and strengthened heart. Courage isn't the absence of fear - it's choosing faith in the face of it. God is calling you into deeper waters, but He is also the One holding you above the waves. This is your month of boldness.

DAY 61 – Stepping Forward in Faith

Prayer:
Father, I come choosing to step forward in faith instead of holding back in fear. Hallowed be Your name; strengthen my heart to trust what You have spoken (Hebrews 11:1). Let Your kingdom come and lead me into the places You have prepared. Let Your will be done as I walk in obedience, even when the path seems uncertain. Give me today my daily bread of courage and conviction. Forgive me for hesitating when You called me forward, and I forgive those who discouraged my faith. Lead me not into the temptation of doubt, but deliver me into bold faith in Your promises (2 Corinthians 5:7). For Thine is the kingdom, and the power, and the glory forever and ever. Amen.

Reflection:
What step of faith is God asking you to take today?

_____

_____

_____

Action:
Write down one step of obedience you will take-big or small.

_____

_____

_____

Scriptures Referenced Today:
Hebrews 11:1 (KJV) - "Now faith is the substance of things hoped for, the evidence of things not seen."
2 Corinthians 5:7 (KJV) - "For we walk by faith, not by sight."

DAY 62 – Courage When You Feel Afraid

Prayer:
Father, I come asking for courage where fear has held me back. Hallowed be Your name; remind me that You go before me and stand beside me (Deuteronomy 31:6). Let Your kingdom come and break the grip of fear over my life. Let Your will be done as You empower me to act with boldness and confidence. Give me today my daily bread of strength and assurance. Forgive me for letting fear silence my faith, and I forgive those whose words reinforced my fears. Lead me not into the temptation of retreating, but deliver me into fearless trust in You (Psalm 27:1). Yours is the kingdom, the power, and the glory forever. Amen.

Reflection:
Where has fear been holding you back from God's best?

_____

_____

_____

Action:
Write one fear you are choosing to confront through God's strength.

_____

_____

_____

Scriptures Referenced Today:
Deuteronomy 31:6 (KJV) - "Be strong and of a good courage, fear not, nor be afraid of them: for the LORD thy God, he it is that doth go with thee; he will not fail thee, nor forsake thee."
Psalm 27:1 (KJV) - "The LORD is my light and my salvation; whom shall I fear? The LORD is the strength of my life; of whom shall I be afraid?"

DAY 63 – Believing God's Promises

Prayer:

Father, I come anchoring my heart in Your unfailing promises. Hallowed be Your name; establish my faith on the certainty of Your Word (Numbers 23:19). Let Your kingdom come and silence every lie that contradicts what You've spoken. Let Your will be done as I choose to believe even when I cannot see the outcome. Give me today my daily bread of confidence, trust, and unwavering hope. Forgive me for doubting Your faithfulness, and I forgive those who weakened my belief. Lead me not into the temptation of unbelief, but deliver me into steadfast faith in Your promises (Joshua 21:45). All glory be to You, forever and ever. Amen.

Reflection:

Which promise of God do you need to believe more deeply today?

_____

_____

_____

Action:

Write one Scripture promise you will meditate on throughout the day.

_____

_____

_____

Scriptures Referenced Today:

Numbers 23:19 (KJV) - "God is not a man, that he should lie; neither the son of man, that he should repent: hath he said, and shall he not do it? Or hath he spoken, and shall he not make it good?"

Joshua 21:45 (KJV) - "There failed not ought of any good thing which the LORD had spoken unto the house of Israel; all came to pass."

DAY 64 – Strength for Spiritual Battles

Prayer:
Father, I come asking for Your strength for the battles I face. Hallowed be Your name; arm me with Your power and steady my spirit (Ephesians 6:10). Let Your kingdom come and fortify me with courage for every challenge. Let Your will be done as You teach me to stand firm in faith. Give me today my daily bread of resilience and spiritual strength. Forgive me for fighting in my own power, and I forgive those who added weight to my battles. Lead me not into the temptation of fear or discouragement, but deliver me into the victory that comes through You (Isaiah 54:17). For Yours alone is the kingdom, the power, and the glory. Amen.

Reflection:
What battle are you facing that requires God's strength?

_____

_____

_____

Action:
Write down one way you will stand firm in God's strength today.

_____

_____

_____

Scriptures Referenced Today:
Ephesians 6:10 (KJV) - "Finally, my brethren, be strong in the Lord, and in the power of his might."
Isaiah 54:17 (KJV) - "No weapon that is formed against thee shall prosper; and every tongue that shall rise against thee in judgment thou shalt condemn. This is the heritage of the servants of the LORD, and their righteousness is of me, saith the LORD."

DAY 65 – Courage to Do What God Has Called You To Do

Prayer:
Father, I come asking for courage to walk boldly in the calling You have placed on my life. Hallowed be Your name; equip me for the work You've prepared for me (Ephesians 2:10). Let Your kingdom come and guide my steps into the assignments You have ordained. Let Your will be done as You strengthen me to obey without hesitation. Give me today my daily bread of confidence and purpose. Forgive me for shrinking back from what You've asked, and I forgive those who doubted or discouraged my calling. Lead me not into the temptation of fear or inadequacy, but deliver me into the boldness of Your Spirit (2 Timothy 1:7). To You be the glory, now and forever. Amen.

Reflection:
What calling or assignment do you need courage to step into?

_____

_____

_____

Action:
Write down one action that moves you closer to walking in your calling.

_____

_____

_____

Scriptures Referenced Today:
Ephesians 2:10 (KJV) - "For we are his workmanship, created in Christ Jesus unto good works, which God hath before ordained that we should walk in them."
2 Timothy 1:7 (KJV) - "For God hath not given us the spirit of fear; but of power, and of love, and of a sound mind."

DAY 66 – Faith to Stand When It's Hard

Prayer:
Father, I come asking for faith that stands firm even when life feels difficult. Hallowed be Your name; strengthen my heart to remain steadfast under pressure (1 Corinthians 16:13). Let Your kingdom come and anchor me when circumstances feel uncertain. Let Your will be done as You steady my feet on the path You've set before me. Give me today my daily bread of courage, endurance, and unwavering trust. Forgive me for wavering when challenges rise, and I forgive those who discouraged my faith. Lead me not into the temptation of giving up, but deliver me into Your strength to stand firm (Psalm 112:7). For Thine is the kingdom, and the power, and the glory forever and ever. Amen.

Reflection:
Where do you need faith to stand firm today?

_____

_____

Action:
Write one situation where you will choose to stand in faith.

_____

_____

Scriptures Referenced Today:
1 Corinthians 16:13 (KJV) - "Watch ye, stand fast in the faith, quit you like men, be strong."
Psalm 112:7 (KJV) - "He shall not be afraid of evil tidings: his heart is fixed, trusting in the LORD."

DAY 67 – Courage to Obey God Immediately

Prayer:
Father, I come asking for the courage to obey You without delay. Hallowed be Your name; give me a willing heart that responds quickly when You speak (Psalm 119:60). Let Your kingdom come and remove every hesitation that slows my obedience. Let Your will be done as You strengthen me to walk boldly in Your commands. Give me today my daily bread of clarity, readiness, and courage. Forgive me for delaying obedience, and I forgive those who pushed me toward fear or doubt. Lead me not into the temptation of procrastination, but deliver me into joyful, immediate obedience (James 1:22). Yours is the kingdom, the power, and the glory forever. Amen.

Reflection:
Where is God asking you to obey promptly and boldly?

_____

_____

_____

Action:
Write one step of obedience you will take today-without delay.

_____

_____

_____

Scriptures Referenced Today:
Psalm 119:60 (KJV) - "I made haste, and delayed not to keep thy commandments."
James 1:22 (KJV) - "But be ye doers of the word, and not hearers only, deceiving your own selves."

DAY 68 – Faith That Overcomes Fear

Prayer:
Father, I come asking for faith that rises above every fear. Hallowed be Your name; strengthen me to trust You more than what frightens me (Isaiah 41:13). Let Your kingdom come and push back the darkness of fear that tries to overwhelm my heart. Let Your will be done as You fill me with confidence in Your nearness and strength. Give me today my daily bread of courage, assurance, and victory. Forgive me for giving fear too much room, and I forgive those whose words fueled my fears. Lead me not into the temptation of fear-driven thinking, but deliver me into bold faith (Psalm 56:4). All glory be to You, forever and ever. Amen.

Reflection:
What fear is God calling you to confront through faith today?

_____

_____

_____

Action:
Write one Scripture truth you will use to stand against fear.

_____

_____

_____

Scriptures Referenced Today:
Isaiah 41:13 (KJV) - "For I the LORD thy God will hold thy right hand, saying unto thee, Fear not; I will help thee."
Psalm 56:4 (KJV) - "In God I will praise his word, in God I have put my trust; I will not fear what flesh can do unto me."

DAY 69 – Courage to Speak Truth Boldly

Prayer:
Father, I come asking for boldness to speak truth with love and confidence. Hallowed be Your name; fill my mouth with Your words and my heart with Your courage (Acts 4:29). Let Your kingdom come and break any fear that keeps me silent when You call me to speak. Let Your will be done as You use my voice to encourage, challenge, and lift others. Give me today my daily bread of boldness and clarity. Forgive me for staying quiet when I should have spoken, and I forgive those who silenced or intimidated me. Lead me not into the temptation of fear-filled silence, but deliver me into faith-filled boldness (Ephesians 6:19–20). For Yours alone is the kingdom, the power, and the glory. Amen.

Reflection:
Where is God asking you to speak truth courageously?

_____

_____

_____

Action:
Write one truth you need to speak-with love and courage.

_____

_____

_____

Scriptures Referenced Today:
Acts 4:29 (KJV) - "And now, Lord, behold their threatenings: and grant unto thy servants, that with all boldness they may speak thy word."
Ephesians 6:19–20 (KJV) - "And for me, that utterance may be given unto me, that I may open my mouth boldly, to make known the mystery of the gospel, for which I am an ambassador in bonds: that therein I may speak boldly, as I ought to speak."

DAY 70 – Faith to Do What Seems Impossible

Prayer:
Father, I come believing that nothing is impossible with You. Hallowed be Your name; strengthen my faith to trust You for what feels beyond my ability (Mark 10:27). Let Your kingdom come and expand my spiritual vision to see what You see. Let Your will be done as You lead me to attempt things that require Your strength, not mine. Give me today my daily bread of bold expectation and unwavering faith. Forgive me for limiting what I thought You could do, and I forgive those who doubted the calling You placed on my life. Lead me not into the temptation of small thinking, but deliver me into God-sized faith (Luke 1:37). To You be the glory, now and forever. Amen.

Reflection:
Where is God asking you to believe Him for something that seems impossible?

_____

_____

_____

Action:
Write down an "impossible" prayer you will believe God for today.

_____

_____

_____

Scriptures Referenced Today:
Mark 10:27 (KJV) - "And Jesus looking upon them saith, With men it is impossible, but not with God: for with God all things are possible."
Luke 1:37 (KJV) - "For with God nothing shall be impossible."

DAY 71 – Courage to Confront Spiritual Opposition

Prayer:
Father, I come asking for the courage to stand strong when spiritual resistance rises. Hallowed be Your name; remind me that greater is He who is in me than he who is in the world (1 John 4:4). Let Your kingdom come and push back every force that tries to intimidate my faith. Let Your will be done as You strengthen me to resist the enemy with bold confidence. Give me today my daily bread of courage, discernment, and spiritual strength. Forgive me for shrinking back in fear, and I forgive those who discouraged my boldness. Lead me not into the temptation of spiritual passivity, but deliver me into victory through Your power (James 4:7). For Thine is the kingdom, and the power, and the glory forever and ever. Amen.

Reflection:
Where do you sense spiritual resistance, and how can you stand firm?

Action:
Write down one declaration of truth you will stand on today.

Scriptures Referenced Today:
1 John 4:4 (KJV) - "Ye are of God, little children, and have overcome them: because greater is he that is in you, than he that is in the world."
James 4:7 (KJV) - "Submit yourselves therefore to God. Resist the devil, and he will flee from you."

DAY 72 – Faith to Persevere Through Delays

Prayer:
Father, I come asking for faith to persevere through delays and waiting. Hallowed be Your name; remind me that delay is not denial (Habakkuk 2:3). Let Your kingdom come and strengthen my heart to trust You when progress feels slow. Let Your will be done as You train me to wait with hope and expectation. Give me today my daily bread of endurance and patience. Forgive me for growing weary in the waiting, and I forgive those who pressured me to lose heart. Lead me not into the temptation of giving up, but deliver me into steadfast faith (Galatians 6:9). All glory be to You, forever and ever. Amen.

Reflection:
What promise or prayer do you need to continue believing for?

_____

_____

_____

Action:
Write one delayed prayer you will continue to trust God to fulfill.

_____

_____

Scriptures Referenced Today:
Habakkuk 2:3 (KJV) - "For the vision is yet for an appointed time, but at the end it shall speak, and not lie: though it tarry, wait for it; because it will surely come, it will not tarry."
Galatians 6:9 (KJV) - "And let us not be weary in well doing: for in due season we shall reap, if we faint not."

DAY 73 – Courage to See Yourself as God Sees You

Prayer:
Father, I come asking for the courage to see myself through Your eyes and not through fear, insecurity, or comparison. Hallowed be Your name; remind me that I am Your workmanship, created with purpose and intention (Ephesians 2:10). Let Your kingdom come and silence every lie that challenges my identity. Let Your will be done as You renew my mind to believe the truth You speak over me. Give me today my daily bread of confidence, identity, and courage. Forgive me for agreeing with false labels, and I forgive those who spoke words that wounded my worth. Lead me not into the temptation of self-doubt, but deliver me into bold confidence in who You created me to be (1 Peter 2:9). Yours is the kingdom, the power, and the glory forever. Amen.

Reflection:
What untrue thought about yourself is God asking you to release?

_____

_____

_____

Action:
Write a truth from Scripture that declares who you really are in Christ.

_____

_____

_____

Scriptures Referenced Today:
Ephesians 2:10 (KJV) - "For we are his workmanship, created in Christ Jesus unto good works, which God hath before ordained that we should walk in them."
1 Peter 2:9 (KJV) - "But ye are a chosen generation, a royal priesthood, an holy nation, a peculiar people; that ye should shew forth the praises of him who hath called you out of darkness into his marvelous light."

DAY 74 – Faith That Speaks to Mountains

Prayer:
Father, I come believing that through faith in You, the mountains in my life can move. Hallowed be Your name; remind me that nothing is too great for Your power (Mark 11:23). Let Your kingdom come and breathe courage into my prayers. Let Your will be done as I speak in faith rather than fear. Give me today my daily bread of bold expectation and unwavering trust. Forgive me for doubting that change is possible, and I forgive those who diminished my faith. Lead me not into the temptation of silent disbelief, but deliver me into mountain-moving faith (Matthew 17:20). For Yours alone is the kingdom, the power, and the glory. Amen.

Reflection:
What "mountain" in your life are you believing God to move?

_____

_____

_____

Action:
Write a prayer of faith declaring God's authority over that mountain.

_____

_____

_____

Scriptures Referenced Today:
Mark 11:23 (KJV) - "For verily I say unto you, That whosoever shall say unto this mountain, Be thou removed, and be thou cast into the sea; and shall not doubt in his heart, but shall believe that those things which he saith shall come to pass; he shall have whatsoever he saith."
Matthew 17:20 (KJV) - "And Jesus said unto them, Because of your unbelief: for verily I say unto you, If ye have faith as a grain of mustard seed, ye shall say unto this mountain, Remove hence to yonder place; and it shall remove; and nothing shall be impossible unto you."

DAY 75 – Courage to Walk Into the Unknown

Prayer:
Father, I come stepping forward into places where I cannot see the full path. Hallowed be Your name; guide me with Your wisdom and steady my heart when the way feels unfamiliar (Psalm 32:8). Let Your kingdom come and illuminate the next steps before me. Let Your will be done as You teach me to trust You more than my need for clarity. Give me today my daily bread of courage, assurance, and guidance. Forgive me for hesitating in uncertainty, and I forgive those who fed my doubts. Lead me not into the temptation of needing to control every detail, but deliver me into peace as I follow You into the unknown (Hebrews 11:8). To You be the glory, now and forever. Amen.

Reflection:
What unknown or uncertain area is God asking you to walk into by faith?

_____

_____

_____

Action:
Write one step you can take into the unknown-trusting God fully.

_____

_____

_____

Scriptures Referenced Today:
Psalm 32:8 (KJV) - "I will instruct thee and teach thee in the way which thou shalt go: I will guide thee with mine eye."
Hebrews 11:8 (KJV) - "By faith Abraham, when he was called to go out into a place which he should after receive for an inheritance, obeyed; and he went out, not knowing whither he went."

DAY 76 – Courage to Pray Bold Prayers

Prayer:
Father, I come asking for courage to pray boldly-to ask for things only
You can accomplish. Hallowed be Your name; expand my faith so I pray
according to Your power, not my limitations (Ephesians 3:20). Let Your
kingdom come and stretch my expectation of what is possible with You.
Let Your will be done as I align my prayers with Your heart and Your
Word. Give me today my daily bread of boldness, conviction, and
expectancy. Forgive me for praying small out of fear or doubt, and I
forgive those who minimized my faith. Lead me not into the temptation
of timid prayers, but deliver me into bold, faith-filled intercession
(Jeremiah 33:3). For Thine is the kingdom, and the power, and the glory
forever and ever. Amen.

Reflection:
What bold prayer has God placed on your heart?

_____

_____

Action:
Write that bold prayer plainly and courageously before God.

_____

_____

Scriptures Referenced Today:
Ephesians 3:20 (KJV) - "Now unto him that is able to do exceeding
abundantly above all that we ask or think, according to the power that
worketh in us,"
Jeremiah 33:3 (KJV) - "Call unto me, and I will answer thee, and show
thee great and mighty things, which thou knowest not."

DAY 77 – Faith When You Feel Unequipped

Prayer:
Father, I come trusting You even when I feel unequipped or inadequate. Hallowed be Your name; remind me that You do not call the qualified; You qualify the called (Exodus 4:10–12). Let Your kingdom come and strengthen me where I feel weak or insecure. Let Your will be done as You equip me with everything I need to do what You've asked. Give me today my daily bread of confidence, ability, and grace. Forgive me for doubting myself, and I forgive those who dismissed or underestimated me. Lead me not into the temptation of self-doubt, but deliver me into courage through Your empowerment (Philippians 4:13). Yours is the kingdom, the power, and the glory forever. Amen.

Reflection:
Where do you feel unequipped-and how is God equipping you?

Action:
Write one way you will rely on God's strength instead of your own.

Scriptures Referenced Today:
Exodus 4:10–12 (KJV) - "And Moses said unto the LORD, O my Lord, I am not eloquent, neither heretofore, nor since thou hast spoken unto thy servant: but I am slow of speech, and of a slow tongue.
And the LORD said unto him, Who hath made man's mouth? or who maketh the dumb, or deaf, or the seeing, or the blind? have not I the LORD? Now therefore go, and I will be with thy mouth, and teach thee what thou shalt say."
Philippians 4:13 (KJV) - "I can do all things through Christ which strengtheneth me."

DAY 78 – Courage to Rise After Failure

Prayer:
Father, I come rising again with courage after my failures and setbacks. Hallowed be Your name; lift me back to my feet and restore my confidence in You (Micah 7:8). Let Your kingdom come and silence the voice of condemnation. Let Your will be done as You turn failure into wisdom and growth. Give me today my daily bread of resilience and renewed hope. Forgive me for giving up on myself, and I forgive those who judged or criticized my failures. Lead me not into the temptation of shame, but deliver me into courage that rises again (Proverbs 24:16). All glory be to You, forever and ever. Amen.

Reflection:
Where have you fallen-and how is God calling you to rise again?

_____

_____

_____

Action:
Write one step forward you will take today, no matter how small.

_____

_____

Scriptures Referenced Today:
Micah 7:8 (KJV) - "Rejoice not against me, O mine enemy: when I fall, I shall arise; when I sit in darkness, the LORD shall be a light unto me."
Proverbs 24:16 (KJV) - "For a just man falleth seven times, and riseth up again: but the wicked shall fall into mischief."

DAY 79 – Faith That Conquers Discouragement

Prayer:
Father, I come asking for faith that conquers discouragement and strengthens my spirit. Hallowed be Your name; lift my eyes above the weight I feel (Psalm 3:3). Let Your kingdom come and breathe fresh encouragement into my heart. Let Your will be done as You remind me that You are my shield, my glory, and the lifter of my head. Give me today my daily bread of joy, strength, and renewed hope. Forgive me for allowing discouragement to take root, and I forgive those who added to my heaviness. Lead me not into the temptation of despair, but deliver me into the encouragement of Your presence (Isaiah 40:31). For Yours alone is the kingdom, the power, and the glory. Amen.

Reflection:
What discouragement do you need God to lift off of you today?

_____

_____

_____

Action:
Write one truth that will encourage your heart today.

_____

_____

_____

Scriptures Referenced Today:
Psalm 3:3 (KJV) - "But thou, O LORD, art a shield for me; my glory, and the lifter up of mine head."
Isaiah 40:31 (KJV) - "But they that wait upon the LORD shall renew their strength; they shall mount up with wings as eagles; they shall run, and not be weary; and they shall walk, and not faint."

DAY 80 – Courage to Follow God Fully

Prayer:
Father, I come asking for the courage to follow You with my whole heart. Hallowed be Your name; strengthen me to walk in wholehearted devotion, not partial obedience (Joshua 14:9). Let Your kingdom come and ignite a faith that follows wherever You lead. Let Your will be done as You refine my desires and steady my steps. Give me today my daily bread of courage, loyalty, and faith. Forgive me for following You half-heartedly at times, and I forgive those who discouraged my commitment. Lead me not into the temptation of divided loyalty, but deliver me into bold, wholehearted obedience (Psalm 86:11). To You be the glory, now and forever. Amen.

Reflection:
Where is God calling you to follow Him more fully?

_____

_____

_____

Action:
Write one area where you will commit to following God wholeheartedly.

_____

_____

_____

Scriptures Referenced Today:
Joshua 14:9 (KJV) - "And Moses sware on that day, saying, Surely the land whereon thy feet have trodden shall be thine inheritance, and thy children's for ever, because thou hast wholly followed the LORD my God."
Psalm 86:11 (KJV) - "Teach me thy way, O LORD; I will walk in thy truth: unite my heart to fear thy name."

DAY 81 – Faith to Pray With Confidence

Prayer:
Father, I come praying with confidence, knowing You hear me when I call. Hallowed be Your name; strengthen my faith to approach You boldly and trust Your heart toward me (1 John 5:14–15). Let Your kingdom come and deepen my assurance that You respond according to Your will. Let Your will be done as You grow my faith through prayer and expectation. Give me today my daily bread of boldness, clarity, and perseverance. Forgive me for doubting Your willingness to answer, and I forgive those who weakened my expectancy. Lead me not into the temptation of faithless prayer, but deliver me into confidence grounded in Your Word (Hebrews 4:16). For Thine is the kingdom, and the power, and the glory forever and ever. Amen.

Reflection:
In what area do you need confidence that God hears your prayers?

_____

_____

_____

Action:
Write a confident prayer request you are bringing before God today.

_____

_____

_____

Scriptures Referenced Today:
1 John 5:14–15 (KJV) - "And this is the confidence that we have in him, that, if we ask any thing according to his will, he heareth us: And if we know that he hear us, whatsoever we ask, we know that we have the petitions that we desired of him."
Hebrews 4:16 (KJV) - "Let us therefore come boldly unto the throne of grace, that we may obtain mercy, and find grace to help in time of need."

DAY 82 – Courage to Trust God's Protection

Prayer:

Father, I come trusting in Your protection over my life. Hallowed be Your name; remind me that You are my refuge, my fortress, and the One who watches over me (Psalm 91:1–2). Let Your kingdom come and quiet every fear that rises against my peace. Let Your will be done as You surround me with Your covering and strengthen my trust. Give me today my daily bread of security, comfort, and assurance. Forgive me for fearing what might happen, and I forgive those who increased my worries. Lead me not into the temptation of living in fear, but deliver me into confidence in Your protection (Psalm 121:7–8). Yours is the kingdom, the power, and the glory forever. Amen.

Reflection:
What fear about safety or protection do you need to place into God's hands?

_____

_____

_____

Action:
Write a declaration of trust in God's protection today.

_____

_____

_____

Scriptures Referenced Today:
Psalm 91:1–2 (KJV) - "He that dwelleth in the secret place of the most High shall abide under the shadow of the Almighty. I will say of the LORD, He is my refuge and my fortress: my God; in him will I trust."
Psalm 121:7–8 (KJV) - "The LORD shall preserve thee from all evil: he shall preserve thy soul. The LORD shall preserve thy going out and thy coming in from this time forth, and even for evermore."

DAY 83 – Faith to Rise Above Discouragement

Prayer:
Father, I come asking for the faith to rise above discouragement and regain my strength. Hallowed be Your name; lift my spirit and renew my hope (Psalm 42:11). Let Your kingdom come and overwhelm

discouragement with truth. Let Your will be done as You remind me that You are my God and my help. Give me today my daily bread of encouragement, endurance, and renewed faith. Forgive me for letting hopelessness overshadow my trust, and I forgive those who contributed to my discouragement. Lead me not into the temptation of despair, but deliver me into hope anchored in You (Romans 15:13). All glory be to You, forever and ever. Amen.

Reflection:

What discouragement do you need God to lift off you today?

Action:

Write one truth or promise that restores your hope.

Scriptures Referenced Today:

Psalm 42:11 (KJV) - "Why art thou cast down, O my soul? and why art thou disquieted within me? Hope thou in God: for I shall yet praise him, who is the health of my countenance, and my God."

Romans 15:13 (KJV) - "Now the God of hope fill you with all joy and peace in believing, that ye may abound in hope, through the power of the Holy Ghost."

DAY 84 – Courage to Break Free From Limiting Beliefs

Prayer:
Father, I come asking for courage to break free from the beliefs that limit my faith and my future. Hallowed be Your name; renew my mind and transform my thinking (Romans 12:2). Let Your kingdom come and silence every false belief that contradicts Your truth. Let Your will be done as You free me from patterns of thought that hold me back. Give me today my daily bread of confidence, clarity, and breakthrough. Forgive me for agreeing with limitations instead of Your promises, and I forgive those who spoke limitations over me. Lead me not into the temptation of small thinking, but deliver me into a renewed mind filled with Your truth (Philippians 4:8). For Yours alone is the kingdom, the power, and the glory. Amen.

Reflection:
What limiting belief is God asking you to surrender today?

_____

_____

_____

Action:
Write a scripture that replaces that limiting belief with God's truth.

_____

_____

_____

Scriptures Referenced Today:
Romans 12:2 (KJV) - "And be not conformed to this world: but be ye transformed by the renewing of your mind, that ye may prove what is that good, and acceptable, and perfect, will of God."
Philippians 4:8 (KJV) - "Finally, brethren, whatsoever things are true, whatsoever things are honest, whatsoever things are just, whatsoever things are pure, whatsoever things are lovely, whatsoever things are of good report; if there be any virtue, and if there be any praise, think on these things."

DAY 85 – Faith to Move Forward After Setbacks

Prayer:
Father, I come believing that setbacks do not cancel Your purpose for my life. Hallowed be Your name; remind me that You are working all things for my good (Romans 8:28). Let Your kingdom come and turn every setback into a setup for growth. Let Your will be done as You lead me forward with renewed strength and confidence. Give me today my daily bread of hope, resilience, and forward motion. Forgive me for letting setbacks define me, and I forgive those who contributed to my discouragement. Lead me not into the temptation of standing still in defeat, but deliver me into courage that moves forward (Philippians 3:13–14). To You be the glory, now and forever. Amen.

Reflection:
What setback is God calling you to move forward from today?

_____

_____

_____

Action:
Write one step-small or large-that moves you forward in faith.

_____

_____

_____

Scriptures Referenced Today:
Romans 8:28 (KJV) - "And we know that all things work together for good to them that love God, to them who are the called according to his purpose."
Philippians 3:13–14 (KJV) - "Brethren, I count not myself to have apprehended: but this one thing I do, forgetting those things which are behind, and reaching forth unto those things which are before, I press toward the mark for the prize of the high calling of God in Christ Jesus."

DAY 86 – Courage to Trust God Beyond Your Comfort Zone

Prayer:
Father, I come stepping beyond what feels comfortable or familiar. Hallowed be Your name; stretch my faith and lead me where I would never go without You (Psalm 18:32–33). Let Your kingdom come and strengthen my feet to walk new paths with confidence. Let Your will be done as You empower me to grow beyond fear and hesitation. Give me today my daily bread of boldness, endurance, and trust. Forgive me for clinging to comfort, and I forgive those who influenced my fear. Lead me not into the temptation of staying where it feels safe, but deliver me into courageous obedience (Joshua 1:9). For Thine is the kingdom, and the power, and the glory forever and ever. Amen.

Reflection:
What comfort zone is God inviting you to step out of?

_____

_____

_____

Action:
Write one bold step outside your comfort zone you will take today.

_____

_____

_____

Scriptures Referenced Today:
Psalm 18:32–33 (KJV) - "It is God that girdeth me with strength, and maketh my way perfect. He maketh my feet like hinds' feet, and setteth me upon my high places."
Joshua 1:9 (KJV) - "Have not I commanded thee? Be strong and of a good courage; be not afraid, neither be thou dismayed: for the LORD thy God is with thee whithersoever thou goest."

DAY 87 – Faith to Overcome Doubt

Prayer:
Father, I come asking You to strengthen my faith where doubt tries to whisper. Hallowed be Your name; remind me that nothing You speak can fail (Luke 1:37). Let Your kingdom come and overthrow every lie that challenges my belief. Let Your will be done as You steady my heart in unwavering trust. Give me today my daily bread of confidence and clarity. Forgive me for entertaining doubt, and I forgive those whose words planted uncertainty in me. Lead me not into the temptation of double-mindedness, but deliver me into faith that stands firm (James 1:6). Yours is the kingdom, the power, and the glory forever. Amen.

Reflection:
What doubt do you need God to replace with faith today?

_____

_____

_____

Action:
Write one truth that speaks louder than your doubt.

_____

_____

_____

Scriptures Referenced Today:
Luke 1:37 (KJV) - "For with God nothing shall be impossible."
James 1:6 (KJV) - "But let him ask in faith, nothing wavering. For he that wavereth is like a wave of the sea driven with the wind and tossed."

DAY 88 – Courage to Take Spirit-Led Risks

Prayer:
Father, I come asking for courage to take the risks You are calling me to take. Hallowed be Your name; lead me into bold obedience that stretches my faith (Matthew 14:29). Let Your kingdom come and empower me to step where only faith can sustain me. Let Your will be done as You guide me into what is uncomfortable but ordained by You. Give me today my daily bread of courage, clarity, and bold trust. Forgive me for avoiding Spirit-led risks, and I forgive those who discouraged me from following You fully. Lead me not into the temptation of playing it safe, but deliver me into bold steps of faith (Hebrews 11:8). All glory be to You, forever and ever. Amen.

Reflection:
What Spirit-led risk is God inviting you to take?

_____

_____

_____

Action:
Write one risky step of obedience you will take with God today.

_____

_____

_____

Scriptures Referenced Today:
Matthew 14:29 (KJV) - "And he said, Come. And when Peter was come down out of the ship, he walked on the water, to go to Jesus."
Hebrews 11:8 (KJV) - "By faith Abraham, when he was called to go out into a place which he should after receive for an inheritance, obeyed; and he went out, not knowing whither he went."

DAY 89 – Faith to Trust God's Voice

Prayer:
Father, I come asking for the faith to recognize and trust Your voice. Hallowed be Your name; tune my ears to hear You clearly (John 10:27). Let Your kingdom come and quiet every competing voice. Let Your will be done as You lead me with clarity and discernment. Give me today my daily bread of wisdom and spiritual sensitivity. Forgive me for ignoring or doubting what You've spoken, and I forgive those whose voices drowned out Yours. Lead me not into the temptation of confusion, but deliver me into clear, confident faith in Your leading (Isaiah 30:21). For Yours alone is the kingdom, the power, and the glory. Amen.

Reflection:
Where do you need to better discern God's voice?

_____

_____

Action:
Write one thing you believe God is speaking to you right now.

_____

_____

Scriptures Referenced Today:
John 10:27 (KJV) - "My sheep hear my voice, and I know them, and they follow me."
Isaiah 30:21 (KJV) - "And thine ears shall hear a word behind thee, saying, This is the way, walk ye in it, when ye turn to the right hand, and when ye turn to the left."

DAY 90 – Courage to Step Into Your God-Given Identity

Prayer:
Father, I come stepping boldly into the identity You have given me. Hallowed be Your name; remind me of who I am in Christ and silence every false label (2 Corinthians 5:17). Let Your kingdom come and restore confidence where insecurity once lived. Let Your will be done as You strengthen me to walk boldly in my calling, gifting, and design. Give me today my daily bread of confidence, boldness, and purpose. Forgive me for living beneath who You created me to be, and I forgive those who spoke against my identity. Lead me not into the temptation of shrinking back, but deliver me into bold, God-given confidence (Romans 8:15). To You be the glory, now and forever. Amen.

Reflection:
What part of your God-given identity is God calling you to embrace today?

Action:
Write a declaration of identity rooted in Scripture.

Scriptures Referenced Today:
2 Corinthians 5:17 (KJV) - "Therefore if any man be in Christ, he is a new creature: old things are passed away; behold, all things are become new."
Romans 8:15 (KJV) - "For ye have not received the spirit of bondage again to fear; but ye have received the Spirit of adoption, whereby we cry, Abba, Father."

DAY 91 – Faith to Stand Firm in Your Calling

Prayer:
Father, I come standing firm in the calling You have placed on my life. Hallowed be Your name; strengthen me to walk faithfully in what You entrusted to me (1 Thessalonians 5:24). Let Your kingdom come and establish me in bold, unwavering obedience. Let Your will be done as You remove every doubt, fear, and hindrance that tries to pull me away from my purpose. Give me today my daily bread of confidence, clarity, and courage. Forgive me for questioning whether I am truly called, and I forgive those who planted doubt or discouragement in my spirit. Lead me not into the temptation of abandoning my purpose, but deliver me into steadfast faithfulness (1 Corinthians 15:58). For Thine is the kingdom, and the power, and the glory forever and ever. Amen.

Reflection:
How is God affirming your calling in this season?

_____

_____

_____

Action:
Write one step you will take to stand firm in the calling God has placed on your life.

_____

_____

_____

Scriptures Referenced Today:
1 Thessalonians 5:24 (KJV) - "Faithful is he that calleth you, who also will do it."
1 Corinthians 15:58 (KJV) - "Therefore, my beloved brethren, be ye steadfast, unmoveable, always abounding in the work of the Lord, forasmuch as ye know that your labour is not in vain in the Lord."

MONTH 3 CLOSING REFLECTION: FAITH & COURAGE

As Month 3 comes to a close, pause and remember where you began: perhaps uncertain, maybe hesitant, possibly afraid of the road ahead. But look at you now-strengthened, stretched, awakened. Courage has grown in you, not because life became easier, but because faith became deeper. This month called you to rise. To believe again. To step forward. To trust God's calling more than your comfort. To let courage silence fear. You learned to:

- Pray bold prayers, not timid ones
- Stand on God's promises when doubt whispered
- Confront discouragement with truth
- Walk into the unknown with God beside you
- Reject the fear that once defined your steps
- Move forward after setbacks
- Remember who you truly are in Christ

Month 3 was not just about doing brave things-

It was about becoming brave. Not by force, not by willpower, but by the Spirit of God strengthening you from the inside out.

As you leave this month, take a moment to reflect:

- Where did faith grow stronger?
- What fear loosened its grip?
- What step of courage surprised even you?
- Where did God meet you, strengthen you, steady you?

Carry these truths forward:

- **Courage is born from trust.**
- **Faith grows when you move, not when you stay still.**
- **God's calling on your life is unshakable, even when you feel shaken.**
- **What God starts in you, He will strengthen, sustain, and complete.**

Month 3 closes with a challenge and a promise:

Step boldly. You are not alone. Believe deeply. God is with you. Walk courageously. His Spirit empowers you.

And as you enter Month 4, you do not step forward as who you were-

You step forward as who God is forming you to become.

MONTH 4 THEME: GROWTH, CHARACTER, & MATURITY

Month 4 leads you into the inner work - the long, faithful work - of spiritual growth and maturity. God is not just shaping your actions; He is shaping your character, your values, your focus, and your internal strength. Growth is rarely glamorous, but it is always transformative. This is where roots deepen, fruit forms, and spiritual endurance develops. Up to this point, God has renewed you, healed you, strengthened you, and awakened your courage. Now He begins to refine you - not through pressure but through process. True maturity is formed through repetition, obedience, and dependence. God builds you inwardly so that what He does through you has a foundation that will not crack.

This month will help you:

- Develop consistency in your spiritual life
- Grow in wisdom, stability, and spiritual insight
- Strengthen your daily habits and disciplines
- Cultivate godly character that lasts
- Align your decisions with godly priorities
- Deepen your dependence on the Holy Spirit
- Mature in your responses, motives, and attitudes
- Build a life that reflects Christ from the inside out

Let the Lord's Prayer shape your growth this month:

- **"Our Father in Heaven"** - Growth begins with identity rooted in Him.
- **"Hallowed be Your name"** - Holiness shapes maturity and deepens desire for God.
- **"Your kingdom come"** - God cultivates purpose as He expands your spiritual capacity.
- **"Your will be done"** - Maturity is formed through obedience and surrender.
- **"Give us this day…"** - Growth happens daily, not instantly - through steady nourishment.
- **"Forgive us…"** - Character is strengthened through humility, repentance, and grace.
- **"Lead us not…"** - Ask God to guard your maturing heart from old patterns and temptations.

- **"Yours is the kingdom…"** - Your growth serves His kingdom, not your platform.

As you begin Month 4, remember this: God develops you in the quiet places long before He displays you in the visible ones. Maturity is slow, steady, and sacred. Trust the process. Let God do the deep work. Who you are becoming matters just as much as what you are doing.

DAY 92 – Growing in Spiritual Maturity

Prayer:
Father, I come asking You to grow me in spiritual maturity. Hallowed be Your name; shape my thoughts, my words, and my actions so they reflect the heart of Christ (Ephesians 4:15). Let Your kingdom come and deepen my roots in Your truth. Let Your will be done as You transform my character through Your Spirit. Give me today my daily bread of wisdom, discipline, and growth. Forgive me for remaining in childish ways of thinking or reacting, and I forgive those who hindered my growth. Lead me not into the temptation of spiritual complacency, but deliver me into maturity and steadfastness (Hebrews 5:13–14). For Thine is the kingdom, and the power, and the glory forever and ever. Amen.

Reflection:
What area of your spiritual life is God maturing right now?

_____

_____

_____

Action:
Write one intentional step you will take toward spiritual growth today.

_____

_____

_____

Scriptures Referenced Today:
Ephesians 4:15 (KJV) - "But speaking the truth in love, may grow up into him in all things, which is the head, even Christ."
Hebrews 5:13–14 (KJV) - "For every one that useth milk is unskillful in the word of righteousness: for he is a babe. But strong meat belongeth to them that are of full age, even those who by reason of use have their senses exercised to discern both good and evil."

DAY 93 – Growing in Wisdom

Prayer:
Father, I come seeking the wisdom that comes from You alone.
Hallowed be Your name; fill my mind with understanding and my heart
with discernment (James 1:5). Let Your kingdom come and lead me to
make choices that honor You. Let Your will be done as You help me
walk wisely, not foolishly, in every area of life. Give me today my daily
bread of insight, clarity, and counsel. Forgive me for leaning on my own
understanding, and I forgive those who advised me poorly. Lead me not
into the temptation of earthly wisdom, but deliver me into wisdom that is
pure, peaceable, gentle, and full of mercy (James 3:17). Yours is the
kingdom, the power, and the glory forever. Amen.

Reflection:
Where do you need God's wisdom most right now?

_____

_____

_____

Action:
Write a decision you need God's wisdom for-and ask Him to guide you.

_____

_____

Scriptures Referenced Today:
James 1:5 (KJV) - "If any of you lack wisdom, let him ask of God, that
giveth to all men liberally, and upbraideth not; and it shall be given him."
James 3:17 (KJV) - "But the wisdom that is from above is first pure, then
peaceable, gentle, and easy to be intreated, full of mercy and good fruits,
without partiality, and without hypocrisy."

DAY 94 – Cultivating Teachability

Prayer:
Father, I come asking for a teachable spirit. Hallowed be Your name; soften my heart to receive correction, truth, and instruction from You (Proverbs 9:9). Let Your kingdom come and shape me into someone who learns eagerly and humbly. Let Your will be done as You train my heart to be responsive, not resistant. Give me today my daily bread of humility and openness. Forgive me for resisting correction, and I forgive those who corrected me in hurtful ways. Lead me not into the temptation of pride, but deliver me into a teachable, receptive spirit (Psalm 25:4–5). All glory be to You, forever and ever. Amen.

Reflection:
Where is God inviting you to be more teachable?

Action:
Write one area where you will intentionally welcome God's instruction.

Scriptures Referenced Today:
Proverbs 9:9 (KJV) - "Give instruction to a wise man, and he will be yet wiser: teach a just man, and he will increase in learning."
Psalm 25:4–5 (KJV) - "Shew me thy ways, O LORD; teach me thy paths. Lead me in thy truth, and teach me: for thou art the God of my salvation; on thee do I wait all the day."

DAY 95 – Growing in Purity of Heart

Prayer:
Father, I come asking You to purify my heart and my motives. Hallowed be Your name; cleanse me of anything that hinders Your presence within me (Psalm 51:10). Let Your kingdom come and refine my desires until they reflect Your holiness. Let Your will be done as You strengthen me to walk in purity of thought, intention, and action. Give me today my daily bread of holiness and integrity. Forgive me for entertaining impure thoughts or motives, and I forgive those who influenced me toward impurity. Lead me not into the temptation of compromise, but deliver me into purity that honors You (Matthew 5:8). For Yours is the kingdom, the power, and the glory. Amen.

Reflection:
What part of your heart or motives needs purification?

_____

_____

_____

Action:
Write one way you will pursue purity of heart today.

_____

_____

_____

Scriptures Referenced Today:
Psalm 51:10 (KJV) - "Create in me a clean heart, O God; and renew a right spirit within me."
Matthew 5:8 (KJV) - "Blessed are the pure in heart: for they shall see God."

DAY 96 – Growing in Love That Looks Like Jesus

Prayer:
Father, I come asking to grow in love that reflects the heart of Jesus.
Hallowed be Your name; teach me to love as You have loved me (John
13:34). Let Your kingdom come and expand my capacity to show grace,
patience, and kindness. Let Your will be done as You shape me into
someone who loves sacrificially, generously, and purely. Give me today
my daily bread of compassion and Christlike affection. Forgive me for
withholding love, and I forgive those who failed to love me well. Lead
me not into the temptation of selfishness, but deliver me into love that
honors and reveals You (1 Corinthians 13:4–7). To You be the glory,
now and forever. Amen.

Reflection:
Where is God calling you to love more like Jesus?

_____

_____

_____

Action:
Write one intentional act of Christlike love you will show today.

_____

_____

Scriptures Referenced Today:
John 13:34 (KJV) - "A new commandment I give unto you, That ye love
one another; as I have loved you, that ye also love one another."
1 Corinthians 13:4–7 (KJV) -
"Charity suffereth long, and is kind; charity envieth not; charity vaunteth
not itself, is not puffed up,
Doth not behave itself unseemly, seeketh not her own, is not easily
provoked, thinketh no evil; Rejoiceth not in iniquity, but rejoiceth in the
truth; Beareth all things, believeth all things, hopeth all things, endureth all
things."

DAY 97 – Growing in Discipline and Consistency

Prayer:
Father, I come asking You to build discipline and spiritual consistency within me. Hallowed be Your name; strengthen my habits, steady my devotion, and anchor my daily walk (1 Corinthians 9:27). Let Your kingdom come and establish rhythms that draw me closer to You. Let Your will be done as You form godly patterns in my thoughts, actions, and priorities. Give me today my daily bread of focus, diligence, and endurance. Forgive me for inconsistency in my walk, and I forgive those who discouraged my spiritual discipline. Lead me not into the temptation of laziness or distraction, but deliver me into steadfast perseverance (Galatians 6:9). For Thine is the kingdom, and the power, and the glory forever and ever. Amen.

Reflection:
What spiritual discipline do you need to strengthen in this season?

_____

_____

Action:
Write one consistent practice you will commit to building today.

_____

_____

Scriptures Referenced Today:
1 Corinthians 9:27 (KJV) - "But I keep under my body, and bring it into subjection: lest that by any means, when I have preached to others, I myself should be a castaway."
Galatians 6:9 (KJV) - "And let us not be weary in well doing: for in due season we shall reap, if we faint not."

DAY 98 – Growing in Patience and Spiritual Endurance

Prayer:
Father, I come asking for patience as You mature my heart and refine my character. Hallowed be Your name; teach me to wait with grace, strength, and trust (James 1:4). Let Your kingdom come and use every trial to deepen my endurance. Let Your will be done as I grow into someone who reflects Your steadfastness. Give me today my daily bread of patience and long-suffering. Forgive me for growing frustrated in the slow work of growth, and I forgive those who tested my patience. Lead me not into the temptation of irritability or discouragement, but deliver me into spiritual endurance (Romans 5:3–4). Yours is the kingdom, the power, and the glory forever. Amen.

Reflection:
Where is God teaching you patience right now?

_____

_____

_____

Action:
Write one situation where you will consciously practice patience today.

_____

_____

_____

Scriptures Referenced Today:
James 1:4 (KJV) - "But let patience have her perfect work, that ye may be perfect and entire, wanting nothing."
Romans 5:3–4 (KJV) - "And not only so, but we glory in tribulations also: knowing that tribulation worketh patience; And patience, experience; and experience, hope."

DAY 99 – Growing in Humility and Christlike Character

Prayer:
Father, I come seeking a deeper humility that reflects the heart of Christ. Hallowed be Your name; shape my character through gentleness, patience, and lowliness of mind (Philippians 2:3–5). Let Your kingdom come and remove every trace of pride within me. Let Your will be done as You form Christlike humility in my thoughts and actions. Give me today my daily bread of compassion, meekness, and selflessness. Forgive me for prideful attitudes, and I forgive those whose pride wounded me. Lead me not into the temptation of self-importance, but deliver me into the beauty of humility (Colossians 3:12). All glory be to You, forever and ever. Amen.

Reflection:
What area of your life is God using to grow humility in you?

_____

_____

_____

Action:
Write one humble action you will take today to reflect Christ's character.

_____

_____

_____

Scriptures Referenced Today:
Philippians 2:3–5 (KJV) - "Let nothing be done through strife or vainglory; but in lowliness of mind let each esteem other better than themselves. Look not every man on his own things, but every man also on the things of others. Let this mind be in you, which was also in Christ Jesus."
Colossians 3:12 (KJV) - "Put on therefore, as the elect of God, holy and beloved, bowels of mercies, kindness, humbleness of mind, meekness, longsuffering;"

DAY 100 – Growing in Spiritual Discernment

Prayer:
Father, I come asking for spiritual discernment to recognize what is from You and what is not. Hallowed be Your name; sharpen my vision and attune my heart to Your truth (Hebrews 5:14). Let Your kingdom come and increase my sensitivity to the leading of Your Spirit. Let Your will be done as You teach me to distinguish between wisdom and deception. Give me today my daily bread of clarity, perception, and spiritual insight. Forgive me for ignoring Your nudges or missing Your warnings, and I forgive those whose influence confused my judgment. Lead me not into the temptation of spiritual dullness, but deliver me into discernment grounded in Your Word (Proverbs 3:21–23). To You be the glory, now and forever. Amen.

Reflection:
Where do you need God's discernment right now?

_____

_____

_____

Action:
Write one decision or area where you will actively seek God's discernment today.

_____

_____

_____

Scriptures Referenced Today:
Hebrews 5:14 (KJV) - "But strong meat belongeth to them that are of full age, even those who by reason of use have their senses exercised to discern both good and evil."
Proverbs 3:21–23 (KJV) -
"My son, let not them depart from thine eyes: keep sound wisdom and discretion: So shall they be life unto thy soul, and grace to thy neck. Then shalt thou walk in thy way safely, and thy foot shall not stumble."

DAY 101 – Growing in Self-Control

Prayer:
Father, I come asking You to strengthen me in self-control through the power of Your Spirit. Hallowed be Your name; teach me to govern my emotions, thoughts, and actions in a way that honors You (Galatians 5:22–23). Let Your kingdom come and bring alignment between my desires and Your will. Let Your will be done as You form discipline and restraint within me. Give me today my daily bread of patience, clarity, and Holy-Spirit empowerment. Forgive me for moments where I lacked self-control, and I forgive those who provoked or pressured me. Lead me not into the temptation of reacting impulsively, but deliver me into calm, steady obedience (Proverbs 25:28). For Thine is the kingdom, and the power, and the glory forever and ever. Amen.

Reflection:
Where do you need God to strengthen your self-control today?

_____

_____

_____

Action:
Write one area where you will practice intentional self-control today.

_____

_____

Scriptures Referenced Today:
Galatians 5:22–23 (KJV) - "But the fruit of the Spirit is love, joy, peace, longsuffering, gentleness, goodness, faith, Meekness, temperance: against such there is no law."
Proverbs 25:28 (KJV) - "He that hath no rule over his own spirit is like a city that is broken down, and without walls."

DAY 102 – Growing in the Fear of the Lord

Prayer:
Father, I come asking You to grow in me a holy fear and reverence for Your name. Hallowed be Your name; teach me to honor You above all else (Proverbs 9:10). Let Your kingdom come and deepen my awe of Your greatness. Let Your will be done as You align my heart with Your holiness and Your truth. Give me today my daily bread of humility, reverence, and understanding. Forgive me for treating holy things lightly, and I forgive those who influenced irreverence in my life. Lead me not into the temptation of casual faith, but deliver me into awe-filled worship (Psalm 111:10). Yours is the kingdom, the power, and the glory forever. Amen.

Reflection:
Where do you need to grow in reverence for God?

_____

_____

_____

Action:
Write one way you will honor God with deeper reverence today.

_____

_____

_____

Scriptures Referenced Today:
Proverbs 9:10 (KJV) - "The fear of the LORD is the beginning of wisdom: and the knowledge of the holy is understanding."
Psalm 111:10 (KJV) - "The fear of the LORD is the beginning of wisdom: a good understanding have all they that do his commandments: his praise endureth for ever."

DAY 103 – Growing in the Word of God

Prayer:
Father, I come asking You to deepen my love for Your Word. Hallowed be Your name; open my eyes to see wondrous things from Your law (Psalm 119:18). Let Your kingdom come and shape my mind through Scripture. Let Your will be done as You root Your truth deeply within me. Give me today my daily bread of revelation, understanding, and delight in Your Word. Forgive me for neglecting Scripture, and I forgive those who distracted me from it. Lead me not into the temptation of spiritual neglect, but deliver me into disciplined, joyful study (Psalm 119:105). All glory be to You, forever and ever. Amen.

Reflection:
What part of Scripture is God drawing you toward right now?

_____

_____

Action:
Write one passage you will meditate on today.

_____

_____

Scriptures Referenced Today:
Psalm 119:18 (KJV) - "Open thou mine eyes, that I may behold wondrous things out of thy law."
Psalm 119:105 (KJV) - "Thy word is a lamp unto my feet, and a light unto my path."

DAY 104 – Growing in Servanthood

Prayer:
Father, I come asking You to grow a servant's heart within me. Hallowed be Your name; teach me to follow the example of Jesus, who served with humility and love (Mark 10:45). Let Your kingdom come and shape me into someone who serves willingly and joyfully. Let Your will be done as You direct my hands, my time, and my heart toward others. Give me today my daily bread of compassion and humility. Forgive me for seeking to be served, and I forgive those who took advantage of my service. Lead me not into the temptation of selfishness, but deliver me into Christlike servanthood (Philippians 2:3–4). For Yours alone is the kingdom, the power, and the glory. Amen.

Reflection:
Where is God calling you to serve others with humility?

_____

_____

_____

Action:
Write one act of service you will practice today.

_____

_____

_____

Scriptures Referenced Today:
Mark 10:45 (KJV) - "For even the Son of man came not to be ministered unto, but to minister, and to give his life a ransom for many."
Philippians 2:3–4 (KJV) - "Let nothing be done through strife or vainglory; but in lowliness of mind let each esteem other better than themselves.
Look not every man on his own things, but every man also on the things of others."

DAY 105 – Growing in the Fruit of the Spirit

Prayer:
Father, I come asking for growth in the fruit of the Spirit in every area of my life. Hallowed be Your name; produce in me love, joy, peace, longsuffering, gentleness, goodness, faith, meekness, and temperance (Galatians 5:22–23). Let Your kingdom come and let these qualities overflow from my heart into my actions. Let Your will be done as You conform me more fully to the likeness of Christ. Give me today my daily bread of spiritual fruitfulness. Forgive me for moments that reflected the flesh instead of the Spirit, and I forgive those whose actions made growth difficult. Lead me not into the temptation of the old nature, but deliver me into the fullness of life in the Spirit (John 15:5). To You be the glory, now and forever. Amen.

Reflection:
Which fruit of the Spirit do you need God to grow in you right now?

_____

_____

Action:
Write one way you will intentionally walk in the Spirit today.

_____

_____

Scriptures Referenced Today:
Galatians 5:22–23 (KJV) - "But the fruit of the Spirit is love, joy, peace, longsuffering, gentleness, goodness, faith, Meekness, temperance: against such there is no law."
John 15:5 (KJV) - "I am the vine, ye are the branches: He that abideth in me, and I in him, the same bringeth forth much fruit: for without me ye can do nothing."

DAY 106 – Growing in Godly Character

Prayer:
Father, I come asking You to grow godly character within me. Hallowed be Your name; form in me the qualities that reflect Jesus in every area of life (Romans 5:4). Let Your kingdom come and shape me through both blessings and trials. Let Your will be done as You refine my motives, strengthen my integrity, and establish Your character in me. Give me today my daily bread of perseverance, depth, and inner transformation. Forgive me for valuing appearance over character, and I forgive those who misjudged or misunderstood my heart. Lead me not into the temptation of superficial living, but deliver me into character that honors You (Galatians 5:22–23). For Thine is the kingdom, and the power, and the glory forever and ever. Amen.

Reflection:
Which part of your character is God strengthening in this season?

_____

_____

_____

Action:
Write one intentional choice you will make today that reflects godly character.

_____

_____

_____

Scriptures Referenced Today:
Romans 5:4 (KJV) - "And patience, experience; and experience, hope."
Galatians 5:22–23 (KJV) - "But the fruit of the Spirit is love, joy, peace, longsuffering, gentleness, goodness, faith, Meekness, temperance: against such there is no law."

DAY 107 – Growing in Perseverance

Prayer:
Father, I come asking You to strengthen my perseverance. Hallowed be
Your name; teach me to endure faithfully through trials and growth
(James 1:12). Let Your kingdom come and fortify my spirit so I do not
grow weary. Let Your will be done as You build resilience and
steadfastness in my soul. Give me today my daily bread of endurance and
hope. Forgive me for giving up too easily at times, and I forgive those
who discouraged my persistence. Lead me not into the temptation of
quitting, but deliver me into perseverance that honors You (Romans
12:12). Yours is the kingdom, the power, and the glory forever. Amen.

Reflection:
Where do you need to persevere instead of giving up?

_____

_____

_____

Action:
Write one step that demonstrates perseverance in something God has
called you to.

_____

_____

_____

Scriptures Referenced Today:
James 1:12 (KJV) - "Blessed is the man that endureth temptation: for
when he is tried, he shall receive the crown of life, which the Lord hath
promised to them that love him."
Romans 12:12 (KJV) - "Rejoicing in hope; patient in tribulation;
continuing instant in prayer."

DAY 108 – Growing in Gratitude

Prayer:
Father, I come asking You to grow gratitude within me, no matter the circumstance. Hallowed be Your name; teach me to give thanks in all things as an act of faith and maturity (1 Thessalonians 5:18). Let Your kingdom come and renew my heart with joy and appreciation. Let Your will be done as You free me from complaining, comparison, and discontentment. Give me today my daily bread of thanksgiving and praise. Forgive me for complaining or focusing on what I lack, and I forgive those who fostered negativity around me. Lead me not into the temptation of discontentment, but deliver me into grateful worship (Psalm 103:2). All glory be to You, forever and ever. Amen.

Reflection:
What blessing or provision are you thanking God for today?

_____

_____

_____

Action:
Write one thing you will intentionally give thanks for today.

_____

_____

_____

Scriptures Referenced Today:
1 Thessalonians 5:18 (KJV) - "In every thing give thanks: for this is the will of God in Christ Jesus concerning you."
Psalm 103:2 (KJV) - "Bless the LORD, O my soul, and forget not all his benefits."

DAY 109 – Growing in Holiness

Prayer:
Father, I come asking You to grow holiness within me-to set me apart for Your purposes. Hallowed be Your name; purify my thoughts, refine my motives, and cleanse my heart (1 Peter 1:15–16). Let Your kingdom come and make me more like Jesus in every area of life. Let Your will be done as You shape me into someone who reflects Your character. Give me today my daily bread of purity, obedience, and reverence. Forgive me for compromise, and I forgive those who influenced me toward sin. Lead me not into the temptation of impurity, but deliver me into holiness fueled by love for You (Psalm 119:9). For Yours alone is the kingdom, the power, and the glory. Amen.

Reflection:
What area of your life is God calling you to deeper holiness?

_____

_____

_____

Action:
Write one practical step you will take toward holiness today.

_____

_____

_____

Scriptures Referenced Today:
1 Peter 1:15–16 (KJV) - "But as he which hath called you is holy, so be ye holy in all manner of conversation; Because it is written, Be ye holy; for I am holy."
Psalm 119:9 (KJV) - "Wherewithal shall a young man cleanse his way? by taking heed thereto according to thy word."

DAY 110 – Growing in Fellowship With God

Prayer:
Father, I come seeking deeper fellowship with You. Hallowed be Your name; draw my heart into consistent communion with Your presence (Psalm 16:11). Let Your kingdom come and strengthen my desire to walk closely with You. Let Your will be done as You teach me to abide in You daily. Give me today my daily bread of closeness, fellowship, and intimacy with Your Spirit. Forgive me for drifting or neglecting communion with You, and I forgive those who distracted me from Your presence. Lead me not into the temptation of spiritual distance, but deliver me into deep and joyful fellowship with You (James 4:8). To You be the glory, now and forever. Amen.

Reflection:
How is God inviting you into deeper fellowship with Him today?

_____

_____

_____

Action:
Write one intentional way you will draw near to God today.

_____

_____

_____

Scriptures Referenced Today:
Psalm 16:11 (KJV) - "Thou wilt show me the path of life: in thy presence is fulness of joy; at thy right hand there are pleasures for evermore."
James 4:8 (KJV) - "Draw nigh to God, and he will draw nigh to you. Cleanse your hands, ye sinners; and purify your hearts, ye double minded."

DAY 111 – Growing in Integrity

Prayer:
Father, I come asking You to grow integrity within me-integrity in my motives, my words, and my actions. Hallowed be Your name; teach me to walk uprightly before You at all times (Proverbs 10:9). Let Your kingdom come and strengthen my character in both public and private moments. Let Your will be done as You align my life with truth and honesty. Give me today my daily bread of purity, honesty, and consistency. Forgive me for compromises in character, and I forgive those who damaged my trust. Lead me not into the temptation of deceit or shortcuts, but deliver me into integrity that honors You (Psalm 25:21). For Thine is the kingdom, and the power, and the glory forever and ever. Amen.

Reflection:
What area of your life is God inviting you to strengthen in integrity?

_____

_____

Action:
Write one choice you will make today that reflects integrity.

_____

_____

Scriptures Referenced Today:
Proverbs 10:9 (KJV) - "He that walketh uprightly walketh surely: but he that perverteth his ways shall be known."
Psalm 25:21 (KJV) - "Let integrity and uprightness preserve me; for I wait on thee."

DAY 112 – Growing in Spiritual Boldness

Prayer:

Father, I come asking You to grow boldness within me-boldness to live out my faith without shrinking back. Hallowed be Your name; fill me with the courage that comes from Your Spirit (Acts 4:31). Let Your kingdom come and remove timidity from my heart. Let Your will be done as You strengthen my witness and my confidence in You. Give me today my daily bread of courage, conviction, and holy confidence. Forgive me for moments when I stayed silent or hid my faith, and I forgive those who pressured me to do so. Lead me not into the temptation of fear, but deliver me into boldness that honors Christ (2 Timothy 1:7–8). Yours is the kingdom, the power, and the glory forever. Amen.

Reflection:

Where is God calling you to walk in greater boldness today?

_____

_____

_____

Action:

Write one way you will show spiritual courage today.

_____

_____

Scriptures Referenced Today:

Acts 4:31 (KJV) - "And when they had prayed, the place was shaken where they were assembled together; and they were all filled with the Holy Ghost, and they spake the word of God with boldness."

2 Timothy 1:7–8 (KJV) - "For God hath not given us the spirit of fear; but of power, and of love, and of a sound mind. Be not thou therefore ashamed of the testimony of our Lord, nor of me his prisoner: but be thou partaker of the afflictions of the gospel according to the power of God;"

DAY 113 – Growing in Spiritual Hunger

Prayer:
Father, I come asking You to deepen my hunger for You and for righteousness. Hallowed be Your name; stir within me a longing for Your presence above all else (Psalm 42:1–2). Let Your kingdom come and awaken spiritual appetite where complacency once lived. Let Your will be done as You draw me into deeper pursuit of Your heart. Give me today my daily bread of passion, desire, and renewed fire. Forgive me for letting distractions dull my desire for You, and I forgive those who weakened my zeal. Lead me not into the temptation of spiritual apathy, but deliver me into hunger that pursues You wholeheartedly (Matthew 5:6). All glory be to You, forever and ever. Amen.

Reflection:
Where is God increasing your hunger for Him?

_____

_____

_____

Action:
Write one way you will intentionally seek God today.

_____

_____

_____

Scriptures Referenced Today:
Psalm 42:1–2 (KJV) - "As the hart panteth after the water brooks, so panteth my soul after thee, O God.
My soul thirsteth for God, for the living God: when shall I come and appear before God?"
Matthew 5:6 (KJV) - "Blessed are they which do hunger and thirst after righteousness: for they shall be filled."

DAY 114 – Growing in Peace

Prayer:
Father, I come asking You to grow peace within me-peace that remains steady regardless of circumstances. Hallowed be Your name; guard my heart and mind with Your perfect peace (Isaiah 26:3). Let Your kingdom come and calm every anxious thought. Let Your will be done as You teach me to rest in Your sovereignty. Give me today my daily bread of calmness, trust, and emotional stillness. Forgive me for letting anxiety rule my thoughts, and I forgive those who added to my stress. Lead me not into the temptation of worry, but deliver me into peace that comes from You alone (John 14:27). For Yours alone is the kingdom, the power, and the glory. Amen.

Reflection:
Where do you need God's peace to settle your heart today?

_____

_____

_____

Action:
Write one anxious thought you are surrendering to God's peace today.

_____

_____

_____

Scriptures Referenced Today:
Isaiah 26:3 (KJV) - "Thou wilt keep him in perfect peace, whose mind is stayed on thee: because he trusteth in thee."
John 14:27 (KJV) - "Peace I leave with you, my peace I give unto you: not as the world giveth, give I unto you. Let not your heart be troubled, neither let it be afraid."

DAY 115 – Growing in Joy

Prayer:
Father, I come asking You to grow joy within me-a joy rooted in Your presence, not my circumstances. Hallowed be Your name; restore to me the joy of Your salvation (Psalm 51:12). Let Your kingdom come and fill me with gladness, strength, and renewed delight in You. Let Your will be done as You teach me to rejoice in all seasons. Give me today my daily bread of joy that strengthens and sustains me. Forgive me for letting heaviness overshadow my joy, and I forgive those who drained or discouraged me. Lead me not into the temptation of sadness or despair, but deliver me into joy overflowing through the Holy Spirit (Romans 15:13). To You be the glory, now and forever. Amen.

Reflection:
What is God restoring joy to in your life right now?

_____

_____

_____

Action:
Write one practice or thought today that will help you walk in joy.

_____

_____

_____

Scriptures Referenced Today:
Psalm 51:12 (KJV) - "Restore unto me the joy of thy salvation; and uphold me with thy free spirit."
Romans 15:13 (KJV) - "Now the God of hope fill you with all joy and peace in believing, that ye may abound in hope, through the power of the Holy Ghost."

DAY 116 – Growing in Faithfulness

Prayer:
Father, I come asking You to grow faithfulness within me-faithfulness in the small things, in the unseen things, and in everything You've entrusted to me. Hallowed be Your name; make me steadfast and dependable in all I do (Proverbs 20:6). Let Your kingdom come and shape my heart to be committed and loyal. Let Your will be done as You develop consistency and reliability in my character. Give me today my daily bread of endurance, devotion, and steady obedience. Forgive me for inconsistency or half-heartedness, and I forgive those who were unfaithful toward me. Lead me not into the temptation of complacency, but deliver me into the beauty of a faithful spirit (Luke 16:10). For Thine is the kingdom, and the power, and the glory forever and ever. Amen.

Reflection:
Where is God calling you to grow in faithfulness today?

_____

_____

_____

Action:
Write one faithful action you will take today, even if it seems small.

_____

_____

_____

Scriptures Referenced Today:
Proverbs 20:6 (KJV) - "Most men will proclaim every one his own goodness: but a faithful man who can find?"
Luke 16:10 (KJV) - "He that is faithful in that which is least is faithful also in much: and he that is unjust in the least is unjust also in much."

DAY 117 – Growing in Spiritual Strength

Prayer:
Father, I come asking You to strengthen me spiritually in my inner man. Hallowed be Your name; renew me with Your power and fortify the deepest parts of my heart (Ephesians 3:16). Let Your kingdom come and restore strength where I feel weak. Let Your will be done as You empower me to endure, to stand, and to overcome. Give me today my daily bread of spiritual might, resilience, and confidence. Forgive me for trying to be strong on my own, and I forgive those who criticized my weakness. Lead me not into the temptation of self-reliance, but deliver me into the strength that comes through Your Spirit (Isaiah 40:29). Yours is the kingdom, the power, and the glory forever. Amen.

Reflection:
Where do you need spiritual strength today?

_____

_____

_____

Action:
Write one way you will rely on God's strength instead of your own.

_____

_____

_____

Scriptures Referenced Today:
Ephesians 3:16 (KJV) - "That he would grant you, according to the riches of his glory, to be strengthened with might by his Spirit in the inner man."
Isaiah 40:29 (KJV) - "He giveth power to the faint; and to them that have no might he increaseth strength."

DAY 118 – Growing in Alignment With God's Will

Prayer:
Father, I come asking You to align my desires and decisions with Your
will. Hallowed be Your name; make Your will clearer than my emotions
or circumstances (Psalm 143:10). Let Your kingdom come and bring
clarity where I've been confused or conflicted. Let Your will be done as
You guide my choices and shape my direction. Give me today my daily
bread of insight, surrender, and obedience. Forgive me for pushing my
own agenda, and I forgive those who pressured me away from Your will.
Lead me not into the temptation of self-willed decisions, but deliver me
into joyful alignment with Your plans (Romans 12:2). All glory be to You,
forever and ever. Amen.

Reflection:
Where is God inviting you to align more fully with His will?

Action:
Write one decision or area you are yielding to God's will today.

Scriptures Referenced Today:
Psalm 143:10 (KJV) - "Teach me to do thy will; for thou art my God: thy
spirit is good; lead me into the land of uprightness."
Romans 12:2 (KJV) - "And be not conformed to this world: but be ye
transformed by the renewing of your mind, that ye may prove what is that
good, and acceptable, and perfect, will of God."

DAY 119 – Growing in Spiritual Focus

Prayer:
Father, I come asking You to grow my focus and sharpen my spiritual attention. Hallowed be Your name; teach me to fix my eyes on things above, not on earthly distractions (Colossians 3:2). Let Your kingdom come and silence the noise that pulls me away from You. Let Your will be done as You center my heart on what truly matters. Give me today my daily bread of clarity, concentration, and steadiness. Forgive me for wandering attention or double-mindedness, and I forgive those who fed distraction in my life. Lead me not into the temptation of spiritual drift, but deliver me into focused devotion (Hebrews 12:2). For Yours alone is the kingdom, the power, and the glory. Amen.

Reflection:
What has been distracting you spiritually, and how is God calling you back?

_____

_____

_____

Action:
Write one distraction you are choosing to lay down today.

_____

_____

Scriptures Referenced Today:
Colossians 3:2 (KJV) - "Set your affection on things above, not on things on the earth."
Hebrews 12:2 (KJV) - "Looking unto Jesus the author and finisher of our faith; who for the joy that was set before him endured the cross, despising the shame, and is set down at the right hand of the throne of God."

DAY 120 – Growing in Transformation

Prayer:
Father, I come asking You to transform me more fully into the likeness of Christ. Hallowed be Your name; renew my mind, purify my heart, and reshape my life through Your Spirit (2 Corinthians 3:18). Let Your kingdom come and continue the lifelong work of sanctification within me. Let Your will be done as You change me from the inside out. Give me today my daily bread of revelation, renewal, and surrendered transformation. Forgive me for resisting change, and I forgive those who tried to mold me into something other than who You called me to be. Lead me not into the temptation of settling for who I was, but deliver me into who You are making me to become (Philippians 1:6). To You be the glory, now and forever. Amen.

Reflection:
What is God transforming in you right now?

_____

_____

_____

Action:
Write one way you will yield to God's transforming work today.

_____

_____

_____

Scriptures Referenced Today:
2 Corinthians 3:18 (KJV) - "But we all, with open face beholding as in a glass the glory of the Lord, are changed into the same image from glory to glory, even as by the Spirit of the Lord."
Philippians 1:6 (KJV) - "Being confident of this very thing, that he which hath begun a good work in you will perform it until the day of Jesus Christ."

MONTH 4 CLOSING REFLECTION: SPIRITUAL GROWTH & MATURITY

As Month 4 draws to a close, pause and notice the quiet but steady work God has been doing within you. This month was not about outward victories or dramatic breakthroughs-it was about the hidden work of the heart. The deeper shaping. The forming of spiritual muscle. The maturing that only comes through time, surrender, discipline, and grace. Spiritual growth doesn't always feel exciting. But it is always sacred. This month invited you to:

- Strengthen your character
- Pursue holiness
- Build discipline and consistency
- Grow in patience and perseverance
- Develop humility and Christlike love
- Learn to discern God's voice
- Deepen your hunger for God
- Walk in joy, peace, integrity, and truth
- Align your life with God's will
- Allow God to transform you from the inside out

Consider what God has done in these past days:

- Where did He stretch you?
- What habits began forming or strengthening?
- What parts of your heart became more teachable?
- Where did you begin to see change-not just in behavior, but in character?
- How has your relationship with God deepened through discipline, surrender, and trust?

Month 4 reminds us of a great truth: **Growth is not accidental. It is intentional, nurtured, and formed by the Spirit over time.**

As you leave this month behind:

- Carry forward the disciplines God awakened.
- Hold onto the humility, wisdom, and perseverance He has cultivated.
- Remember that maturity is a lifelong journey-and God is faithful to complete the work He began.

Let this truth settle in your soul as you prepare for Month 5:

You are stronger than you were. You are more rooted than you realized.

You are being shaped into the image of Christ-day by day, prayer by prayer, surrender by surrender.

Month 4 ends with a quiet confidence:

God is not finished with you. He is growing you, stretching you, refining you-

and He will complete every good work He started.

MONTH 5 THEME: SPIRITUAL WARFARE & GOD'S PROTECTION

Month 5 leads you into one of the most misunderstood but essential parts of the Christian life: spiritual warfare. This month teaches you that the battles you face are not just physical, emotional, or circumstantial-they are deeply spiritual. You have an enemy who wants to intimidate, confuse, exhaust, and discourage you. But you also have a Savior who has already won, already conquered, and already established victory on your behalf. Spiritual warfare is not about living in fear-it is about learning to stand firm in the authority Jesus purchased for you.

This month helps you see the unseen.

It teaches you where the real battle is happening and how to recognize when you're being spiritually opposed-not to scare you, but to prepare you. The enemy works through subtle whispers, old wounds, lies, temptations, and pressure points. But God equips you with clarity, truth, protection, and strength. He does not send you into battle unarmed; He covers you, leads you, shields you, and strengthens you.

Spiritual warfare is not about shouting at darkness; it's about refusing to give darkness a place in your heart. It is learning to confront lies with truth, replace fear with faith, shut doors the enemy wants open, and walk in the power of the Spirit. This month teaches you that every spiritual attack is an opportunity to grow deeper roots, develop spiritual maturity, and experience the protection of God in real, tangible ways.

This month will help you:

• Recognize spiritual attacks when they show up in thoughts, emotions, or circumstances

• Discern the enemy's strategies-confusion, fear, isolation, temptation, distraction

• Understand your authority in Christ and how to use it

• Identify spiritual "open doors" that need to be closed

• Replace lies with God's truth in every area of life

• Pray with confidence, clarity, and boldness

• Learn how to "stand firm" instead of being shaken

• Trust God's protection in battles you can't see

• Break patterns the enemy tries to use against you

• Rest in the victory Jesus already won on your behalf

Spiritual warfare is not about being strong on your own-it's about staying surrendered to the One who is strong for you. God's protection is not fragile. His authority is not partial. His covering is not temporary. When you stand in His strength, you are fighting from victory, not for victory.

Let the Lord's Prayer be your spiritual battle plan this month:

• **"Our Father in Heaven"** - Warfare begins with belonging. You fight from identity, not insecurity.

• **"Hallowed be Your name"** - Worship breaks intimidation and exposes lies.

• **"Your kingdom come"** - Declare God's authority over every area where darkness tries to reign.

• **"Your will be done"** - Surrender aligns you with God's strategy, not your own strength.

• **"Give us this day our daily bread"** - Receive fresh strength for each battle you face.

• **"Forgive us…"** - Unforgiveness is a spiritual entry point-close it quickly.

• **"Lead us not into temptation"** - Ask God for discernment, purity, and spiritual awareness.

• **"Yours is the kingdom…"** - Remind your soul that God reigns, God wins, and God protects.

This month is an invitation to stand-not in anxiety, but in authority.

To fight-not with fear, but with faith.

To resist-not in your own power, but in the strength of the Spirit.

To walk-not intimidated, but covered.

And to remember daily that the One who lives in you is greater than anything that comes against you.

As you step into Month 5, let this truth settle deeply in your spirit:

The enemy may attack, but he cannot win.

God fights for you, covers you, strengthens you, and surrounds you with victory.

DAY 121 – Standing Firm in God's Armor

Prayer:
Father, I come putting on the full armor of God. Hallowed be Your name; strengthen me to stand against every scheme of the enemy (Ephesians 6:11). Let Your kingdom come and clothe me with Your truth, righteousness, peace, faith, salvation, and the sword of the Spirit. Let Your will be done as You teach me to fight spiritual battles with spiritual weapons. Give me today my daily bread of courage, clarity, and protection. Forgive me for trying to fight in my own strength, and I forgive those who led me into unhealthy battles. Lead me not into the temptation of spiritual passivity, but deliver me into vigilant, Spirit-filled readiness (2 Corinthians 10:4). For Thine is the kingdom, and the power, and the glory forever and ever. Amen.

Reflection:
Where do you need to stand firm today instead of shrinking back?

_____

_____

_____

Action:
Write one piece of God's armor you will consciously "put on" today.

_____

_____

_____

Scriptures Referenced Today:
Ephesians 6:11 (KJV) - "Put on the whole armour of God, that ye may be able to stand against the wiles of the devil."
2 Corinthians 10:4 (KJV) - "For the weapons of our warfare are not carnal, but mighty through God to the pulling down of strong holds."

DAY 122 – God's Protection in Spiritual Battle

Prayer:
Father, I come declaring that You are my shield and my defender.
Hallowed be Your name; cover me with Your protection and surround
me with Your strength (Psalm 3:3). Let Your kingdom come and push
back every force of darkness seeking to harm, distract, or deceive me. Let
Your will be done as You teach me to trust Your covering in every
circumstance. Give me today my daily bread of peace, confidence, and
divine protection. Forgive me for fearing the enemy more than honoring
Your power, and I forgive those who opened doors to spiritual harm.
Lead me not into the temptation of fear, but deliver me into the safety of
Your presence (Psalm 91:4). Yours is the kingdom, the power, and the
glory forever. Amen.

Reflection:
Where do you need God's protection most today?

_____

_____

_____

Action:
Write a declaration of God's protection over yourself or your household.

_____

_____

_____

Scriptures Referenced Today:
Psalm 3:3 (KJV) - "But thou, O LORD, art a shield for me; my glory,
and the lifter up of mine head."
Psalm 91:4 (KJV) - "He shall cover thee with his feathers, and under his
wings shalt thou trust: his truth shall be thy shield and buckler."

DAY 123 – Resisting the Enemy

Prayer:
Father, I come submitting myself to You and resisting the enemy's influence. Hallowed be Your name; strengthen me to stand in purity, truth, and obedience (James 4:7). Let Your kingdom come and expose every lie or temptation aimed at weakening my walk. Let Your will be done as You empower me to resist every attack through the power of the Holy Spirit. Give me today my daily bread of discernment, endurance, and spiritual clarity. Forgive me for agreeing with lies or temptations, and I forgive those who led me toward sin. Lead me not into the temptation of spiritual compromise, but deliver me into victory and steadfastness (1 Peter 5:8–9). All glory be to You, forever and ever. Amen.

Reflection:
What lie, temptation, or attack do you need to actively resist today?

_____

_____

_____

Action:
Write one Scripture truth you will use to resist the enemy.

_____

_____

_____

Scriptures Referenced Today:
James 4:7 (KJV) - "Submit yourselves therefore to God. Resist the devil, and he will flee from you."
1 Peter 5:8–9 (KJV) - "Be sober, be vigilant; because your adversary the devil, as a roaring lion, walketh about, seeking whom he may devour: Whom resist stedfast in the faith, knowing that the same afflictions are accomplished in your brethren that are in the world."

DAY 124 – Strength in Times of Spiritual Attack

Prayer:
Father, I come seeking Your strength when I am weary from spiritual battle. Hallowed be Your name; uphold me when I feel pressed, attacked, or overwhelmed (Isaiah 59:19). Let Your kingdom come and raise a standard against every force that comes against me. Let Your will be done as You guard my mind, steady my heart, and strengthen my spirit. Give me today my daily bread of resilience, courage, and divine help. Forgive me for fear or discouragement in battle, and I forgive those who contributed to my weakness. Lead me not into the temptation of giving up, but deliver me into supernatural endurance (Psalm 18:32). For Thine is the kingdom, and the power, and the glory forever and ever. Amen.

Reflection:
Where do you feel spiritually under attack today?

_____

_____

_____

Action:
Write one way you will lean into God's strength instead of your own.

_____

_____

_____

Scriptures Referenced Today:
Isaiah 59:19 (KJV) - "When the enemy shall come in like a flood, the Spirit of the LORD shall lift up a standard against him."
Psalm 18:32 (KJV) - "It is God that girdeth me with strength, and maketh my way perfect."

DAY 125 – Victory Through the Power of Christ

Prayer:
Father, I come declaring victory through the finished work of Jesus Christ. Hallowed be Your name; remind me that the battle is already won through His blood and authority (Revelation 12:11). Let Your kingdom come and fill me with confidence in Christ's power over all darkness. Let Your will be done as You teach me to walk in victory, not fear. Give me today my daily bread of courage, certainty, and spiritual triumph. Forgive me for living as though I am defeated, and I forgive those who spoke defeat over me. Lead me not into the temptation of despair, but deliver me into the victory purchased by Christ (Romans 8:37). To You be the glory, now and forever. Amen.

Reflection:
Where do you need to walk in Christ's victory instead of defeat?

_____

_____

_____

Action:
Write a victory declaration rooted in Scripture for today.

_____

_____

_____

Scriptures Referenced Today:
Revelation 12:11 (KJV) - "And they overcame him by the blood of the Lamb, and by the word of their testimony; and they loved not their lives unto the death."
Romans 8:37 (KJV) - "Nay, in all these things we are more than conquerors through him that loved us."

DAY 126 – Guarding Your Mind in Christ

Prayer:
Father, I come asking You to guard my mind with Your peace and Your truth. Hallowed be Your name; protect my thoughts from fear, deception, and confusion (Philippians 4:7). Let Your kingdom come and fortify my mind with Scripture and discernment. Let Your will be done as You help me take every thought captive to Christ. Give me today my daily bread of clarity, focus, and mental strength. Forgive me for entertaining thoughts that oppose Your truth, and I forgive those who spoke lies into my mind. Lead me not into the temptation of mental anxiety or spiraling thoughts, but deliver me into a sound mind anchored in You (2 Corinthians 10:5). For Thine is the kingdom, and the power, and the glory forever and ever. Amen.

Reflection:
What thought or mental battle do you need to surrender to God today?

Action:
Write one Scripture that will guard your mind today.

Scriptures Referenced Today:
Philippians 4:7 (KJV) - "And the peace of God, which passeth all understanding, shall keep your hearts and minds through Christ Jesus."
2 Corinthians 10:5 (KJV) - "Casting down imaginations, and every high thing that exalteth itself against the knowledge of God, and bringing into captivity every thought to the obedience of Christ."

DAY 127 – Strength to Stand During Temptation

Prayer:
Father, I come asking for strength to stand firm when temptation comes. Hallowed be Your name; remind me that You always provide a way of escape (1 Corinthians 10:13). Let Your kingdom come and break the power of anything that tries to pull me away from You. Let Your will be done as You strengthen my conviction and purify my desires. Give me today my daily bread of discipline, vigilance, and purity. Forgive me for moments when I gave in, and I forgive those who influenced temptation in my life. Lead me not into the temptation of sinful desires, but deliver me into holiness and victory (James 4:7). Yours is the kingdom, the power, and the glory forever. Amen.

Reflection:
What temptation do you need God's strength to resist today?

_____

_____

_____

Action:
Write one step you will take to avoid or withstand this temptation.

_____

_____

_____

Scriptures Referenced Today:
1 Corinthians 10:13 (KJV) - "There hath no temptation taken you but such as is common to man: but God is faithful, who will not suffer you to be tempted above that ye are able; but will with the temptation also make a way to escape, that ye may be able to bear it."
James 4:7 (KJV) - "Submit yourselves therefore to God. Resist the devil, and he will flee from you."

DAY 128 – God's Deliverance From Every Attack

Prayer:
Father, I come trusting in Your power to deliver me from every spiritual attack. Hallowed be Your name; You are my refuge, fortress, and strong deliverer (Psalm 91:2). Let Your kingdom come and break the grip of every scheme formed against me. Let Your will be done as You rescue me from the traps, lies, and snares of the enemy. Give me today my daily bread of safety, victory, and freedom. Forgive me for allowing fear to intimidate me, and I forgive those who opened doors to attack in my life. Lead me not into the temptation of fear or retreat, but deliver me into confident trust in Your deliverance (Psalm 34:19). For Thine is the kingdom, and the power, and the glory forever and ever. Amen.

Reflection:
Where do you need God's deliverance right now?

_____

_____

_____

Action:
Write one declaration of deliverance you are believing God for.

_____

_____

_____

Scriptures Referenced Today:
Psalm 91:2 (KJV) - "I will say of the LORD, He is my refuge and my fortress: my God; in him will I trust."
Psalm 34:19 (KJV) - "Many are the afflictions of the righteous: but the LORD delivereth him out of them all."

DAY 129 – Victory Over Fear

Prayer:
Father, I come asking for victory over every form of fear-fear of the future, fear of people, fear of failure, fear of attack. Hallowed be Your name; fill me with the boldness that comes from Your perfect love (1 John 4:18). Let Your kingdom come and uproot every fear that has taken hold in my heart. Let Your will be done as You strengthen me to walk in courage and security. Give me today my daily bread of peace, assurance, and steadfast faith. Forgive me for partnering with fear, and I forgive those who instilled fear in me. Lead me not into the temptation of fearful thinking, but deliver me into courage rooted in Your truth (Psalm 27:1). All glory be to You, forever and ever. Amen.

Reflection:
What fear do you need God to break today?

Action:
Write a bold declaration of faith over that fear.

Scriptures Referenced Today:
1 John 4:18 (KJV) - "There is no fear in love; but perfect love casteth out fear: because fear hath torment. He that feareth is not made perfect in love."
Psalm 27:1 (KJV) - "The LORD is my light and my salvation; whom shall I fear? the LORD is the strength of my life; of whom shall I be afraid?"

DAY 130 – Walking in Authority in Christ

Prayer:
Father, I come walking in the authority You have given me through Jesus Christ. Hallowed be Your name; remind me that all power in heaven and earth belongs to Him (Matthew 28:18). Let Your kingdom come and empower me to stand against darkness with boldness and clarity. Let Your will be done as You strengthen my confidence in the authority of Christ within me. Give me today my daily bread of courage, dominion, and spiritual confidence. Forgive me for living beneath the authority You've given, and I forgive those who diminished my spiritual identity. Lead me not into the temptation of timidity, but deliver me into bold authority rooted in Christ (Luke 10:19). To You be the glory, now and forever. Amen.

Reflection:
Where do you need to walk in Christ-given authority today?

_____

_____

_____

Action:
Write one way you will exercise spiritual authority through prayer today.

_____

_____

_____

Scriptures Referenced Today:
Matthew 28:18 (KJV) - "And Jesus came and spake unto them, saying, All power is given unto me in heaven and in earth."
Luke 10:19 (KJV) - "Behold, I give unto you power to tread on serpents and scorpions, and over all the power of the enemy: and nothing shall by any means hurt you."

DAY 131 – Strength to Stand in Trials

Prayer:
Father, I come asking for strength to stand firm when trials feel heavy. Hallowed be Your name; remind me that the testing of my faith produces endurance (James 1:3). Let Your kingdom come and turn every trial into spiritual strengthening. Let Your will be done as You steady my heart when pressure rises. Give me today my daily bread of resilience, courage, and unshakable trust. Forgive me for letting trials overwhelm me, and I forgive those who contributed to my distress. Lead me not into the temptation of discouragement, but deliver me into steadfast faith that endures (1 Peter 1:6–7). For Thine is the kingdom, and the power, and the glory forever and ever. Amen.

Reflection:
What trial are you trusting God to strengthen you through today?

_____

_____

_____

Action:
Write one way you will stand firm in faith during this trial.

_____

_____

_____

Scriptures Referenced Today:
James 1:3 (KJV) - "Knowing this, that the trying of your faith worketh patience."
1 Peter 1:6–7 (KJV) - "Wherein ye greatly rejoice, though now for a season, if need be, ye are in heaviness through manifold temptations: That the trial of your faith, being much more precious than of gold that perisheth, though it be tried with fire, might be found unto praise and honour and glory at the appearing of Jesus Christ."

DAY 132 – God's Presence in the Battle

Prayer:

Father, I come resting in the truth that I do not fight alone. Hallowed be Your name; You go before me, stand beside me, and cover me with Your presence (Deuteronomy 31:8). Let Your kingdom come and fill every battle with the assurance of Your nearness. Let Your will be done as You remind me that You will never leave nor forsake me. Give me today my daily bread of confidence, peace, and courage. Forgive me for acting as though I must fight in my own strength, and I forgive those who abandoned me in my battles. Lead me not into the temptation of fearfulness, but deliver me into boldness through Your presence (Psalm 46:1). Yours is the kingdom, the power, and the glory forever. Amen.

Reflection:

Where do you need to feel God's presence in your battle?

Action:

Write a declaration reminding yourself that God is with you.

Scriptures Referenced Today:

Deuteronomy 31:8 (KJV) - "And the LORD, he it is that doth go before thee; he will be with thee, he will not fail thee, neither forsake thee: fear not, neither be dismayed."

Psalm 46:1 (KJV) - "God is our refuge and strength, a very present help in trouble."

DAY 133 – Overcoming the Enemy Through Prayer

Prayer:
Father, I come stepping into the authority of prayer, believing that You move when I call on Your name. Hallowed be Your name; teach me to war in prayer with persistence and faith (Colossians 4:2). Let Your kingdom come and overthrow every scheme formed against me. Let Your will be done as You train my hands for spiritual battle and my heart for intercession. Give me today my daily bread of boldness, perseverance, and heavenly perspective. Forgive me for neglecting the power of prayer, and I forgive those who discouraged my prayer life. Lead me not into the temptation of prayerlessness, but deliver me into victory through prayer (Ephesians 6:18). All glory be to You, forever and ever. Amen.

Reflection:
What battle do you need to bring before God in prayer today?

_____

_____

_____

Action:
Write one specific prayer you will persist in until breakthrough comes.

_____

_____

_____

Scriptures Referenced Today:
Colossians 4:2 (KJV) - "Continue in prayer, and watch in the same with thanksgiving."
Ephesians 6:18 (KJV) - "Praying always with all prayer and supplication in the Spirit, and watching thereunto with all perseverance and supplication for all saints."

DAY 134 – God's Light in Spiritual Darkness

Prayer:
Father, I come asking for Your light to shine in every place where darkness tries to hide. Hallowed be Your name; expose every lie, every scheme, and every hidden attack (Psalm 27:1). Let Your kingdom come and illuminate every shadow with Your truth. Let Your will be done as You guide my steps and guard my heart. Give me today my daily bread of clarity, revelation, and spiritual sight. Forgive me for tolerating things that opposed Your light, and I forgive those who led me toward darkness. Lead me not into the temptation of confusion or secrecy, but deliver me into the light of Your presence (Ephesians 5:11). For Thine is the kingdom, and the power, and the glory forever and ever. Amen.

Reflection:
Where do you need God's light to expose darkness?

_____

_____

_____

Action:
Write one area where you will intentionally choose light over darkness today.

_____

_____

_____

Scriptures Referenced Today:
Psalm 27:1 (KJV) - "The LORD is my light and my salvation; whom shall I fear? the LORD is the strength of my life; of whom shall I be afraid?"
Ephesians 5:11 (KJV) - "And have no fellowship with the unfruitful works of darkness, but rather reprove them."

DAY 135 – Secure in God's Covering

Prayer:
Father, I come resting securely in Your divine covering. Hallowed be
Your name; thank You for being my refuge, my fortress, and my safe
dwelling place (Psalm 91:1). Let Your kingdom come and surround my
life with Your protection and peace. Let Your will be done as You hide
me under the shadow of Your wings. Give me today my daily bread of
calmness, safety, and strength. Forgive me for running to lesser forms of
security, and I forgive those who made me feel unsafe. Lead me not into
the temptation of fear or self-reliance, but deliver me into complete trust
in Your covering (Psalm 121:3–4). To You be the glory, now and forever.
Amen.

Reflection:
Where do you need to rest in God's protection rather than your own
strength?

Action:
Write a declaration of trust in God's covering for today.

Scriptures Referenced Today:
Psalm 91:1 (KJV) - "He that dwelleth in the secret place of the most
High shall abide under the shadow of the Almighty."
Psalm 121:3–4 (KJV) - "He will not suffer thy foot to be moved: he that
keepeth thee will not slumber.
Behold, he that keepeth Israel shall neither slumber nor sleep."

DAY 136 – Protected by God's Faithfulness

Prayer:
Father, I come resting in the truth that Your faithfulness is my shield.
Hallowed be Your name; cover me with Your unwavering protection
(Psalm 91:4). Let Your kingdom come and surround me with Your
steadfast love. Let Your will be done as You teach me to rely fully on
Your faithfulness in every trial. Give me today my daily bread of courage,
trust, and confidence in Your protection. Forgive me for doubting Your
care, and I forgive those who made me feel abandoned or unsafe. Lead
me not into the temptation of fear or mistrust, but deliver me into steady
faith grounded in Your character (2 Thessalonians 3:3). For Thine is the
kingdom, and the power, and the glory forever and ever. Amen.

Reflection:
Where do you need to trust in God's faithfulness for protection today?

_____

_____

_____

Action:
Write a statement declaring God's faithfulness over your situation.

_____

_____

_____

Scriptures Referenced Today:
Psalm 91:4 (KJV) - "He shall cover thee with his feathers, and under his
wings shalt thou trust: his truth shall be thy shield and buckler."
2 Thessalonians 3:3 (KJV) - "But the Lord is faithful, who shall stablish
you, and keep you from evil."

DAY 137 – Strength Against Spiritual Fatigue

Prayer:
Father, I come asking for renewed strength where I feel spiritually tired or worn down. Hallowed be Your name; fill me again with the power of Your Spirit (Isaiah 40:31). Let Your kingdom come and revive areas of my heart that feel weary. Let Your will be done as You lift every heaviness and restore my courage. Give me today my daily bread of spiritual vitality and renewed strength. Forgive me for trying to push forward in my own power, and I forgive those who drained or discouraged me. Lead me not into the temptation of spiritual burnout, but deliver me into refreshing and renewal through Your Spirit (Psalm 23:3). Yours is the kingdom, the power, and the glory forever. Amen.

Reflection:
Where do you feel spiritually fatigued and in need of renewal?

Action:
Write one way you will rest in God's strength today instead of striving.

Scriptures Referenced Today:
Isaiah 40:31 (KJV) - "But they that wait upon the LORD shall renew their strength; they shall mount up with wings as eagles; they shall run, and not be weary; and they shall walk, and not faint."
Psalm 23:3 (KJV) - "He restoreth my soul: he leadeth me in the paths of righteousness for his name's sake."

DAY 138 – Guarding Your Heart With Diligence

Prayer:
Father, I come asking You to guard my heart from every attack, distraction, and influence that seeks to harm me. Hallowed be Your name; teach me to keep my heart with all diligence (Proverbs 4:23). Let Your kingdom come and purify the motives, desires, and affections within me. Let Your will be done as You strengthen my heart against spiritual interference. Give me today my daily bread of wisdom, vigilance, and purity. Forgive me for letting unguarded places become points of attack, and I forgive those who wounded my heart. Lead me not into the temptation of emotional carelessness, but deliver me into a guarded, steadfast heart (Psalm 51:10). All glory be to You, forever and ever. Amen.

Reflection:
What area of your heart needs guarding or healing today?

_____

_____

_____

Action:
Write one way you will guard your heart with wisdom today.

_____

_____

_____

Scriptures Referenced Today:
Proverbs 4:23 (KJV) - "Keep thy heart with all diligence; for out of it are the issues of life."
Psalm 51:10 (KJV) - "Create in me a clean heart, O God; and renew a right spirit within me."

DAY 139 – Victory Over Spiritual Strongholds

Prayer:
Father, I come asking You to tear down every stronghold-every lie, habit, or pattern-exalting itself against Your truth. Hallowed be Your name; replace every bondage with freedom and clarity (2 Corinthians 10:4). Let Your kingdom come and break every chain that seeks to hold me captive. Let Your will be done as You renew my mind and restore my strength. Give me today my daily bread of breakthrough, freedom, and transformation. Forgive me for agreeing with lies or strongholds, and I forgive those whose words or actions contributed to them. Lead me not into the temptation of resignation, but deliver me into total victory and freedom (John 8:36). For Thine is the kingdom, and the power, and the glory forever. Amen.

Reflection:
What stronghold (lie, habit, fear, or pattern) do you need God to break?

_____

_____

_____

Action:
Write a declaration of truth to replace the stronghold you're confronting.

_____

_____

_____

Scriptures Referenced Today:
2 Corinthians 10:4 (KJV) - "For the weapons of our warfare are not carnal, but mighty through God to the pulling down of strong holds."
John 8:36 (KJV) - "If the Son therefore shall make you free, ye shall be free indeed."

DAY 140 – Resting in God's Victory

Prayer:
Father, I come resting in the truth that victory belongs to You. Hallowed be Your name; remind me that the battle is not mine, but Yours (2 Chronicles 20:15). Let Your kingdom come and strengthen my faith as I stand still and watch You work. Let Your will be done as You calm my spirit and quiet every anxious thought. Give me today my daily bread of rest, assurance, and confidence in Your power. Forgive me for striving in battles that belong to You, and I forgive those who pushed me into unnecessary conflict. Lead me not into the temptation of fighting in my own strength, but deliver me into the rest of Your victory (Exodus 14:14). To You be the glory, now and forever. Amen.

Reflection:
What battle do you need to stop fighting alone and trust God with?

_____

_____

_____

Action:
Write a statement releasing that battle fully into God's hands today.

_____

_____

_____

Scriptures Referenced Today:
2 Chronicles 20:15 (KJV) - "Thus saith the LORD unto you, Be not afraid nor dismayed by reason of this great multitude; for the battle is not yours, but God's."
Exodus 14:14 (KJV) - "The LORD shall fight for you, and ye shall hold your peace."

DAY 141 – Strength to Stand Against Deception

Prayer:
Father, I come asking You to protect me from deception-subtle, spiritual, emotional, or relational. Hallowed be Your name; anchor me in truth so I will not be moved (John 8:32). Let Your kingdom come and expose every lie the enemy has tried to plant in my mind. Let Your will be done as You sharpen my discernment and open my eyes to what is real and what is false. Give me today my daily bread of clarity, wisdom, and spiritual vision. Forgive me for believing lies that were not from You, and I forgive those who deceived or misled me. Lead me not into the temptation of confusion, but deliver me into truth that sets me free (1 John 4:1). For Thine is the kingdom, and the power, and the glory forever and ever. Amen.

Reflection:
What area of your life needs the light of God's truth today?

Action:
Write one truth from Scripture that defeats a lie you have believed.

Scriptures Referenced Today:
John 8:32 (KJV) - "And ye shall know the truth, and the truth shall make you free."
1 John 4:1 (KJV) - "Beloved, believe not every spirit, but try the spirits whether they are of God: because many false prophets are gone out into the world."

DAY 142 – God's Strength When You Feel Weak

Prayer:
Father, I come acknowledging my weakness and leaning on Your strength. Hallowed be Your name; remind me that Your strength is made perfect in weakness (2 Corinthians 12:9). Let Your kingdom come and empower me where I feel unable or exhausted. Let Your will be done as You turn my weakness into a testimony of Your power. Give me today my daily bread of endurance, grace, and inner strength. Forgive me for despising my own weakness, and I forgive those who shamed me for it. Lead me not into the temptation of self-reliance, but deliver me into a life strengthened by Your Spirit (Psalm 28:7). Yours is the kingdom, the power, and the glory forever. Amen.

Reflection:
Where do you feel weak-and how is God strengthening you in that place?

Action:
Write one area where you will rely on God's strength today.

Scriptures Referenced Today:
2 Corinthians 12:9 (KJV) - "And he said unto me, My grace is sufficient for thee: for my strength is made perfect in weakness."
Psalm 28:7 (KJV) - "The LORD is my strength and my shield; my heart trusted in him, and I am helped: therefore my heart greatly rejoiceth; and with my song will I praise him."

DAY 143 – Protected From the Enemy's Snares

Prayer:
Father, I come asking You to protect me from the snares, traps, and hidden strategies of the enemy. Hallowed be Your name; deliver me from every assignment meant to harm, confuse, or mislead me (Psalm 124:7). Let Your kingdom come and break every hidden trap before it springs. Let Your will be done as You guide my steps safely and wisely. Give me today my daily bread of discernment, alertness, and spiritual protection. Forgive me for walking carelessly at times, and I forgive those who laid traps for me. Lead me not into the temptation of spiritual carelessness, but deliver me into the safety of Your path (Psalm 91:3). For Thine is the kingdom, and the power, and the glory forever. Amen.

Reflection:
What "snare" or hidden danger do you need God to reveal or dismantle?

_____

_____

_____

Action:
Write one way you will walk more wisely and alertly today.

_____

_____

_____

Scriptures Referenced Today:
Psalm 124:7 (KJV) - "Our soul is escaped as a bird out of the snare of the fowlers: the snare is broken, and we are escaped."
Psalm 91:3 (KJV) - "Surely he shall deliver thee from the snare of the fowler, and from the noisome pestilence."

DAY 144 – God's Justice in Spiritual Battle

Prayer:
Father, I come trusting in Your justice when the enemy comes against me. Hallowed be Your name; remind me that vengeance belongs to You alone (Romans 12:19). Let Your kingdom come and silence every voice of accusation, oppression, and opposition. Let Your will be done as You fight for me in ways I cannot see. Give me today my daily bread of peace, trust, and confidence in Your righteous judgment. Forgive me for trying to defend myself in my own strength, and I forgive those who wronged me. Lead me not into the temptation of bitterness, but deliver me into the rest of trusting Your justice (Isaiah 54:17). All glory be to You, forever and ever. Amen.

Reflection:
Where do you need to trust God's justice instead of fighting back?

_____

_____

_____

Action:
Write a declaration releasing justice into God's hands.

_____

_____

_____

Scriptures Referenced Today:
Romans 12:19 (KJV) - "Dearly beloved, avenge not yourselves, but rather give place unto wrath: for it is written, Vengeance is mine; I will repay, saith the Lord."
Isaiah 54:17 (KJV) - "No weapon that is formed against thee shall prosper; and every tongue that shall rise against thee in judgment thou shalt condemn. This is the heritage of the servants of the Lord, and their righteousness is of me, saith the Lord."

DAY 145 – Strength to Persevere in Warfare

Prayer:
Father, I come asking for strength to persevere when spiritual warfare lasts longer than I expected. Hallowed be Your name; remind me that those who endure will overcome (Galatians 6:9). Let Your kingdom come and renew my determination to stand, pray, and believe. Let Your will be done as You strengthen my hands for battle and my heart for endurance. Give me today my daily bread of perseverance, hope, and steadfast faith. Forgive me for wanting to quit before breakthrough came, and I forgive those who discouraged my endurance. Lead me not into the temptation of giving up, but deliver me into the victory that comes through persistence (Ephesians 6:13). To You be the glory, now and forever. Amen.

Reflection:
Where do you need perseverance in ongoing spiritual battles?

_____

_____

_____

Action:
Write one commitment you will hold onto until God brings breakthrough.

_____

_____

_____

Scriptures Referenced Today:
Galatians 6:9 (KJV) - "And let us not be weary in well doing: for in due season we shall reap, if we faint not."
Ephesians 6:13 (KJV) - "Wherefore take unto you the whole armour of God, that ye may be able to withstand in the evil day, and having done all, to stand."

DAY 146 – Victory Over Emotional Attacks

Prayer:
Father, I come asking You to protect my emotions from the enemy's attacks. Hallowed be Your name; steady my heart when fear, anger, or heaviness tries to overtake me (Psalm 34:17–18). Let Your kingdom come and calm every storm swirling inside me. Let Your will be done as You guard my heart with Your peace and truth. Give me today my daily bread of stability, comfort, and Spirit-filled calmness. Forgive me for letting emotions control me, and I forgive those who wounded or provoked me. Lead me not into the temptation of emotional chaos, but deliver me into the steadiness of Your presence (Philippians 4:7). For Thine is the kingdom, and the power, and the glory forever and ever. Amen.

Reflection:
What emotion is most vulnerable to spiritual attack right now?

_____

_____

_____

Action:
Write one Scripture you will speak over your emotions today.

_____

_____

_____

Scriptures Referenced Today:
Psalm 34:17–18 (KJV) - "The righteous cry, and the LORD heareth, and delivereth them out of all their troubles. The LORD is nigh unto them that are of a broken heart; and saveth such as be of a contrite spirit."
Philippians 4:7 (KJV) - "And the peace of God, which passeth all understanding, shall keep your hearts and minds through Christ Jesus."

DAY 147 – Protected From Spiritual Exhaustion

Prayer:
Father, I come asking for Your strength when spiritual battles leave me weary. Hallowed be Your name; renew my soul and restore my strength when I feel emptied (Psalm 73:26). Let Your kingdom come and revive every place where I feel spiritually drained. Let Your will be done as You refresh my spirit and quiet my mind. Give me today my daily bread of renewal, rest, and revitalization. Forgive me for pushing beyond the grace You've given, and I forgive those who wore down my spirit. Lead me not into the temptation of burnout, but deliver me into rest that comes from trusting You (Matthew 11:28). Yours is the kingdom, the power, and the glory forever. Amen.

Reflection:
Where are you spiritually exhausted?

_____

_____

_____

Action:
Write one way you will rest in God instead of striving today.

_____

_____

_____

Scriptures Referenced Today:
Psalm 73:26 (KJV) - "My flesh and my heart faileth: but God is the strength of my heart, and my portion for ever."
Matthew 11:28 (KJV) - "Come unto me, all ye that labour and are heavy laden, and I will give you rest."

DAY 148 – Protected From the Enemy's Lies

Prayer:
Father, I come asking You to guard me from every lie the enemy speaks. Hallowed be Your name; silence every voice that contradicts Your Word (John 10:5). Let Your kingdom come and expose every deceptive thought before it takes root. Let Your will be done as You renew my mind with truth. Give me today my daily bread of strong discernment, clarity, and spiritual insight. Forgive me for agreeing with lies spoken over me, and I forgive those who spoke them. Lead me not into the temptation of self-doubt or confusion, but deliver me into truth that sets me free (Psalm 119:160). For Thine is the kingdom, and the power, and the glory forever. Amen.

Reflection:
What lie about yourself or your situation do you need God to silence?

_____

_____

_____

Action:
Write a truth from Scripture that replaces that lie.

_____

_____

_____

Scriptures Referenced Today:
John 10:5 (KJV) - "And a stranger will they not follow, but will flee from him: for they know not the voice of strangers."
Psalm 119:160 (KJV) - "Thy word is true from the beginning: and every one of thy righteous judgments endureth for ever."

DAY 149 – God's Strength When You Face Opposition

Prayer:
Father, I come asking for strength when I face opposition or resistance. Hallowed be Your name; remind me that You are my defender and my strong tower (Proverbs 18:10). Let Your kingdom come and silence every opposition that rises against Your purpose for my life. Let Your will be done as You give me courage to stand firm in truth. Give me today my daily bread of boldness, stability, and divine help. Forgive me for shrinking back in fear, and I forgive those who opposed or attacked me. Lead me not into the temptation of retaliation, but deliver me into steadfast confidence in You (Isaiah 41:10). All glory be to You, forever and ever. Amen.

Reflection:
Where are you facing opposition, and how is God strengthening you?

_____

_____

_____

Action:
Write one way you will stand firm in God's strength today.

_____

_____

_____

Scriptures Referenced Today:
Proverbs 18:10 (KJV) - "The name of the LORD is a strong tower: the righteous runneth into it, and is safe."
Isaiah 41:10 (KJV) - "Fear thou not; for I am with thee: be not dismayed; for I am thy God: I will strengthen thee; yea, I will help thee; yea, I will uphold thee with the right hand of my righteousness."

DAY 150 – Victory Through God's Promises

Prayer:

Father, I come standing on the promises of Your Word. Hallowed be Your name; remind me that every promise of Yours is sure, steadfast, and unfailing (2 Peter 1:4). Let Your kingdom come and strengthen my faith to believe what You have spoken. Let Your will be done as You align my heart with Your unchanging truth. Give me today my daily bread of courage, endurance, and confident expectation. Forgive me for doubting Your promises, and I forgive those who mocked or discouraged my faith. Lead me not into the temptation of unbelief, but deliver me into victory through Your promises (Joshua 21:45). To You be the glory, now and forever. Amen.

Reflection:

What promise of God do you need to stand on today?

_____

_____

_____

Action:

Write the promise you will cling to until you see God fulfill it.

_____

_____

_____

Scriptures Referenced Today:

2 Peter 1:4 (KJV) - "Whereby are given unto us exceeding great and precious promises: that by these ye might be partakers of the divine nature, having escaped the corruption that is in the world through lust."

Joshua 21:45 (KJV) - "There failed not ought of any good thing which the LORD had spoken unto the house of Israel; all came to pass."

DAY 151 – Covered by God's Peace in Battle

Prayer:
Father, I come asking You to cover my heart with Your peace in every battle. Hallowed be Your name; remind me that Your peace guards my heart and mind like a fortress (Philippians 4:7). Let Your kingdom come and silence the chaos around me. Let Your will be done as You steady my spirit and calm every anxious thought. Give me today my daily bread of rest, courage, and inner quiet. Forgive me for letting turmoil rule my heart, and I forgive those who stirred fear or unrest in my life. Lead me not into the temptation of panic, but deliver me into peace that stands firm even in warfare (John 14:27). For Thine is the kingdom, and the power, and the glory forever and ever. Amen.

Reflection:
Where do you most need God's peace to guard your heart today?

_____

_____

_____

Action:
Write one declaration of peace you will hold onto today.

_____

_____

_____

Scriptures Referenced Today:
Philippians 4:7 (KJV) - "And the peace of God, which passeth all understanding, shall keep your hearts and minds through Christ Jesus."
John 14:27 (KJV) - "Peace I leave with you, my peace I give unto you: not as the world giveth, give I unto you. Let not your heart be troubled, neither let it be afraid."

MONTH 5 CLOSING REFLECTION: SPIRITUAL WARFARE & PROTECTION

Month 5 brought you into the reality of spiritual battle-but also into the far greater reality of God's victory, His covering, and His presence. This month was not meant to create fear; it was meant to produce awareness, strength, and confidence in who fights for you.

You learned to:

- Put on the full armor of God
- Stand firm when attacked
- Resist temptation and deception
- Fight with spiritual, not fleshly weapons
- Trust God's protection over your mind, heart, and home
- Walk in Christ's authority
- Rest in the truth that the battle belongs to the Lord
- Recognize the enemy's schemes while refusing to be intimidated
- Rely on God's justice, not your own strength
- Persevere when warfare lasts longer than expected

This month revealed something important:

You are not powerless. You are not alone. And you are not fighting from defeat-you are fighting from victory.

The Lord has:

- Covered you
- Strengthened you
- Delivered you
- Armed you
- Guarded you
- Gone before you

Warfare didn't break you-it built you. It sharpened your discernment. It strengthened your endurance. It deepened your dependence on God. It awakened your authority in Christ.

As you close this month, take time to reflect:

- Where did God fight for you?
- Where did He protect you from what you could not see?
- What attacks did He turn into testimonies?
- What chains did He break?
- What lies did He expose and replace with truth?

Month 5 sends you forward with this core truth:

You belong to the One who commands the armies of heaven, and He is committed to your protection, your freedom, and your victory. Now, you step into Month 6 with fresh strength-not afraid of the battle, but confident in the God who wins them.

MONTH 6 THEME: PROVISION, DEPENDENCE, & DAILY BREAD

Month 6 invites you into one of the most transformative lessons in the Christian walk: learning to depend on God daily, consistently, and confidently. This month teaches you that God is not distant from your needs-He is deeply present in every detail, every longing, every burden, and every place where you feel lack. Provision is not just about money or resources; it is about the steady, faithful presence of God meeting you in every need of every day.

This is the month where God shifts you from self-reliance to God-reliance. From anxiety to trust. From pressure to peace. From carrying everything on your own shoulders to learning how to rest under His covering. God does not want you living exhausted, fearful, or stretched thin. He wants you rooted in the truth that **He alone is your Source**, and He is faithful to provide everything you need-spiritually, emotionally, mentally, relationally, and practically.

This month will help you:

- Recognize where you've carried what God never asked you to carry
- Let go of the belief that you must supply for yourself
- Trust God with daily needs instead of worrying about tomorrow
- Break free from fear around finances, resources, or provision
- Identify where anxiety has replaced dependence
- Rest in God's timing instead of striving for control
- Ask boldly for what you need, without guilt or hesitation
- Notice God's hand in the small, quiet provisions of each day
- Develop gratitude that strengthens faith
- Build confidence in God's character as Provider

Provision is not about getting everything you want-it's about receiving everything God knows you need. And often, the greatest provision is peace, clarity, courage, and strength in the exact moment you need them. Month 6 teaches you that "daily bread" is not just physical; it is the grace, wisdom, guidance, and support that sustains your heart day by day.

Let the Lord's Prayer guide your dependence this month:

- **"Our Father in Heaven"** - Provision flows from identity. You are God's child, not His burden.

- **"Hallowed be Your name"** - His character is your confidence. He provides because He is faithful.
- **"Your kingdom come"** - Invite God into every decision involving resources, energy, and needs.
- **"Your will be done"** - Trust His timing, His process, and His methods-even when different from yours.
- **"Give us this day our daily bread"** - Ask boldly for today's needs; God cares about every detail.
- **"Forgive us…"** - Release envy, comparison, fear of lack, or the pressure to prove yourself.
- **"Lead us not into temptation"** - Ask God to guard your heart from anxiety, self-reliance, or scarcity thinking.
- **"Yours is the kingdom…"** - Remember everything belongs to Him, comes from Him, and flows through Him.

This month is an invitation to rest, not strive; to trust, not fear; to receive, not hoard; to walk with open hands instead of clenched fists.

As you step into Month 6, breathe deeply and let this truth settle in your heart:

You are not responsible for being your own provider.

God is. And He delights in taking care of you.

DAY 152 – Trusting God for Today's Bread

Prayer:
Father, I come trusting You for everything I need today. Hallowed be Your name; remind me that You are my Provider, not my circumstances, not my strength, not my plans (Matthew 6:11). Let Your kingdom come and quiet every anxious thought about tomorrow. Let Your will be done as You teach me to rely on Your daily provision. Give me today my daily bread-wisdom, strength, peace, and the practical needs of this day. Forgive me for trying to carry tomorrow in my own power, and I forgive those who made me feel I must provide for myself alone. Lead me not into the temptation of self-reliance, but deliver me into trust and dependence on You (Philippians 4:19). For Thine is the kingdom, and the power, and the glory forever and ever. Amen.

Reflection:
What area of your life requires trust in God for today's needs?

_____

_____

_____

Action:
Write one practical need you are trusting God to provide today.

_____

_____

_____

Scriptures Referenced Today:
Matthew 6:11 (KJV) - "Give us this day our daily bread."
Philippians 4:19 (KJV) - "But my God shall supply all your need according to his riches in glory by Christ Jesus."

DAY 153 – God's Faithfulness in Every Season

Prayer:
Father, I come thanking You for Your faithfulness in every season-plenty or lack, clarity or confusion. Hallowed be Your name; remind me that You do not change with my circumstances (Hebrews 13:8). Let Your kingdom come and settle my heart in the truth that You are faithful in all things. Let Your will be done as You teach me to trust You with each changing season. Give me today my daily bread of stability, gratitude, and steady faith. Forgive me for doubting You in difficult seasons, and I forgive those who spoke fear into my situation. Lead me not into the temptation of mistrust, but deliver me into confidence in Your unchanging character (Lamentations 3:22–23). Yours is the kingdom, the power, and the glory forever. Amen.

Reflection:
What season are you currently in, and how is God faithful in it?

Action:
Write one way you will acknowledge God's faithfulness today.

Scriptures Referenced Today:
Hebrews 13:8 (KJV) - "Jesus Christ the same yesterday, and to day, and for ever."
Lamentations 3:22–23 (KJV) - "It is of the LORD'S mercies that we are not consumed, because his compassions fail not. They are new every morning: great is thy faithfulness."

DAY 154 – Receiving Strength for the Day

Prayer:
Father, I come asking You for the strength I need for this day-no more, no less. Hallowed be Your name; be my strength in weakness and my energy when I feel drained (Isaiah 40:29). Let Your kingdom come and fill me with the grace necessary for today's tasks. Let Your will be done as You help me walk in Your strength, not my own. Give me today my daily bread of endurance, peace, and spiritual strength. Forgive me for striving in my own power, and I forgive those who placed unrealistic demands on me. Lead me not into the temptation of exhaustion, but deliver me into Your sustaining presence (Psalm 46:1). All glory be to You, forever and ever. Amen.

Reflection:
Where do you most need God's strength today?

_____

_____

_____

Action:
Write one way you will rely on God's strength instead of your own.

_____

_____

_____

Scriptures Referenced Today:
Isaiah 40:29 (KJV) - "He giveth power to the faint; and to them that have no might he increaseth strength."
Psalm 46:1 (KJV) - "God is our refuge and strength, a very present help in trouble."

DAY 155 – God Provides in Unexpected Ways

Prayer:
Father, I come asking You to open my eyes to the unexpected ways You provide. Hallowed be Your name; remind me that Your provision often comes from places I did not see coming (Isaiah 43:19). Let Your kingdom come and teach me to recognize Your hand in the ordinary and the surprising. Let Your will be done as You free me from narrow expectations. Give me today my daily bread of trust, openness, and spiritual awareness. Forgive me for limiting how I think You can provide, and I forgive those who taught me to expect little from You. Lead me not into the temptation of unbelief, but deliver me into joyful expectation of Your goodness (Ephesians 3:20). To You be the glory, now and forever. Amen.

Reflection:
Where might God be providing for you in unexpected ways?

_____

_____

Action:
Write one area where you will look for God's unexpected provision today.

_____

_____

Scriptures Referenced Today:
Isaiah 43:19 (KJV) - "Behold, I will do a new thing; now it shall spring forth; shall ye not know it? I will even make a way in the wilderness, and rivers in the desert."
Ephesians 3:20–21 (KJV) - "Now unto him that is able to do exceeding abundantly above all that we ask or think, according to the power that worketh in us, Unto him be glory in the church by Christ Jesus throughout all ages, world without end. Amen."

DAY 156 – God's Faithfulness in Every Season

Prayer:
Father, I thank You that Your faithfulness does not change with my circumstances. Hallowed be Your name; remind me that even when seasons shift, You remain steady and sure (Malachi 3:6). Let Your kingdom come and anchor my heart in Your unchanging nature. Let Your will be done as You help me trust You in every season-whether joyful, uncertain, or difficult. Give me today my daily bread of stability, confidence, and peace. Forgive me for doubting Your consistency, and I forgive those who made me feel abandoned or forgotten. Lead me not into the temptation of fear, but deliver me into the assurance that You are faithful to perform what You promised (1 Thessalonians 5:24). To You be the glory forever. Amen.

Reflection:
Where do you need to be reminded of God's faithfulness today?

_____

_____

_____

Action:
Write one area of your life where you will trust God's unchanging character today.

_____

_____

_____

Scriptures Referenced Today:
Malachi 3:6 (KJV) - "For I am the Lord, I change not; therefore ye sons of Jacob are not consumed."
1 Thessalonians 5:24 (KJV) - "Faithful is he that calleth you, who also will do it."

DAY 157 – God Speaks Peace Into Anxiety

Prayer:
Father, thank You for speaking peace over every anxious thought in me. Hallowed be Your name; quiet the noise in my mind and calm the storms in my heart (Philippians 4:6–7). Let Your kingdom come and bring a holy stillness over my fears. Let Your will be done as I surrender every worry into Your hands. Give me today my daily bread of calmness, clarity, and confidence in You. Forgive me for trying to manage anxiety on my own, and I forgive those who contributed to my stress or fear. Lead me not into the temptation of panic, but deliver me into Your perfect peace that guards my heart and mind (John 14:27). To You be glory, now and forever. Amen.

Reflection:
What anxious thought do you need God to speak peace over today?

_____

_____

_____

Action:
Write down the worry you will release into God's hands today.

_____

_____

_____

Scriptures Referenced Today:
Philippians 4:6–7 (KJV) - "Be careful for nothing; but in every thing by prayer and supplication with thanksgiving let your requests be made known unto God.
And the peace of God, which passeth all understanding, shall keep your hearts and minds through Christ Jesus."
John 14:27 (KJV) - "Peace I leave with you, my peace I give unto you: not as the world giveth, give I unto you. Let not your heart be troubled, neither let it be afraid."

DAY 158 – God Calms the Storm Within You

Prayer:
Father, thank You for being the One who speaks peace into every storm in my heart. Hallowed be Your name; quiet my fears and still every anxious thought as You speak, "Peace, be still" (Mark 4:39). Let Your kingdom come and bring calm where there has been inner turmoil. Let Your will be done as You steady my emotions and strengthen my trust. Give me today my daily bread of peace, clarity, and a mind stayed on You. Forgive me for letting worry rule my heart, and I forgive those whose actions added to my anxiety. Lead me not into the temptation of fear, but deliver me into the perfect peace You promise (Isaiah 26:3). To You be glory forever. Amen.

Reflection:
What storm in your life needs Jesus to speak "Peace, be still"?

_____

_____

_____

Action:
Write down one fear you release to God today.

_____

_____

_____

Scriptures Referenced Today:
Mark 4:39 (KJV) - "And he arose, and rebuked the wind, and said unto the sea, Peace, be still. And the wind ceased, and there was a great calm."
Isaiah 26:3 (KJV) - "Thou wilt keep him in perfect peace, whose mind is stayed on thee: because he trusteth in thee."

DAY 159 – God Restores Your Strength

Prayer:
Father, thank You for renewing my strength when I grow weary.
Hallowed be Your name; restore my soul and refresh my spirit when I feel
worn down (Psalm 23:3). Let Your kingdom come into the places where
exhaustion has settled. Let Your will be done as You lift my head, renew
my energy, and fill me with hope. Give me today my daily bread of rest,
renewal, and joy. Forgive me for pushing myself beyond what You asked,
and I forgive those who placed unrealistic expectations on me. Lead me
not into the temptation of burnout, but deliver me into the rest and
restoration You promised (Matthew 11:28–30). To You be honor and
praise. Amen.

Reflection:
Where do you need God to restore your strength today?

_____

_____

_____

Action:
Identify one step of rest or recovery you will honor today.

_____

_____

_____

Scriptures Referenced Today:
Psalm 23:3 (KJV) - "He restoreth my soul: he leadeth me in the paths of
righteousness for his name's sake."
Matthew 11:28–30 (KJV) -"Come unto me, all ye that labour and are
heavy laden, and I will give you rest.
Take my yoke upon you, and learn of me; for I am meek and lowly in
heart: and ye shall find rest unto your souls.
For my yoke is easy, and my burden is light."

DAY 160 – God Guides Your Steps

Prayer:
Father, thank You for guiding me even when I see only one step at a time. Hallowed be Your name; shine Your light on the path before me and steady my steps according to Your Word (Psalm 119:105). Let Your kingdom come into every decision I need to make. Let Your will be done as You lead me with wisdom, patience, and courage. Give me today my daily bread of discernment, clarity, and a willing heart. Forgive me for running ahead of You, and I forgive those who pressured me to move before I was ready. Lead me not into the temptation of fear or haste, but deliver me into the confidence that You order my steps (Psalm 37:23–24). Yours is the way, the truth, and the life. Amen.

Reflection:
What is the next step-not the whole journey-that God is asking you to take?

_____

_____

_____

Action:
Write the one step you will take today in obedience.

_____

_____

_____

Scriptures Referenced Today:
Psalm 119:105 (KJV) - "Thy word is a lamp unto my feet, and a light unto my path."
Psalm 37:23–24 (KJV) -
"The steps of a good man are ordered by the Lord: and he delighteth in his way.
Though he fall, he shall not be utterly cast down: for the Lord upholdeth him with his hand."

DAY 161 – God Heals the Wounds You Don't Talk About

Prayer:
Father, thank You for seeing the hidden wounds I carry. Hallowed be Your name; bring healing to the places in me that I rarely speak of, the places only You truly know (Psalm 147:3). Let Your kingdom come and touch every area of hurt, fear, or disappointment. Let Your will be done as You bring restoration, wholeness, and comfort. Give me today my daily bread of courage, honesty, and emotional healing. Forgive me for burying pain instead of bringing it to You, and I forgive those who contributed to the wounds I carry. Lead me not into the temptation of hiding, but deliver me into Your healing and freedom (Jeremiah 30:17). To You be all the glory. Amen.

Reflection:
What wound are you inviting God to heal today?

_____

_____

_____

Action:
Write down one step you will take to bring an unspoken hurt into God's presence.

_____

_____

_____

Scriptures Referenced Today:
Psalm 147:3 (KJV) - "He healeth the broken in heart, and bindeth up their wounds."
Jeremiah 30:17 (KJV) - "For I will restore health unto thee, and I will heal thee of thy wounds, saith the Lord; because they called thee an Outcast, saying, This is Zion, whom no man seeketh after."

DAY 162 – God Gives Strength to Keep Moving Forward

Prayer:
Father, thank You for giving strength when I feel like stopping. Hallowed be Your name; renew my resolve and remind me that You are the One who empowers me to continue (Isaiah 40:29). Let Your kingdom come and breathe life into weary places. Let Your will be done as You help me run with endurance and walk with perseverance. Give me today my daily bread of energy, hope, and forward momentum. Forgive me for wanting to quit, and I forgive those who discouraged me. Lead me not into the temptation of giving up, but deliver me into steadfastness that comes from You (Galatians 6:9). Yours is the strength that sustains me. Amen.

Reflection:
Where do you need God's strength to keep moving forward?

_____

_____

Action:
Write the next step-just one-that you will take today.

_____

_____

Scriptures Referenced Today:
Isaiah 40:29 (KJV) - "He giveth power to the faint; and to them that have no might he increaseth strength."
Galatians 6:9 (KJV) - "And let us not be weary in well doing: for in due season we shall reap, if we faint not."

DAY 163 – God's Peace Guards Your Heart

Prayer:
Father, thank You for surrounding my heart with Your peace. Hallowed be Your name; guard my emotions and steady my thoughts when I feel unsettled (Philippians 4:7). Let Your kingdom come and replace anxiety with confidence in Your presence. Let Your will be done as Your peace rules over every concern in my mind. Give me today my daily bread of calmness, perspective, and trust. Forgive me for letting fear take over, and I forgive those who brought chaos into my life. Lead me not into the temptation of worry, but deliver me into Your peace that passes all understanding (John 16:33). To You be glory forever. Amen.

Reflection:
What situation needs God's guarding peace today?

_____

_____

_____

Action:
Write down what you will entrust entirely into God's peace today.

_____

_____

_____

Scriptures Referenced Today:
Philippians 4:7 (KJV) - "And the peace of God, which passeth all understanding, shall keep your hearts and minds through Christ Jesus."
John 16:33 (KJV) - "These things I have spoken unto you, that in me ye might have peace. In the world ye shall have tribulation: but be of good cheer; I have overcome the world."

DAY 164 – God Gives Wisdom When You Ask

Prayer:
Father, thank You for promising wisdom when I seek You. Hallowed be Your name; open my understanding and guide my decisions with clarity and discernment (James 1:5). Let Your kingdom come into my thoughts and choices. Let Your will be done as You align my mind with Your truth. Give me today my daily bread of insight, direction, and sound judgment. Forgive me for acting without asking You, and I forgive those who pressured me into unwise decisions. Lead me not into the temptation of confusion, but deliver me into wisdom that comes from above (Proverbs 2:6). All glory to You. Amen.

Reflection:
In what area do you need God's wisdom right now?

_____

_____

_____

Action:
Write the specific question you are bringing to God for wisdom today.

_____

_____

_____

Scriptures Referenced Today:
James 1:5 (KJV) - "If any of you lack wisdom, let him ask of God, that giveth to all men liberally, and upbraideth not; and it shall be given him."
Proverbs 2:6 (KJV) - "For the Lord giveth wisdom: out of his mouth cometh knowledge and understanding."

DAY 165 – God Fights Battles You Cannot See

Prayer:
Father, thank You for fighting battles on my behalf-those I see and those I don't. Hallowed be Your name; remind me that You go before me and surround me on every side (Deuteronomy 20:4). Let Your kingdom come and give me courage, knowing that I never fight alone. Let Your will be done as You defend, protect, and strengthen me. Give me today my daily bread of confidence, faith, and courage. Forgive me for trying to win battles in my own strength, and I forgive those who opposed or mistreated me. Lead me not into the temptation of fear, but deliver me into the victory You provide (Exodus 14:14). To You be praise forever. Amen.

Reflection:
What battle do you need to trust God with today?

_____

_____

_____

Action:
Write down the battle you will stop carrying alone.

_____

_____

_____

Scriptures Referenced Today:
Deuteronomy 20:4 (KJV) - "For the Lord your God is he that goeth with you, to fight for you against your enemies, to save you."
Exodus 14:14 (KJV) - "The Lord shall fight for you, and ye shall hold your peace."

DAY 166 – God Protects Your Mind

Prayer:
Father, thank You for guarding my thoughts and renewing my mind. Hallowed be Your name; fill my thinking with truth, clarity, and peace (Romans 12:2). Let Your kingdom come and reshape the patterns of my mind according to Your Word. Let Your will be done as You filter out every lie, fear, and distraction. Give me today my daily bread of focus, discernment, and mental strength. Forgive me for agreeing with thoughts that did not come from You, and I forgive those who spoke words that damaged my confidence. Lead me not into the temptation of negative thinking, but deliver me into a mind transformed by Your Spirit (2 Corinthians 10:5). To You be the glory forever. Amen.

Reflection:
What thought or belief needs to be renewed by God today?

_____

_____

_____

Action:
Write down one thought you will intentionally replace with God's truth.

_____

_____

_____

Scriptures Referenced Today:
Romans 12:2 (KJV) - "And be not conformed to this world: but be ye transformed by the renewing of your mind, that ye may prove what is that good, and acceptable, and perfect, will of God."
2 Corinthians 10:5 (KJV) - "Casting down imaginations, and every high thing that exalteth itself against the knowledge of God, and bringing into captivity every thought to the obedience of Christ."

DAY 167 – God Restores What Was Lost

Prayer:
Father, thank You for being the God who restores. Hallowed be Your name; renew what has been broken, lost, or taken from my life (Joel 2:25). Let Your kingdom come and bring healing to every place of loss. Let Your will be done as You rebuild what I cannot restore on my own. Give me today my daily bread of hope, patience, and trust in Your timing. Forgive me for losing heart, and I forgive those who contributed to the losses I've experienced. Lead me not into the temptation of despair, but deliver me into the expectation that You make all things new (Revelation 21:5). To You be honor and praise. Amen.

Reflection:
What area of your life do you need God to restore?

_____

_____

Action:
Write one loss you are placing into God's hands for restoration.

_____

_____

Scriptures Referenced Today:
Joel 2:25 (KJV) - "And I will restore to you the years that the locust hath eaten, the cankerworm, and the caterpiller, and the palmerworm, my great army which I sent among you."
Revelation 21:5 (KJV) - "And he that sat upon the throne said, Behold, I make all things new. And he said unto me, Write: for these words are true and faithful."

DAY 168 – God Strengthens You to Stand Firm

Prayer:
Father, thank You for giving me strength to stand when life feels overwhelming. Hallowed be Your name; hold me steady and firm in Your power (Ephesians 6:10). Let Your kingdom come and make me strong in the battles of life. Let Your will be done as You help me stand my ground in faith and courage. Give me today my daily bread of resilience, boldness, and spiritual strength. Forgive me for relying on my own strength, and I forgive those who tried to weaken or discourage me. Lead me not into the temptation to retreat, but deliver me into steadfastness through Your mighty power (Psalm 27:1). All glory to You. Amen.

Reflection:
What area of your life requires you to stand firm today?

_____

_____

_____

Action:
Write down the stand you will take in faith today.

_____

_____

_____

Scriptures Referenced Today:
Ephesians 6:10 (KJV) - "Finally, my brethren, be strong in the Lord, and in the power of his might."
Psalm 27:1 (KJV) - "The Lord is my light and my salvation; whom shall I fear? The Lord is the strength of my life; of whom shall I be afraid?"

DAY 169 – God Listens When You Call

Prayer:
Father, thank You for hearing me every time I call out to You. Hallowed be Your name; remind me that You are near and attentive to my prayer (Psalm 34:17). Let Your kingdom come and draw close to me as I seek You. Let Your will be done as You answer, guide, and comfort me. Give me today my daily bread of confidence in Your nearness. Forgive me for doubting that You hear me, and I forgive those who dismissed or ignored me. Lead me not into the temptation of silence or withdrawal, but deliver me into boldness and honesty in prayer (Jeremiah 33:3). To You be the glory forever. Amen.

Reflection:
What prayer do you need to bring boldly before God today?

_____

_____

_____

Action:
Write down one request you will bring to God without hesitation.

_____

_____

_____

Scriptures Referenced Today:
Psalm 34:17 (KJV) - "The righteous cry, and the Lord heareth, and delivereth them out of all their troubles."
Jeremiah 33:3 (KJV) - "Call unto me, and I will answer thee, and show thee great and mighty things, which thou knowest not."

DAY 170 – God Renews Your Hope

Prayer:
Father, thank You for renewing my hope when it grows dim. Hallowed be Your name; lift my head and fill my heart with expectation again (Romans 15:13). Let Your kingdom come and revive every place where hope has faded. Let Your will be done as You stir up faith, joy, and confidence in Your promises. Give me today my daily bread of hope, encouragement, and spiritual refreshment. Forgive me for allowing discouragement to settle in my heart, and I forgive those who contributed to my hopelessness. Lead me not into the temptation of giving up, but deliver me into renewed hope through Your Spirit (Lamentations 3:22–23). To You be all praise. Amen.

Reflection:
What hope do you need God to renew today?

_____

_____

_____

Action:
Write one promise of God that you will stand on today.

_____

_____

_____

Scriptures Referenced Today:
Romans 15:13 (KJV) - "Now the God of hope fill you with all joy and peace in believing, that ye may abound in hope, through the power of the Holy Ghost."

Lamentations 3:22–23 (KJV) -
"It is of the Lord's mercies that we are not consumed, because his compassions fail not.

They are new every morning: great is thy faithfulness."

DAY 171 – God Lights the Path Ahead

Prayer:
Father, thank You for lighting my path when I cannot see what is ahead. Hallowed be Your name; shine Your wisdom and clarity on every step I need to take (Psalm 119:105). Let Your kingdom come and illuminate the places that feel confusing or unsure. Let Your will be done as You guide me with steady direction. Give me today my daily bread of insight, discernment, and spiritual understanding. Forgive me for trying to navigate life on my own, and I forgive those who led me into confusion or uncertainty. Lead me not into the temptation of walking in darkness, but deliver me into the light of Your guidance (Proverbs 3:6). To You be the glory forever. Amen.

Reflection:
Where do you need God's light and direction today?

_____

_____

_____

Action:
Write down one step where you need God to guide your path.

_____

_____

_____

Scriptures Referenced Today:
Psalm 119:105 (KJV) - "Thy word is a lamp unto my feet, and a light unto my path."
Proverbs 3:6 (KJV) - "In all thy ways acknowledge him, and he shall direct thy paths."

DAY 172 – God Holds You Steady in Uncertainty

Prayer:
Father, thank You for holding me steady when life feels uncertain.
Hallowed be Your name; remind me that You are my solid foundation
and firm anchor (Psalm 18:2). Let Your kingdom come and bring stability
to every area of my life that feels shaky. Let Your will be done as You
strengthen my heart and settle my spirit. Give me today my daily bread of
courage, calmness, and unwavering trust. Forgive me for letting fear
control my decisions, and I forgive those who contributed to my
instability. Lead me not into the temptation of panic, but deliver me into
the security of Your unfailing strength (Isaiah 41:10). To You be honor
and praise. Amen.

Reflection:
What area of your life feels unstable and needs God's steadying hand?

_____

_____

_____

Action:
Write down the fear or uncertainty you are entrusting to God today.

_____

_____

_____

Scriptures Referenced Today:
Psalm 18:2 (KJV) - "The Lord is my rock, and my fortress, and my
deliverer; my God, my strength, in whom I will trust; my buckler, and the
horn of my salvation, and my high tower."
Isaiah 41:10 (KJV) - "Fear thou not; for I am with thee: be not dismayed;
for I am thy God: I will strengthen thee; yea, I will help thee; yea, I will
uphold thee with the right hand of my righteousness."

DAY 173 – God Brings Peace to Your Decisions

Prayer:

Father, thank You for bringing peace to the decisions I face. Hallowed be Your name; give me clarity, stillness, and the assurance of Your leading (Colossians 3:15). Let Your kingdom come and rule over my thoughts as I discern what is right. Let Your will be done as You help me choose according to Your wisdom. Give me today my daily bread of direction, calmness, and spiritual sensitivity. Forgive me for rushing ahead without seeking You, and I forgive those who pushed me into choices I wasn't prepared to make. Lead me not into the temptation of confusion, but deliver me into the peace that confirms Your will (Psalm 32:8). All glory to You. Amen.

Reflection:

What decision do you need God's peace to confirm?

Action:

Write the decision you will surrender to God's peace today.

Scriptures Referenced Today:

Colossians 3:15 (KJV) - "And let the peace of God rule in your hearts, to the which also ye are called in one body; and be ye thankful."

Psalm 32:8 (KJV) - "I will instruct thee and teach thee in the way which thou shalt go: I will guide thee with mine eye."

DAY 174 – God Gives Courage for the Unknown

Prayer:

Father, thank You for giving me courage to face the unknown. Hallowed be Your name; strengthen my heart and remind me that You go before me (Deuteronomy 31:8). Let Your kingdom come and remove every fear about tomorrow. Let Your will be done as You fill me with boldness and confidence in Your presence. Give me today my daily bread of bravery, assurance, and unwavering trust. Forgive me for shrinking back in fear, and I forgive those who fueled my anxieties. Lead me not into the temptation of hesitation, but deliver me into courage that comes from You alone (Joshua 1:9). To You be the praise forever. Amen.

Reflection:

What unknown or uncertain situation requires courage from God?

Action:

Write down how you will step forward in courage today.

Scriptures Referenced Today:

Deuteronomy 31:8 (KJV) - "And the Lord, he it is that doth go before thee; he will be with thee, he will not fail thee, neither forsake thee: fear not, neither be dismayed."

Joshua 1:9 (KJV) - "Have not I commanded thee? Be strong and of a good courage; be not afraid, neither be thou dismayed: for the Lord thy God is with thee whithersoever thou goest."

DAY 175 – God Lifts Your Head When You Feel Low

Prayer:
Father, thank You for lifting my head when life weighs me down.
Hallowed be Your name; remind me that You are the One who
strengthens, restores, and encourages me (Psalm 3:3). Let Your kingdom
come and replace sadness with hope. Let Your will be done as You
breathe new life into discouraged places. Give me today my daily bread
of comfort, joy, and renewed perspective. Forgive me for letting
heaviness take root, and I forgive those who contributed to my
discouragement. Lead me not into the temptation of hopelessness, but
deliver me into the joy that comes from Your presence (Psalm 16:11). To
You be all the glory. Amen.

Reflection:
Where do you need God to lift your spirit today?

_____

_____

_____

Action:
Write down one source of discouragement you surrender to God.

_____

_____

_____

Scriptures Referenced Today:
Psalm 3:3 (KJV) - "But thou, O Lord, art a shield for me; my glory, and
the lifter up of mine head."
Psalm 16:11 (KJV) - "Thou wilt show me the path of life: in thy presence
is fulness of joy; at thy right hand there are pleasures for evermore."

DAY 176 – God Gives You Rest When You Are Weary

Prayer:
Father, thank You for offering rest when my soul feels worn down. Hallowed be Your name; invite me into the rest that only You can provide (Matthew 11:28). Let Your kingdom come and refresh every weary place within me. Let Your will be done as You restore my strength and renew my peace. Give me today my daily bread of calmness, renewal, and quiet trust. Forgive me for trying to carry burdens alone, and I forgive those who placed heavy expectations on me. Lead me not into the temptation of striving, but deliver me into the rest that comes from Your presence (Psalm 62:1). To You be the glory forever. Amen.

Reflection:
Where are you carrying something God is asking you to lay down?

_____

_____

Action:
Write down the burden you will release into God's rest today.

_____

_____

Scriptures Referenced Today:
Matthew 11:28 (KJV) - "Come unto me, all ye that labour and are heavy laden, and I will give you rest."
Psalm 62:1 (KJV) - "Truly my soul waiteth upon God: from him cometh my salvation."

DAY 177 – God Is Your Refuge in Times of Trouble

Prayer:
Father, thank You for being my safe place when life feels overwhelming. Hallowed be Your name; remind me that I can run to You and find shelter (Psalm 46:1). Let Your kingdom come and surround me with Your strength. Let Your will be done as You protect me and give me courage. Give me today my daily bread of security, comfort, and confidence. Forgive me for trying to hide in lesser things, and I forgive those who contributed to my fear. Lead me not into the temptation of running to the wrong places for safety, but deliver me into the refuge of Your presence (Psalm 91:2). To You be honor and praise. Amen.

Reflection:
Where do you need God's protection and refuge today?

_____

_____

_____

Action:
Write down one fear you will bring under God's covering today.

_____

_____

_____

Scriptures Referenced Today:
Psalm 46:1 (KJV) - "God is our refuge and strength, a very present help in trouble."
Psalm 91:2 (KJV) - "I will say of the Lord, He is my refuge and my fortress: my God; in him will I trust."

DAY 178 – God Renews Your Joy

Prayer:
Father, thank You for restoring joy to my heart. Hallowed be Your name; revive my spirit and remind me of the gladness that comes from knowing You (Psalm 51:12). Let Your kingdom come and fill every empty place with Your presence. Let Your will be done as You bring joy where sadness once lived. Give me today my daily bread of laughter, lightness, and renewed hope. Forgive me for letting discouragement linger, and I forgive those who drained joy from my life. Lead me not into the temptation of dwelling on negativity, but deliver me into the joy that comes from Your salvation (Nehemiah 8:10). To You be the glory. Amen.

Reflection:
Where do you need God to restore joy in your life?

_____

_____

_____

Action:
Write one thing you will thank God for today to stir up joy.

_____

_____

_____

Scriptures Referenced Today:
Psalm 51:12 (KJV) - "Restore unto me the joy of thy salvation; and uphold me with thy free spirit."
Nehemiah 8:10 (KJV) - "Then he said unto them, Go your way, eat the fat, and drink the sweet, and send portions unto them for whom nothing is prepared: for this day is holy unto our Lord: neither be ye sorry; for the joy of the Lord is your strength."

DAY 179 – God Gives You Grace for Today

Prayer:
Father, thank You for giving me grace that is sufficient for whatever today brings. Hallowed be Your name; remind me that Your strength is made perfect in my weakness (2 Corinthians 12:9). Let Your kingdom come and fill me with the grace I need moment by moment. Let Your will be done as You sustain me through challenges and uncertainties. Give me today my daily bread of patience, endurance, and unwavering trust. Forgive me for trying to earn what You freely give, and I forgive those who demanded perfection from me. Lead me not into the temptation of self-reliance, but deliver me into the grace that carries me (Hebrews 4:16). To You be honor and praise. Amen.

Reflection:
Where do you need God's grace the most today?

_____

_____

_____

Action:
Write down one area where you will rely on God's grace instead of your own strength.

_____

_____

_____

Scriptures Referenced Today:
2 Corinthians 12:9 (KJV) - "And he said unto me, My grace is sufficient for thee: for my strength is made perfect in weakness. Most gladly therefore will I rather glory in my infirmities, that the power of Christ may rest upon me."
Hebrews 4:16 (KJV) - "Let us therefore come boldly unto the throne of grace, that we may obtain mercy, and find grace to help in time of need."

DAY 180 – God Lifts You When You Feel Overwhelmed

Prayer:
Father, thank You for lifting me when the weight of life feels too heavy. Hallowed be Your name; remind me that You are the One who upholds me and strengthens me (Psalm 145:14). Let Your kingdom come and replace overwhelm with peace. Let Your will be done as You carry what I cannot. Give me today my daily bread of calmness, resilience, and renewed strength. Forgive me for trying to handle everything myself, and I forgive those who added to the burdens I carry. Lead me not into the temptation of collapsing under pressure, but deliver me into the strength that comes from trusting You (Isaiah 41:13). To You be all the glory. Amen.

Reflection:
What area of life feels the heaviest right now?

_____

_____

_____

Action:
Write down what you will allow God to carry for you today.

_____

_____

_____

Scriptures Referenced Today:
Psalm 145:14 (KJV) - "The Lord upholdeth all that fall, and raiseth up all those that be bowed down."
Isaiah 41:13 (KJV) - "For I the Lord thy God will hold thy right hand, saying unto thee, Fear not; I will help thee."

DAY 181 – God Strengthens You in Times of Waiting

Prayer:
Father, thank You for strengthening me in seasons where I must wait. Hallowed be Your name; teach me to trust Your timing and Your wisdom, even when the answers feel delayed (Psalm 27:14). Let Your kingdom come and fill my waiting with purpose, peace, and expectation. Let Your will be done as You refine my character and deepen my faith. Give me today my daily bread of patience, endurance, and hope. Forgive me for growing frustrated in the waiting, and I forgive those who pressured me to rush ahead. Lead me not into the temptation of discouragement, but deliver me into renewed strength as I wait upon You (Isaiah 40:31). To You be the glory forever. Amen.

Reflection:
Where is God asking you to wait and trust Him today?

_____

_____

_____

Action:
Write one thing you will stop trying to force and choose to wait on God for.

_____

_____

_____

Scriptures Referenced Today:
Psalm 27:14 (KJV) - "Wait on the Lord: be of good courage, and he shall strengthen thine heart: wait, I say, on the Lord."
Isaiah 40:31 (KJV) - "But they that wait upon the Lord shall renew their strength; they shall mount up with wings as eagles; they shall run, and not be weary; and they shall walk, and not faint."

DAY 182 – God Sees Your Effort and Honors Your Faithfulness

Prayer:
Father, thank You for seeing every effort I make, even the ones no one else notices. Hallowed be Your name; remind me that nothing done for You is ever wasted (1 Corinthians 15:58). Let Your kingdom come and strengthen my hands to keep doing what is right. Let Your will be done as You reward faithfulness, perseverance, and integrity. Give me today my daily bread of encouragement, motivation, and unwavering commitment. Forgive me for feeling unseen or unappreciated, and I forgive those who overlooked my efforts. Lead me not into the temptation of giving up, but deliver me into steadfastness through Your Spirit (Hebrews 6:10). All glory belongs to You. Amen.

Reflection:
Where have you been faithful that you need reassurance God sees?

_____

_____

_____

Action:
Write down one faithful effort you will continue-not for recognition, but for God.

_____

_____

_____

Scriptures Referenced Today:
1 Corinthians 15:58 (KJV) - "Therefore, my beloved brethren, be ye steadfast, unmoveable, always abounding in the work of the Lord, forasmuch as ye know that your labour is not in vain in the Lord."
Hebrews 6:10 (KJV) - "For God is not unrighteous to forget your work and labour of love, which ye have showed toward his name, in that ye have ministered to the saints, and do minister."

MONTH 6 CLOSING REFLECTION: STRENGTH, STABILITY & THE GOD WHO SUSTAINS YOU

Month 6 led you through a season of learning how God strengthens you-not just in the big, dramatic moments, but in the ordinary, exhausting, overwhelming, and uncertain spaces of life. This month was about discovering a God who doesn't merely rescue you occasionally… but sustains you continually.

Throughout these days, you learned to recognize His steady hand in the places where you felt your weakest. You learned that God is not disappointed by your limitations-He meets you there with power, patience, and peace.

This month taught you to:

- Receive strength instead of pretending you don't need it
- Let God steady your heart when everything around you shifts
- Trust Him with the steps you cannot yet see
- Release discouragement and embrace renewed joy
- Rest without guilt, knowing God is not asking you to carry everything
- Find refuge in Him rather than in temporary escapes
- Let go of fear and pick up faith
- Allow God to restore what was lost or broken
- Accept His grace instead of striving in your own effort
- Wait with expectation rather than frustration

Month 6 revealed something deeply important:

God does not grow tired of you. He does not get worn out by your needs. He does not back away when your strength runs out.

Instead…

He *renews* you. He *upholds* you. He *covers* you. He *refreshes* you. He *guides* you. He *carries* you when you can't carry yourself.

This month was a reminder that you are not supposed to be strong all the time-

you are supposed to be connected to the One who is strength itself.

As you reflect, ask yourself:

- Where did God strengthen me this month?
- What burden did He carry that I couldn't?
- Where did He give clarity, when I only saw confusion?

- How did He lift me when discouragement pressed in?
- What situation showed me His faithfulness again?
- What place of waiting became a place of renewal?

Month 6 sends you forward with this truth:

Your strength does not come from your capacity-it comes from your connection.

And your Father is committed to sustaining you, stabilizing you, and strengthening you for every step ahead.

Now, you step into Month 7 with a deeper identity, steadier confidence, and a renewed awareness of the God who walks with you-every moment, every season, every day.

MONTH 7 THEME: IDENTITY, CALLING, & BECOMING WHO GOD SAYS YOU ARE

Month 7 invites you into the sacred work of becoming-becoming rooted, becoming whole, becoming aligned with the truth of who God says you are. Up to this point, God has healed wounds, reshaped your faith, strengthened your prayer life, restored your dependence, and equipped you for spiritual battle. Now the focus shifts from what God is doing *around* you to what He is building *within* you. This month is about identity, purpose, calling, and spiritual formation. It's about stepping into the person God envisioned when He created you.

Identity is not something you earn; it is something God declares.

Calling is not something you chase; it is something God reveals.

Purpose is not something you manufacture; it is something God forms within you as you walk with Him.

Month 7 helps you confront the voices, lies, fears, and labels that have tried to define you-and replace them with the truth of who God says you are. You are not the sum of your mistakes, your insecurities, your past, or what others have spoken over you. You are who God says you are, and He is shaping you day by day into a reflection of His heart, His character, and His purpose.

This month will help you:

• Understand the difference between identity and performance

• Reject false labels, lies, and identities the world has placed on you

• Recognize the gifts, strengths, and calling God uniquely placed within you

• Release the pressure to become something in your own strength

• Overcome impostor syndrome, insecurity, and comparison

• See yourself through the lens of Scripture, not circumstance

• Walk in confidence rooted in who God is-not how you feel

• Allow God to refine areas of character, attitude, and maturity

• Understand your calling as a journey, not a destination

• Embrace the person God is forming you into day by day

Identity is formed in relationship, not isolation.

Calling is strengthened in obedience, not striving.

Purpose unfolds in seasons, not moments.

And spiritual maturity is the slow, steady work of God shaping you from the inside out.

Let the Lord's Prayer guide your becoming this month:

• **"Our Father in Heaven"** - Identity begins with knowing whose child you are.

• **"Hallowed be Your name"** - Worship shapes who you are becoming as you behold who He is.

• **"Your kingdom come"** - Calling flows from His kingdom, not your ambition.

• **"Your will be done"** - Becoming who God created you to be requires surrender, trust, and alignment.

• **"Give us this day…"** - Identity grows through daily obedience and daily dependence.

• **"Forgive us…"** - You cannot walk confidently in purpose while carrying shame, guilt, or comparison.

• **"Lead us not…"** - God strengthens you to leave old patterns and step boldly into new ones.

• **"Yours is the kingdom…"** - Your life is part of a bigger story-and God is the One writing it.

Month 7 is an invitation to stop living according to who you were-and to rise into who you are becoming.

It is an invitation to agree with Heaven's truth, silence the lies that have shaped you, and step into the identity and purpose God has always had for your life.

As you begin this month, take a deep breath and lean in:

You are not who you used to be.

You are becoming who God created you to be.

DAY 183 – God Declares Who You Are

Prayer:
Father, thank You for speaking identity over my life. Hallowed be Your name; remind me that who I am begins with who You say I am, not what others have called me (1 John 3:1). Let Your kingdom come and shape my identity according to Your truth. Let Your will be done as You silence every false label that has clung to me. Give me today my daily bread of confidence, clarity, and a grounded sense of belonging. Forgive me for believing lies about myself, and I forgive those who spoke words that wounded my identity. Lead me not into the temptation of defining myself by circumstances, but deliver me into the identity of a child of God (Ephesians 1:5). To You be the glory forever. Amen.

Reflection:
What false identity or old label do you need God to remove?

Action:
Write one truth God speaks about who you are.

Scriptures Referenced Today:
1 John 3:1 (KJV) - "Behold, what manner of love the Father hath bestowed upon us, that we should be called the sons of God: therefore the world knoweth us not, because it knew him not."

Ephesians 1:5 (KJV) - "Having predestinated us unto the adoption of children by Jesus Christ to himself, according to the good pleasure of his will."

DAY 184 – God Calls You by Name

Prayer:
Father, thank You for knowing me personally-my name, my story, and my calling. Hallowed be Your name; remind me that You call me not by my failures, but by my future (Isaiah 43:1). Let Your kingdom come and awaken the purpose You placed inside me. Let Your will be done as You guide me into who You created me to be. Give me today my daily bread of courage, clarity, and willingness to follow. Forgive me for running from my calling, and I forgive those who tried to define my path for me. Lead me not into the temptation of shrinking back, but deliver me into bold obedience (Jeremiah 1:5). To You be praise and honor. Amen.

Reflection:
What is God calling you *toward* in this season?

Action:
Write one step of obedience toward the calling God is highlighting.

Scriptures Referenced Today:
Isaiah 43:1 (KJV) - "But now thus saith the Lord that created thee, O Jacob, and he that formed thee, O Israel, Fear not: for I have redeemed thee, I have called thee by thy name; thou art mine."
Jeremiah 1:5 (KJV) - "Before I formed thee in the belly I knew thee; and before thou camest forth out of the womb I sanctified thee, and I ordained thee a prophet unto the nations."

DAY 185 – God Forms Your Character Before Your Calling

Prayer:
Father, thank You for shaping my character before expanding my calling. Hallowed be Your name; do the inner work in me that prepares me for the outer work You've assigned (Psalm 139:23–24). Let Your kingdom come and refine my motives, desires, and intentions. Let Your will be done as You build integrity, humility, and spiritual maturity within me. Give me today my daily bread of teachability, patience, and surrender. Forgive me for wanting the assignment without the transformation, and I forgive those who pressured me to perform instead of grow. Lead me not into the temptation of rushing ahead, but deliver me into the steady shaping of Your hands (Philippians 1:6). To You be all glory. Amen.

Reflection:
What part of your character is God strengthening or refining right now?

_____

_____

_____

Action:
Write one area where you will allow God to shape you today.

_____

_____

_____

Scriptures Referenced Today:
Psalm 139:23–24 (KJV) - "Search me, O God, and know my heart: try me, and know my thoughts:
And see if there be any wicked way in me, and lead me in the way everlasting."
Philippians 1:6 (KJV) - "Being confident of this very thing, that he which hath begun a good work in you will perform it until the day of Jesus Christ."

DAY 186 – God Gives You a New Mindset for a New Season

Prayer:
Father, thank You for renewing my mind as You lead me into a new season. Hallowed be Your name; transform my thinking so I can see myself the way You see me (Romans 12:2). Let Your kingdom come and shift every thought that holds me back. Let Your will be done as You replace doubt with confidence, fear with faith, and lies with truth. Give me today my daily bread of clarity, strength, and renewed perspective. Forgive me for holding onto old ways of thinking, and I forgive those who shaped mindsets that limited me. Lead me not into the temptation of returning to old patterns, but deliver me into the renewed mind You promise (Ephesians 4:23–24). To You be the glory. Amen.

Reflection:
What mindset or belief must change for you to step into the next season?

_____

_____

_____

Action:
Write one truth-based mindset you will embrace starting today.

_____

_____

Scriptures Referenced Today:
Romans 12:2 (KJV) - "And be not conformed to this world: but be ye transformed by the renewing of your mind, that ye may prove what is that good, and acceptable, and perfect, will of God."
Ephesians 4:23–24 (KJV) - "And be renewed in the spirit of your mind; And that ye put on the new man, which after God is created in righteousness and true holiness."

DAY 187 – God Breaks the Power of Shame

Prayer:

Father, thank You for breaking the weight of shame that has tried to follow me. Hallowed be Your name; remind me that there is no condemnation for those who are in Christ Jesus (Romans 8:1). Let Your kingdom come and lift off the burdens of guilt, regret, and accusations. Let Your will be done as You heal the memories that still speak shame over me. Give me today my daily bread of freedom, forgiveness, and restored dignity. Forgive me for holding onto sins You've already forgiven, and I forgive those who used shame as a weapon against me. Lead me not into the temptation of self-condemnation, but deliver me into the freedom of being fully forgiven (Isaiah 54:4). To You be honor and praise. Amen.

Reflection:

What shame or regret is God inviting you to release?

Action:

Write down the truth God speaks over the shame you're letting go of today.

Scriptures Referenced Today:

Romans 8:1 (KJV) - "There is therefore now no condemnation to them which are in Christ Jesus, who walk not after the flesh, but after the Spirit."

Isaiah 54:4 (KJV) - "Fear not; for thou shalt not be ashamed: neither be thou confounded; for thou shalt not be put to shame: for thou shalt forget the shame of thy youth, and shalt not remember the reproach of thy widowhood any more."

DAY 188 – God Heals the Way You See Yourself

Prayer:

Father, thank You for healing the places in me where my self-image has been damaged. Hallowed be Your name; teach me to see myself through the lens of Your love and truth, not through the opinions of people (Psalm 139:14). Let Your kingdom come and restore every part of me that has been distorted by comparison, criticism, or past hurts. Let Your will be done as You reshape my identity according to Your Word. Give me today my daily bread of confidence, worth, and renewed identity. Forgive me for agreeing with lies about myself, and I forgive those who spoke words that wounded how I see myself. Lead me not into the temptation of self-rejection, but deliver me into the freedom of knowing I am wonderfully made (Ephesians 2:10). To You be all glory. Amen.

Reflection:

What negative belief about yourself is God asking you to lay down?

_____

_____

_____

Action:

Write one truth about your identity that you will choose to believe today.

_____

_____

_____

Scriptures Referenced Today:
Psalm 139:14 (KJV) -
"I will praise thee; for I am fearfully and wonderfully made: marvelous are thy works; and that my soul knoweth right well."
Ephesians 2:10 (KJV) -
"For we are his workmanship, created in Christ Jesus unto good works, which God hath before ordained that we should walk in them."

DAY 189 – God Calls You Into Purpose, Not Performance

Prayer:
Father, thank You that my calling is rooted in purpose-not pressure, perfection, or performance. Hallowed be Your name; remind me that

You care more about my heart than my accomplishments (Micah 6:8). Let Your kingdom come and free me from striving to prove myself. Let Your will be done as You lead me into the purpose You designed uniquely for me. Give me today my daily bread of focus, surrender, and peace. Forgive me for trying to earn what You freely give, and I forgive those who made me feel that my worth was tied to performance. Lead me not into the temptation of comparison or striving, but deliver me into the simplicity of walking humbly with You (Psalm 57:2). To You be praise forever. Amen.

Reflection:
Where have you been performing instead of walking in purpose?

Action:
Write one area where you will shift from striving to surrender.

Scriptures Referenced Today:
Micah 6:8 (KJV) -
"He hath showed thee, O man, what is good; and what doth the Lord require of thee, but to do justly, and to love mercy, and to walk humbly with thy God?"
Psalm 57:2 (KJV) -
"I will cry unto God most high; unto God that performeth all things for me."

DAY 190 – God Gives You Boldness to Step Into Calling

Prayer:
Father, thank You for giving me boldness to step into what You have called me to. Hallowed be Your name; remind me that You have not given me the spirit of fear, but of power, love, and a sound mind (2 Timothy 1:7). Let Your kingdom come and remove hesitation, timidity,

and insecurity. Let Your will be done as You strengthen my heart to walk confidently in the calling You've placed on my life. Give me today my daily bread of courage, conviction, and holy confidence. Forgive me for shrinking back, and I forgive those who discouraged or doubted me. Lead me not into the temptation of fear, but deliver me into bold obedience (Joshua 1:9). To You be glory and honor. Amen.

Reflection:

What step of obedience requires boldness from God right now?

Action:

Write the one bold step you will take today toward your calling.

Scriptures Referenced Today:

2 Timothy 1:7 (KJV) - "For God hath not given us the spirit of fear; but of power, and of love, and of a sound mind."

Joshua 1:9 (KJV) - "Have not I commanded thee? Be strong and of a good courage; be not afraid, neither be thou dismayed: for the Lord thy God is with thee whithersoever thou goest."

DAY 191 – God Removes the Old So You Can Step Into the New

Prayer:
Father, thank You for removing old patterns, habits, and identities that no longer belong to who You are shaping me to be. Hallowed be Your name; teach me to put off the old self and put on the new (Colossians 3:9–10). Let Your kingdom come and break every cycle that has tried to limit my growth. Let Your will be done as You lead me into the new things You are calling me to. Give me today my daily bread of strength, renewal, and transformation. Forgive me for holding onto what You're asking me to release, and I forgive those who kept me tied to old versions of myself. Lead me not into the temptation of returning to old ways, but deliver me into the new life You prepared for me (Isaiah 43:18–19). To You be all praise. Amen.

Reflection:
What "old thing" is God asking you to release in this season?

_____

_____

_____

Action:
Write one old pattern or mindset you will replace with God's truth today.

_____

_____

_____

Scriptures Referenced Today:
Colossians 3:9–10 (KJV) -
"Lie not one to another, seeing that ye have put off the old man with his deeds;
And have put on the new man, which is renewed in knowledge after the image of him that created him."
Isaiah 43:18–19 (KJV) - "Remember ye not the former things, neither consider the things of old.
Behold, I will do a new thing; now it shall spring forth; shall ye not know it? I will even make a way in the wilderness, and rivers in the desert."

DAY 192 – God Equips You With Everything You Need

Prayer:
Father, thank You for equipping me with everything I need for the purpose You've given me. Hallowed be Your name; remind me that You supply every resource, every gift, and every ounce of strength required (2 Peter 1:3). Let Your kingdom come and activate the abilities You placed in me. Let Your will be done as You prepare me for every good work. Give me today my daily bread of confidence, readiness, and spiritual empowerment. Forgive me for doubting my abilities, and I forgive those who underestimated me. Lead me not into the temptation of feeling inadequate, but deliver me into the confidence that You fully equip those You call (Hebrews 13:21). To You be the glory forever. Amen.

Reflection:
Where do you need to trust that God has already equipped you?

_____

_____

_____

Action:
Write one way you will step forward today with confidence in God's equipping.

_____

_____

_____

Scriptures Referenced Today:
2 Peter 1:3 (KJV) - "According as his divine power hath given unto us all things that pertain unto life and godliness, through the knowledge of him that hath called us to glory and virtue:"

Hebrews 13:21 (KJV) - "Make you perfect in every good work to do his will, working in you that which is well pleasing in his sight, through Jesus Christ; to whom be glory for ever and ever. Amen."

DAY 193 – God Teaches You to Walk in Confidence

Prayer:

Father, thank You for teaching me to walk in the confidence that comes from knowing I belong to You. Hallowed be Your name; remind me that my confidence is not in myself but in Christ within me (Philippians 4:13). Let Your kingdom come and strengthen my steps with boldness. Let Your will be done as You remove insecurity and build holy confidence in its place. Give me today my daily bread of courage, stability, and assurance in Your calling. Forgive me for doubting the gifts You placed in me, and I forgive those who spoke words that undermined my confidence. Lead me not into the temptation of self-doubt, but deliver me into boldness rooted in who You are (Hebrews 10:35). To You be the glory forever. Amen.

Reflection:
Where do you need God-given confidence to rise up in you?

_____

_____

Action:
Write one area where you will walk with confidence today-not in yourself, but in Him.

_____

_____

Scriptures Referenced Today:
Philippians 4:13 (KJV) - "I can do all things through Christ which strengtheneth me."
Hebrews 10:35 (KJV) - "Cast not away therefore your confidence, which hath great recompence of reward."

DAY 194 – God Makes You a New Creation

Prayer:
Father, thank You for making me a new creation through Christ. Hallowed be Your name; remind me that the old has passed away and the new has begun (2 Corinthians 5:17). Let Your kingdom come and restore every part of my life that still reflects old patterns or old pain. Let Your will be done as You help me live fully in the identity You have given me. Give me today my daily bread of renewal, transformation, and spiritual clarity. Forgive me for holding onto old versions of myself, and I forgive those who still treat me according to who I used to be. Lead me not into the temptation of returning to old habits, but deliver me into the fullness of new life in Christ (Ezekiel 36:26). All glory to You. Amen.

Reflection:
What part of your "old self" is God asking you to leave behind?

_____

_____

_____

Action:
Write down one way you will walk in your new identity today.

_____

_____

_____

Scriptures Referenced Today:
2 Corinthians 5:17 (KJV) - "Therefore if any man be in Christ, he is a new creature: old things are passed away; behold, all things are become new."

Ezekiel 36:26 (KJV) - "A new heart also will I give you, and a new spirit will I put within you: and I will take away the stony heart out of your flesh, and I will give you an heart of flesh."

DAY 195 – God Strengthens You to Overcome Insecurity

Prayer:
Father, thank You for strengthening me in the places where insecurity has lived far too long. Hallowed be Your name; remind me that You are the source of my worth and confidence (Psalm 27:1). Let Your kingdom come and uproot every fear that has held me back. Let Your will be done as You replace insecurity with courage and assurance. Give me today my daily bread of boldness, stability, and inner strength. Forgive me for letting insecurity speak louder than Your truth, and I forgive those who contributed to my self-doubt. Lead me not into the temptation of shrinking back, but deliver me into the courage to step forward in faith (Isaiah 41:10). To You be honor and glory. Amen.

Reflection:
What insecurity is God helping you overcome in this season?

_____

_____

_____

Action:
Write one truth you will declare over insecurity today.

_____

_____

_____

Scriptures Referenced Today:
Psalm 27:1 (KJV) - "The Lord is my light and my salvation; whom shall I fear? The Lord is the strength of my life; of whom shall I be afraid?"
Isaiah 41:10 (KJV) - "Fear thou not; for I am with thee: be not dismayed; for I am thy God: I will strengthen thee; yea, I will help thee; yea, I will uphold thee with the right hand of my righteousness."

DAY 196 – God Helps You Discover Your Gifts

Prayer:
Father, thank You for the gifts, abilities, and strengths You placed within me. Hallowed be Your name; help me recognize what You've invested in me and how You want those gifts used (1 Peter 4:10). Let Your kingdom come and activate the gifts that have been dormant or overlooked. Let Your will be done as You teach me to serve others with joy and humility. Give me today my daily bread of discernment, clarity, and confidence in the gifts You've given. Forgive me for minimizing or ignoring the gifts You placed in me, and I forgive those who dismissed or undervalued them. Lead me not into the temptation of hiding my gifts, but deliver me into bold, faithful stewardship (Romans 12:6). To You be the glory. Amen.

Reflection:
What gift or ability do you sense God is drawing your attention to?

_____

_____

_____

Action:
Write one small way you will use or practice that gift today.

_____

_____

_____

Scriptures Referenced Today:
1 Peter 4:10 (KJV) - "As every man hath received the gift, even so minister the same one to another, as good stewards of the manifold grace of God."
Romans 12:6 (KJV) - "Having then gifts differing according to the grace that is given to us, whether prophecy, let us prophesy according to the proportion of faith;"

DAY 197 – God Teaches You to Walk Worthy of Your Calling

Prayer:
Father, thank You for calling me into a life of purpose and meaning. Hallowed be Your name; teach me to walk worthy of the calling You have placed on my life (Ephesians 4:1). Let Your kingdom come and shape my character, decisions, and relationships according to Your will. Let Your will be done as You form humility, gentleness, and patience within me. Give me today my daily bread of direction, maturity, and grace. Forgive me for taking Your calling lightly, and I forgive those who tried to distract or derail my purpose. Lead me not into the temptation of living beneath my calling, but deliver me into a life that honors You fully (Colossians 1:10). To You be praise and glory. Amen.

Reflection:
What part of your calling do you need to walk more intentionally today?

_____

_____

_____

Action:
Write one practical way you will walk worthy of God's calling today.

_____

_____

_____

Scriptures Referenced Today:
Ephesians 4:1 (KJV) - "I therefore, the prisoner of the Lord, beseech you that ye walk worthy of the vocation wherewith ye are called,"
Colossians 1:10 (KJV) - "That ye might walk worthy of the Lord unto all pleasing, being fruitful in every good work, and increasing in the knowledge of God;"

DAY 198 – God Gives You Clarity About Your Calling

Prayer:
Father, thank You for giving clarity to my calling and purpose. Hallowed be Your name; illuminate the path You have prepared for me and speak clearly to my heart (Psalm 32:8). Let Your kingdom come and reveal what You are asking me to pursue in this season. Let Your will be done as You align my desires with Your assignments. Give me today my daily bread of direction, discernment, and holy focus. Forgive me for the times I've ignored Your leading, and I forgive those who tried to pull me off course. Lead me not into the temptation of confusion, but deliver me into the clarity and purpose You promise (Proverbs 16:3). To You be all glory. Amen.

Reflection:
What part of your calling is God bringing clarity to right now?

_____

_____

_____

Action:
Write one step you will take today in obedience to the clarity God is giving.

_____

_____

_____

Scriptures Referenced Today:
Psalm 32:8 (KJV) - "I will instruct thee and teach thee in the way which thou shalt go: I will guide thee with mine eye."
Proverbs 16:3 (KJV) - "Commit thy works unto the Lord, and thy thoughts shall be established."

DAY 199 – God Teaches You to Hear His Voice

Prayer:
Father, thank You for speaking to me with clarity, patience, and love. Hallowed be Your name; teach me to recognize Your voice above every other voice in my life (John 10:27). Let Your kingdom come and quiet every distraction that competes for my attention. Let Your will be done as You train my ears and heart to respond immediately to Your leading. Give me today my daily bread of spiritual sensitivity, discernment, and peace. Forgive me for ignoring Your voice, and I forgive those who taught me to doubt Your ability to speak. Lead me not into the temptation of confusion, but deliver me into the confidence that I am Yours and You guide me (Isaiah 30:21). All glory to You. Amen.

Reflection:
What area of your life do you most need to hear God's voice right now?

_____

_____

_____

Action:
Write one way you will make space today to listen for God's voice.

_____

_____

_____

Scriptures Referenced Today:
John 10:27 (KJV) - "My sheep hear my voice, and I know them, and they follow me."
Isaiah 30:21 (KJV) - "And thine ears shall hear a word behind thee, saying, This is the way, walk ye in it, when ye turn to the right hand, and when ye turn to the left."

DAY 200 – God Opens Doors No One Can Shut

Prayer:
Father, thank You for opening doors that no one can close. Hallowed be Your name; remind me that favor, opportunity, and calling come from Your hand alone (Revelation 3:8). Let Your kingdom come and open the right doors for my life while closing the ones that are not of You. Let Your will be done as You lead me into the assignments You have prepared. Give me today my daily bread of divine opportunity, boldness, and discernment. Forgive me for forcing doors that You were never in, and I forgive those who tried to block or hinder my progress. Lead me not into the temptation of striving, but deliver me into confidence in Your timing and Your favor (Isaiah 22:22). To You be praise forever. Amen.

Reflection:
What door do you sense God opening-or closing-in this season?

_____

_____

_____

Action:
Write one step of obedience you'll take toward the door God is opening.

_____

_____

_____

Scriptures Referenced Today:
Revelation 3:8 (KJV) - "I know thy works: behold, I have set before thee an open door, and no man can shut it: for thou hast a little strength, and hast kept my word, and hast not denied my name."
Isaiah 22:22 (KJV) - "And the key of the house of David will I lay upon his shoulder; so he shall open, and none shall shut; and he shall shut, and none shall open."

DAY 201 – God Establishes Your Steps

Prayer:
Father, thank You for establishing my steps according to Your plan.
Hallowed be Your name; remind me that every path You lead me on is
intentional and aligned with Your purpose (Psalm 37:23). Let Your
kingdom come and order my decisions with wisdom and clarity. Let Your
will be done as You steady my heart and remove hesitation. Give me
today my daily bread of direction, confidence, and peace. Forgive me for
resisting Your guidance, and I forgive those who tried to steer me away
from Your calling. Lead me not into the temptation of going my own
way, but deliver me into the path You have prepared for me (Proverbs
4:26). To You be all honor. Amen.

Reflection:
Where do you need God to establish your steps today?

_____

_____

_____

Action:
Write one step you will take today that aligns with God's direction.

_____

_____

_____

Scriptures Referenced Today:
Psalm 37:23 (KJV) - "The steps of a good man are ordered by the Lord:
and he delighteth in his way."
Proverbs 4:26 (KJV) - "Ponder the path of thy feet, and let all thy ways
be established."

DAY 202 – God Prepares You for the Work Ahead

Prayer:
Father, thank You for preparing me for the work You've assigned to my life. Hallowed be Your name; equip me with everything I need to fulfill Your purpose with excellence and humility (2 Timothy 3:17). Let Your kingdom come and shape my character as deeply as You shape my calling. Let Your will be done as You train, develop, and strengthen me for the journey ahead. Give me today my daily bread of readiness, resilience, and spiritual maturity. Forgive me for doubting that You have prepared me, and I forgive those who questioned my calling. Lead me not into the temptation of feeling unqualified, but deliver me into confidence that You prepare, equip, and empower me (Ephesians 2:10). To You be glory forever. Amen.

Reflection:
What part of your calling do you sense God preparing you for right now?

_____

_____

_____

Action:
Write one way you will cooperate with God's preparation today.

_____

_____

_____

Scriptures Referenced Today:
2 Timothy 3:17 (KJV) - "That the man of God may be perfect, throughly furnished unto all good works."
Ephesians 2:10 (KJV) - "For we are his workmanship, created in Christ Jesus unto good works, which God hath before ordained that we should walk in them."

DAY 203 – God Teaches You to Trust His Timing

Prayer:
Father, thank You for teaching me to trust Your timing in every part of my calling. Hallowed be Your name; remind me that everything You do is purposeful and perfectly timed (Ecclesiastes 3:11). Let Your kingdom come and quiet the impatience in my heart. Let Your will be done as You align my pace with Yours. Give me today my daily bread of patience, trust, and calm confidence. Forgive me for rushing ahead, and I forgive those who pressured me to move before I was ready. Lead me not into the temptation of frustration, but deliver me into peace as I wait on You (Psalm 37:7). To You be the glory forever. Amen.

Reflection:
Where is God asking you to trust His timing instead of your own?

_____

_____

_____

Action:
Write one area where you will slow down and trust God's timing today.

_____

_____

_____

Scriptures Referenced Today:
Ecclesiastes 3:11 (KJV) - "He hath made every thing beautiful in his time: also he hath set the world in their heart, so that no man can find out the work that God maketh from the beginning to the end."
Psalm 37:7 (KJV) - "Rest in the Lord, and wait patiently for him: fret not thyself because of him who prospereth in his way, because of the man who bringeth wicked devices to pass."

DAY 204 – God Strengthens You to Overcome Opposition

Prayer:
Father, thank You for strengthening me when opposition rises against my calling. Hallowed be Your name; remind me that no weapon formed against me shall prosper (Isaiah 54:17). Let Your kingdom come and fill me with courage when resistance appears. Let Your will be done as You help me endure with faith, humility, and steadfastness. Give me today my daily bread of strength, resilience, and unwavering confidence in You. Forgive me for becoming discouraged by resistance, and I forgive those who opposed or misunderstood my calling. Lead me not into the temptation of retaliation, but deliver me into peace and perseverance (Psalm 27:3). To You be honor and praise. Amen.

Reflection:
Where are you facing opposition that you need God's strength to overcome?

_____

_____

_____

Action:
Write one way you will trust God when you face resistance today.

_____

_____

_____

Scriptures Referenced Today:
Isaiah 54:17 (KJV) - "No weapon that is formed against thee shall prosper; and every tongue that shall rise against thee in judgment thou shalt condemn. This is the heritage of the servants of the Lord, and their righteousness is of me, saith the Lord."
Psalm 27:3 (KJV) - "Though an host should encamp against me, my heart shall not fear: though war should rise against me, in this will I be confident."

DAY 205 – God Develops Your Character for Your Calling

Prayer:
Father, thank You for developing my character to sustain the calling You've placed on my life. Hallowed be Your name; remind me that godly character is a greater treasure than any achievement (Proverbs 22:1). Let Your kingdom come and shape the quiet, unseen parts of my heart. Let Your will be done as You build humility, integrity, patience, and self-control within me. Give me today my daily bread of growth, maturity, and teachability. Forgive me for resisting Your refining process, and I forgive those who highlighted my flaws more than my progress. Lead me not into the temptation of focusing on image over character, but deliver me into the depth of who You are forming me to be (Romans 5:3–4). To You be all glory. Amen.

Reflection:
What character trait is God developing in you right now?

_____

_____

_____

Action:
Write one practical choice today that reflects the character God is building in you.

_____

_____

_____

Scriptures Referenced Today:
Proverbs 22:1 (KJV) - "A good name is rather to be chosen than great riches, and loving favour rather than silver and gold."
Romans 5:3–4 (KJV) - "And not only so, but we glory in tribulations also: knowing that tribulation worketh patience;
And patience, experience; and experience, hope."

DAY 206 – God Establishes Your Identity in Christ

Prayer:
Father, thank You for establishing my identity firmly in Christ. Hallowed be Your name; remind me that my life is hidden with Christ in God (Colossians 3:3). Let Your kingdom come and quiet every false identity that tries to speak over me. Let Your will be done as You root me deeply in who You say I am. Give me today my daily bread of confidence, security, and spiritual grounding. Forgive me for finding my identity in people or achievements, and I forgive those who misdefined or mislabeled me. Lead me not into the temptation of living from old identities, but deliver me into the truth that I am Yours (1 Peter 2:9). To You be praise and honor. Amen.

Reflection:
What identity do you need to release-and what identity in Christ do you need to embrace?

_____

_____

_____

Action:
Write one identity statement from God's Word that you will walk in today.

_____

_____

_____

Scriptures Referenced Today:
Colossians 3:3 (KJV) - "For ye are dead, and your life is hid with Christ in God."
1 Peter 2:9 (KJV) - "But ye are a chosen generation, a royal priesthood, an holy nation, a peculiar people; that ye should show forth the praises of him who hath called you out of darkness into his marvelous light;"

DAY 207 – God Prepares You to Influence Others

Prayer:
Father, thank You for preparing me to influence others for Your glory.
Hallowed be Your name; remind me that I am called to be salt and light in
this world (Matthew 5:14). Let Your kingdom come and shape my
influence with wisdom, humility, and love. Let Your will be done as You
open opportunities for me to reflect Christ to those around me. Give me
today my daily bread of courage, clarity, and compassion. Forgive me for
hiding the light You placed within me, and I forgive those who tried to
silence my influence. Lead me not into the temptation of seeking
approval, but deliver me into the freedom of living for Your glory
(Philippians 2:15). To You be all glory. Amen.

Reflection:
Where is God inviting you to be an influence in someone's life today?

_____

_____

Action:
Write one way you will reflect Christ's light to someone today.

_____

_____

Scriptures Referenced Today:
Matthew 5:14 (KJV) - "Ye are the light of the world. A city that is set on
an hill cannot be hid."
Philippians 2:15 (KJV) - "That ye may be blameless and harmless, the
sons of God, without rebuke, in the midst of a crooked and perverse
nation, among whom ye shine as lights in the world;"

DAY 208 – God Teaches You to Walk in Humility

Prayer:
Father, thank You for teaching me to walk in humility as You shape my calling. Hallowed be Your name; remind me that greatness in Your kingdom is rooted in a humble heart (James 4:10). Let Your kingdom come and remove pride, comparison, and self-exaltation from my life. Let Your will be done as You strengthen my character to reflect Christ. Give me today my daily bread of gentleness, patience, and a teachable spirit. Forgive me for elevating myself or seeking recognition, and I forgive those who expected perfection instead of growth. Lead me not into the temptation of pride, but deliver me into the humility that honors You (Micah 6:8). To You be the glory forever. Amen.

Reflection:
Where is God inviting you to walk more humbly today?

_____

_____

_____

Action:
Write one humble choice you will make today that reflects Christ's heart.

_____

_____

_____

Scriptures Referenced Today: James 4:10 (KJV) - "Humble yourselves in the sight of the Lord, and he shall lift you up."
Micah 6:8 (KJV) - "He hath showed thee, O man, what is good; and what doth the Lord require of thee, but to do justly, and to love mercy, and to walk humbly with thy God?"

DAY 209 – God Uses Your Story for His Glory

Prayer:
Father, thank You for using my story-even the painful chapters-for Your glory. Hallowed be Your name; remind me that all things work together for good for those who love You (Romans 8:28). Let Your kingdom come and redeem every part of my past. Let Your will be done as You use my experiences to encourage, strengthen, and inspire others. Give me today my daily bread of courage, healing, and vulnerability. Forgive me for hiding my story out of fear or shame, and I forgive those who misjudged my past. Lead me not into the temptation of silence, but deliver me into boldness to share what You have done (Psalm 66:16). To You be honor and praise. Amen.

Reflection:
What part of your story might God be inviting you to share for His glory?

_____

_____

_____

Action:
Write one way you can encourage someone using your testimony today.

_____

_____

_____

Scriptures Referenced Today:
Romans 8:28 (KJV) - "And we know that all things work together for good to them that love God, to them who are the called according to his purpose."
Psalm 66:16 (KJV) - "Come and hear, all ye that fear God, and I will declare what he hath done for my soul."

DAY 210 – God Gives You Wisdom to Walk Out Your Purpose

Prayer:
Father, thank You for giving me wisdom to walk out the purpose You have placed on my life. Hallowed be Your name; grant me the wisdom that comes from above, pure and peaceable (James 3:17). Let Your kingdom come and guide every decision I make. Let Your will be done as You lead me into choices that align with Your calling. Give me today my daily bread of insight, discernment, and wise judgment. Forgive me for leaning on my own understanding, and I forgive those who influenced me toward unwise decisions. Lead me not into the temptation of acting without seeking You, but deliver me into Your wisdom and clarity (Proverbs 2:6). To You be the glory. Amen.

Reflection:
Where do you need God's wisdom as you walk out your calling?

_____

_____

_____

Action:
Write one decision you will bring before God for wisdom today.

_____

_____

_____

Scriptures Referenced Today:
James 3:17 (KJV) - "But the wisdom that is from above is first pure, then peaceable, gentle, and easy to be entreated, full of mercy and good fruits, without partiality, and without hypocrisy."
Proverbs 2:6 (KJV) - "For the Lord giveth wisdom: out of his mouth cometh knowledge and understanding."

DAY 211 – God Strengthens You to Persevere in Purpose

Prayer:
Father, thank You for strengthening me to persevere when my purpose requires endurance. Hallowed be Your name; remind me that steadfastness is forged through faith and reliance on You (James 1:12). Let Your kingdom come and fortify my spirit when the journey grows difficult. Let Your will be done as You strengthen me to keep going. Give me today my daily bread of endurance, resilience, and spiritual fortitude. Forgive me for wanting to quit when things became hard, and I forgive those who discouraged me. Lead me not into the temptation of giving up, but deliver me into perseverance that honors You (Galatians 6:9). To You be praise forever. Amen.

Reflection:
What area of your calling requires perseverance right now?

_____

_____

_____

Action:
Write one step you will take today to persevere with faith.

_____

_____

_____

Scriptures Referenced Today:
James 1:12 (KJV) - "Blessed is the man that endureth temptation: for when he is tried, he shall receive the crown of life, which the Lord hath promised to them that love him."
Galatians 6:9 (KJV) - "And let us not be weary in well doing: for in due season we shall reap, if we faint not."

DAY 212 – God Helps You Discern Your Next Season

Prayer:

Father, thank You for helping me discern the season I am stepping into. Hallowed be Your name; open my eyes to what You are doing in and around me (Isaiah 43:19). Let Your kingdom come and guide me with spiritual understanding. Let Your will be done as You reveal what to continue, what to release, and what to prepare for. Give me today my daily bread of clarity, wisdom, and sensitivity to Your Spirit. Forgive me for misreading seasons in the past, and I forgive those who influenced me in the wrong direction. Lead me not into the temptation of confusion, but deliver me into discernment and confidence in Your leading (Ecclesiastes 3:1). To You be the glory forever. Amen.

Reflection:

What season does it feel like God is leading you into now?

_____

_____

_____

Action:

Write one thing you sense God asking you to continue-or begin-this season.

_____

_____

_____

Scriptures Referenced Today:

Isaiah 43:19 (KJV) - "Behold, I will do a new thing; now it shall spring forth; shall ye not know it? I will even make a way in the wilderness, and rivers in the desert."

Ecclesiastes 3:1 (KJV) - "To every thing there is a season, and a time to every purpose under the heaven:"

DAY 213 – God Teaches You to Walk in Your True Identity

Prayer:
Father, thank You for teaching me to walk boldly in the identity You have given me. Hallowed be Your name; remind me daily that I am chosen, loved, and called by You (Ephesians 1:4). Let Your kingdom come and silence every voice that competes with Your truth. Let Your will be done as You root my heart deeply in who You say I am. Give me today my daily bread of confidence, security, and spiritual assurance. Forgive me for accepting identities that were never mine, and I forgive those who labeled me wrongly. Lead me not into the temptation of living beneath my identity, but deliver me into the fullness of who I am in Christ (1 Peter 2:9). To You be all glory. Amen.

Reflection:
What false identity do you need to completely release today?

_____

_____

Action:
Write one identity truth from God's Word that you will walk in boldly today.

_____

_____

Scriptures Referenced Today:
Ephesians 1:4 (KJV) - "According as he hath chosen us in him before the foundation of the world, that we should be holy and without blame before him in love:"
1 Peter 2:9 (KJV) -
"But ye are a chosen generation, a royal priesthood, an holy nation, a peculiar people; that ye should show forth the praises of him who hath called you out of darkness into his marvelous light;"

MONTH 7 CLOSING REFLECTION: IDENTITY & CALLING

Month 7 has taken you deep into the reality of **who you are in Christ** and **who you are becoming**. This month was about more than encouragement - it was about *transformation*. The Lord peeled back old labels, old expectations, old voices, and old identities so that you could finally walk in the identity He authored for you long before the world ever named you.

This month, you learned that:

You are chosen, adopted, redeemed, and deeply known.

- Identity is not achieved - it is received.
- Calling is not discovered through striving - it unfolds through obedience.
- God shapes character before He expands assignment.
- Confidence grows not from self-belief, but from God's presence.
- Discernment is essential to walking your calling with clarity.
- Purpose flows from identity - never the other way around.
- God breaks shame, insecurity, comparison, and self-doubt as He forms your new identity.
- Boldness rises when fear loses its authority.
- Calling requires endurance, maturity, and a heart rooted in truth.

This month revealed a critical truth:

You are becoming the person God always intended you to be.

Your Father has:

- Rewritten your identity
- Strengthened your confidence
- Clarified your calling
- Purified your motives
- Refined your character
- Sharpened your discernment
- Expanded your insight
- Restored your dignity
- Renewed your mind
- Rebuilt your foundation

Month 7 wasn't just about learning - it was about *becoming*.
As you close this month, take time to reflect:

- What identity lies did God silence?
- What truths did He root deep within you?
- Where has your confidence grown?
- What part of your calling has become clearer?
- What old version of yourself finally fell away?
- Where do you feel more aligned, more grounded, and more confident in Him?

Month 7 sends you forward with this truth:

Your identity is secure. Your calling is real. Your Father is leading you.

Now you step into Month 8 - where identity becomes **action**, calling becomes **responsibility**, and maturity becomes **stewardship**.

MONTH 8 THEME: STEWARDSHIP, FAITHFULNESS & LIVING YOUR CALLING OUTWARDLY

Month 7 established **who you are**.

Month 8 teaches you **what to do with who you are**.

This month is about **stewardship** - managing your gifts, your influence, your opportunities, your time, your character, and your calling with excellence and intentionality. God doesn't just shape identity so you can feel whole; He shapes identity so you can **walk out your purpose with power and faithfulness**.

Month 8 focuses on:

- stewarding your gifts
- developing discipline
- managing opportunities wisely
- cultivating healthy habits
- aligning actions with calling
- strengthening influence and witness
- walking responsibly in spiritual authority
- honoring God with your decisions
- investing your time with purpose
- becoming faithful in both the small and significant

Through the Lord's Prayer framework:

- **"Give us this day..."** - You learn daily stewardship.
- **"Your kingdom come..."** - You manage what God entrusts to you.
- **"Forgive us..."** - You steward relationships with grace.
- **"Lead us..."** - You steward decisions with wisdom.

This month asks you to live intentionally, to take ownership of your growth, to honor God with your habits, and to carry your calling with responsibility, consistency, and excellence.

DAY 214 – God Sharpens Your Discernment

Prayer:
Father, thank You for sharpening my discernment as You grow me into my calling. Hallowed be Your name; teach me to distinguish Your voice from every other voice (Hebrews 5:14). Let Your kingdom come and bring clarity where there has been confusion. Let Your will be done as You train my heart to recognize truth, direction, and spiritual wisdom. Give me today my daily bread of insight, awareness, and sensitivity to Your Spirit. Forgive me for ignoring Your nudges, and I forgive those who influenced me away from Your path. Lead me not into the temptation of deception, but deliver me into spiritual discernment and truth (1 Kings 3:9). To You be the glory. Amen.

Reflection:
Where do you need stronger spiritual discernment today?

_____

_____

_____

Action:
Write one practical step you will take to quiet distractions and listen to God.

_____

_____

_____

Scriptures Referenced Today:
Hebrews 5:14 (KJV) -
"But strong meat belongeth to them that are of full age, even those who by reason of use have their senses exercised to discern both good and evil."
1 Kings 3:9 (KJV) -
"Give therefore thy servant an understanding heart to judge thy people, that I may discern between good and bad: for who is able to judge this thy so great a people?"

DAY 215 – God Aligns Your Desires With His Will

Prayer:
Father, thank You for aligning my desires with Your will. Hallowed be Your name; shape my heart so that I long for what pleases You (Psalm 37:4). Let Your kingdom come and reorder every desire that pulls me away from Your purpose. Let Your will be done as You draw my heart into deeper alignment with Yours. Give me today my daily bread of purity, focus, and surrendered desire. Forgive me for pursuing things outside Your will, and I forgive those who influenced my desires in the wrong direction. Lead me not into the temptation of chasing empty things, but deliver me into delighting fully in You (Philippians 2:13). To You be honor and praise. Amen.

Reflection:
What desire needs to be realigned with God's heart today?

_____

_____

_____

Action:
Write one desire you will surrender to God for alignment.

_____

_____

_____

Scriptures Referenced Today:
Psalm 37:4 (KJV) -
"Delight thyself also in the Lord: and he shall give thee the desires of thine heart."
Philippians 2:13 (KJV) -
"For it is God which worketh in you both to will and to do of his good pleasure."

DAY 216 – God Makes You Bold in the Face of Fear

Prayer:
Father, thank You for making me bold when fear tries to hold me back.
Hallowed be Your name; remind me that You are my light, my salvation,
and my strength (Psalm 27:1). Let Your kingdom come and drive out
every fear that contradicts Your purpose for my life. Let Your will be
done as You fill me with courage to take steps that stretch my faith. Give
me today my daily bread of boldness, strength, and holy confidence.
Forgive me for allowing fear to shape my choices, and I forgive those
who instilled fear in me. Lead me not into the temptation of shrinking
back, but deliver me into fearless obedience (Isaiah 41:13). To You be all
glory. Amen.

Reflection:
What fear must bow to God's presence in your life today?

_____

_____

_____

Action:
Write the bold step you will take today in defiance of fear.

_____

_____

_____

Scriptures Referenced Today:
Psalm 27:1 (KJV) -"The Lord is my light and my salvation; whom shall I
fear? The Lord is the strength of my life; of whom shall I be afraid?"
Isaiah 41:13 (KJV) - "For I the Lord thy God will hold thy right hand,
saying unto thee, Fear not; I will help thee."

DAY 217 – God Cultivates Integrity Within You

Prayer:
Father, thank You for cultivating integrity within me as You shape my calling. Hallowed be Your name; remind me that a life of integrity honors You and protects my purpose (Proverbs 10:9). Let Your kingdom come and purify my motives, my thoughts, and my actions. Let Your will be done as You form consistency and truth within me. Give me today my daily bread of honesty, purity, and steadfast character. Forgive me for compromising in small things, and I forgive those who encouraged or excused compromise. Lead me not into the temptation of cutting corners or hiding truth, but deliver me into a life marked by integrity (Psalm 25:21). To You be the glory. Amen.

Reflection:
What area of your life is God strengthening in integrity?

Action:
Write one decision today that reflects integrity and honors God.

Scriptures Referenced Today:
Proverbs 10:9 (KJV) - "He that walketh uprightly walketh surely: but he that perverteth his ways shall be known."
Psalm 25:21 (KJV) - "Let integrity and uprightness preserve me; for I wait on thee."

DAY 218 – God Strengthens Your Inner Life

Prayer:
Father, thank You for strengthening my inner life so that I can walk confidently in my calling. Hallowed be Your name; renew me in the inner man by Your Spirit (Ephesians 3:16). Let Your kingdom come and fortify the unseen places within me. Let Your will be done as You deepen my faith, refine my motives, and strengthen my spirit. Give me today my daily bread of resilience, depth, and spiritual maturity. Forgive me for neglecting the inner work, and I forgive those who only valued my outward performance. Lead me not into the temptation of focusing on the external, but deliver me into the strength that grows from the inside out (Psalm 51:6). To You be the glory forever. Amen.

Reflection:
Where is God strengthening you internally in this season?

_____

_____

_____

Action:
Write one inner habit or discipline you will cultivate today.

_____

_____

_____

Scriptures Referenced Today:
Ephesians 3:16 (KJV) - "That he would grant you, according to the riches of his glory, to be strengthened with might by his Spirit in the inner man."
Psalm 51:6 (KJV) - "Behold, thou desirest truth in the inward parts: and in the hidden part thou shalt make me to know wisdom."

DAY 219 – God Helps You Let Go of People-Pleasing

Prayer:
Father, thank You for freeing me from the pressure to please people. Hallowed be Your name; remind me that my approval comes from You alone (Galatians 1:10). Let Your kingdom come and silence every fear of disappointing others. Let Your will be done as You teach me to live for Your glory, not human applause. Give me today my daily bread of courage, confidence, and focus. Forgive me for letting the opinions of others shape my choices, and I forgive those who pressured me to meet their expectations. Lead me not into the temptation of people-pleasing, but deliver me into obedience that comes from a pure heart (Colossians 3:23). To You be honor and praise. Amen.

Reflection:
Where is people-pleasing holding you back from God's calling?

_____

_____

_____

Action:
Write one area where you will choose God's approval over people's today.

_____

_____

_____

Scriptures Referenced Today:
Galatians 1:10 (KJV) - "For do I now persuade men, or God? or do I seek to please men? for if I yet pleased men, I should not be the servant of Christ."
Colossians 3:23 (KJV) - "And whatsoever ye do, do it heartily, as to the Lord, and not unto men;"

DAY 220 – God Helps You Break Free From Comparison

Prayer:
Father, thank You for breaking the power of comparison in my life. Hallowed be Your name; remind me that You made me intentionally and uniquely (Psalm 139:13–14). Let Your kingdom come and free me from measuring myself against others. Let Your will be done as You help me embrace my own path, pace, and purpose. Give me today my daily bread of contentment, confidence, and gratitude. Forgive me for comparing myself to others, and I forgive those who made me feel "less than." Lead me not into the temptation of comparison, but deliver me into the joy of being who You created me to be (2 Corinthians 10:12). To You be glory. Amen.

Reflection:
Where has comparison stolen your joy or confidence?

_____

_____

_____

Action:
Write one way you will celebrate who God made you to be today.

_____

_____

_____

Scriptures Referenced Today:
Psalm 139:13–14 (KJV) - "For thou hast possessed my reins: thou hast covered me in my mother's womb.
I will praise thee; for I am fearfully and wonderfully made: marvelous are thy works; and that my soul knoweth right well."
2 Corinthians 10:12 (KJV) - "For we dare not make ourselves of the number, or compare ourselves with some that commend themselves: but they measuring themselves by themselves, and comparing themselves among themselves, are not wise."

DAY 221 – God Calls You to Walk in Freedom

Prayer:
Father, thank You for calling me into true freedom. Hallowed be Your name; remind me that where Your Spirit is, there is liberty (2 Corinthians 3:17). Let Your kingdom come and break every chain that has held me back. Let Your will be done as You lead me out of bondage and into abundant life. Give me today my daily bread of courage, deliverance, and renewed strength. Forgive me for settling for captivity, and I forgive those who contributed to my bondage. Lead me not into the temptation of returning to old chains, but deliver me into the freedom Jesus purchased for me (John 8:36). To You be praise forever. Amen.

Reflection:
Where is God inviting you to walk in greater freedom?

_____

_____

_____

Action:
Write one step you will take today that reflects freedom, not bondage.

_____

_____

_____

Scriptures Referenced Today:
2 Corinthians 3:17 (KJV) - "Now the Lord is that Spirit: and where the Spirit of the Lord is, there is liberty."
John 8:36 (KJV) - "If the Son therefore shall make you free, ye shall be free indeed."

DAY 222 – God Teaches You to Live With Purpose

Prayer:
Father, thank You for teaching me to live with purpose each day. Hallowed be Your name; remind me that You have plans for me, plans for peace and hope (Jeremiah 29:11). Let Your kingdom come and awaken purpose in every part of my life. Let Your will be done as You show me how to live intentionally and meaningfully. Give me today my daily bread of clarity, direction, and intentionality. Forgive me for drifting or wasting time, and I forgive those who distracted me from Your purpose. Lead me not into the temptation of aimlessness, but deliver me into a life directed by You (Proverbs 19:21). To You be glory forever. Amen.

Reflection:
What part of your life needs greater intentionality and purpose?

_____

_____

_____

Action:
Write one purposeful action you will take today in alignment with God's will.

_____

_____

_____

Scriptures Referenced Today:
Jeremiah 29:11 (KJV) - "For I know the thoughts that I think toward you, saith the Lord, thoughts of peace, and not of evil, to give you an expected end."
Proverbs 19:21 (KJV) - "There are many devices in a man's heart; nevertheless the counsel of the Lord, that shall stand."

DAY 223 – God Calls You to Walk in Courage

Prayer:
Father, thank You for calling me into a life of courage. Hallowed be Your name; remind me that You have not given me the spirit of fear, but of power, love, and a sound mind (2 Timothy 1:7). Let Your kingdom come and drive out every fear that tries to limit my calling. Let Your will be done as You strengthen my heart to stand boldly in faith. Give me today my daily bread of courage, confidence, and spiritual boldness. Forgive me for letting fear hold me back, and I forgive those who instilled fear in me. Lead me not into the temptation of shrinking back, but deliver me into fearless obedience (Deuteronomy 31:6). To You be the glory forever. Amen.

Reflection:
Where do you need God's courage to rise in you today?

_____

_____

_____

Action:
Write one bold step you will take today with God's courage.

_____

_____

_____

Scriptures Referenced Today:
2 Timothy 1:7 (KJV) - "For God hath not given us the spirit of fear; but of power, and of love, and of a sound mind."
Deuteronomy 31:6 (KJV) - "Be strong and of a good courage, fear not, nor be afraid of them: for the Lord thy God, he it is that doth go with thee; he will not fail thee, nor forsake thee."

DAY 224 – God Helps You Live a Life of Meaning

Prayer:
Father, thank You for calling me to a life of meaning and impact.
Hallowed be Your name; teach me to redeem the time and live wisely
(Ephesians 5:15–16). Let Your kingdom come and awaken purpose in
every part of my life. Let Your will be done as You guide my choices,
habits, and priorities. Give me today my daily bread of intention, focus,
and alignment. Forgive me for wasting days in distraction, and I forgive
those who pulled me into meaningless pursuits. Lead me not into the
temptation of living aimlessly, but deliver me into the life of meaning You
designed (Psalm 90:12). To You be the glory. Amen.

Reflection:
What area of your life needs more intentional purpose?

_____

_____

_____

Action:
Write one intentional action you will take today to align with God's
purpose.

_____

_____

_____

Scriptures Referenced Today:
Ephesians 5:15–16 (KJV) - "See then that ye walk circumspectly, not as
fools, but as wise,
Redeeming the time, because the days are evil."
Psalm 90:12 (KJV) - "So teach us to number our days, that we may apply
our hearts unto wisdom."

DAY 225 – God Gives You Vision for the Future

Prayer:
Father, thank You for giving me a God-shaped vision for the future.
Hallowed be Your name; help me see beyond what is and glimpse what
You are preparing (Proverbs 29:18). Let Your kingdom come and awaken
vision, direction, and holy expectation. Let Your will be done as You
align my dreams and plans with Your purpose. Give me today my daily
bread of clarity, inspiration, and forward focus. Forgive me for settling
for less than Your vision, and I forgive those who discouraged the dreams
You placed in me. Lead me not into the temptation of small thinking, but
deliver me into the fullness of Your vision (Habakkuk 2:2–3). To You be
honor and praise. Amen.

Reflection:
What vision or dream is God stirring in your heart?

_____

_____

_____

Action:
Write one step you can take today toward the vision God has given you.

_____

_____

_____

Scriptures Referenced Today:
Proverbs 29:18 (KJV) - "Where there is no vision, the people perish: but
he that keepeth the law, happy is he."
Habakkuk 2:2–3 (KJV) - "And the Lord answered me, and said, Write
the vision, and make it plain upon tables, that he may run that readeth it.
For the vision is yet for an appointed time, but at the end it shall speak,
and not lie: though it tarry, wait for it; because it will surely come, it will
not tarry."

DAY 226 – God Teaches You to Guard Your Heart

Prayer:
Father, thank You for teaching me to guard my heart as You develop my calling. Hallowed be Your name; remind me that out of the heart flow the issues of life (Proverbs 4:23). Let Your kingdom come and protect my heart from bitterness, jealousy, pride, and discouragement. Let Your will be done as You create a pure and steadfast heart within me. Give me today my daily bread of emotional strength, spiritual sensitivity, and purity of heart. Forgive me for letting harmful things shape my heart, and I forgive those who wounded it. Lead me not into the temptation of offense or negativity, but deliver me into the wholeness You desire (Psalm 51:10). To You be the glory. Amen.

Reflection:
What does your heart need from God today-healing, protection, or cleansing?

_____

_____

_____

Action:
Write one way you will guard your heart with intention today.

_____

_____

_____

Scriptures Referenced Today:
Proverbs 4:23 (KJV) - "Keep thy heart with all diligence; for out of it are the issues of life."
Psalm 51:10 (KJV) - "Create in me a clean heart, O God; and renew a right spirit within me."

DAY 227 – God Calls You to Walk in Faith, Not Fear

Prayer:
Father, thank You for calling me to live by faith and not by fear. Hallowed be Your name; strengthen my trust and deepen my confidence in You (2 Corinthians 5:7). Let Your kingdom come and dismantle every fear that fights against Your will in my life. Let Your will be done as You build a faith that stands firm in every season. Give me today my daily bread of courage, trust, and unwavering belief in Your promises. Forgive me for allowing fear to control my decisions, and I forgive those who fed fear in me. Lead me not into the temptation of living by sight alone, but deliver me into bold, active faith (Hebrews 11:6). To You be the glory forever. Amen.

Reflection:
Where do you need to step out in faith rather than fear?

_____

_____

_____

Action:
Write one step of faith you will take today-trusting God with the outcome.

_____

_____

_____

Scriptures Referenced Today:
2 Corinthians 5:7 (KJV) - "For we walk by faith, not by sight:"
Hebrews 11:6 (KJV) - "But without faith it is impossible to please him: for he that cometh to God must believe that he is, and that he is a rewarder of them that diligently seek him."

DAY 228 – God Leads You Into Maturity

Prayer:
Father, thank You for leading me into spiritual maturity. Hallowed be Your name; remind me that growing in You is part of walking in my calling (Ephesians 4:15). Let Your kingdom come and develop wisdom, stability, and strength within me. Let Your will be done as You grow me beyond old patterns and childish ways. Give me today my daily bread of understanding, discernment, and spiritual depth. Forgive me for resisting growth, and I forgive those who kept me tied to an old version of myself. Lead me not into the temptation of immaturity or stagnation, but deliver me into the fullness of who You're forming me to be (Hebrews 5:12–14). To You be the glory. Amen.

Reflection:
What area of your life is God inviting into deeper maturity?

Action:
Write one mature choice you will make today that reflects who God is shaping you to be.

Scriptures Referenced Today:
Ephesians 4:15 (KJV) - "But speaking the truth in love, may grow up into him in all things, which is the head, even Christ:"
Hebrews 5:12–14 (KJV) - "For when for the time ye ought to be teachers, ye have need that one teach you again which be the first principles of the oracles of God; and are become such as have need of milk, and not of strong meat.

For every one that useth milk is unskilful in the word of righteousness: for he is a babe.

But strong meat belongeth to them that are of full age, even those who by reason of use have their senses exercised to discern both good and evil."

DAY 229 – God Trains Your Hands for the Work Ahead

Prayer:
Father, thank You for training my hands, mind, and heart for the work You've assigned to me. Hallowed be Your name; prepare me with skill, wisdom, and confidence (Psalm 144:1). Let Your kingdom come and develop the abilities I need for my calling. Let Your will be done as You sharpen my skills and strengthen my resolve. Give me today my daily bread of focus, diligence, and excellence. Forgive me for doubting my abilities, and I forgive those who questioned my capability. Lead me not into the temptation of laziness or fear, but deliver me into readiness and strength (Proverbs 22:29). To You be honor and praise. Amen.

Reflection:
What skill or ability is God developing in you for the future?

_____

_____

Action:
Write one way you will practice or improve that skill today.

_____

_____

Scriptures Referenced Today:
Psalm 144:1 (KJV) - "Blessed be the Lord my strength, which teacheth my hands to war, and my fingers to fight:"
Proverbs 22:29 (KJV) - "Seest thou a man diligent in his business? he shall stand before kings; he shall not stand before mean men."

DAY 230 – God Reveals Your Strength Through Trials

Prayer:
Father, thank You for revealing the strength You've built in me through the trials I've faced. Hallowed be Your name; remind me that the testing of my faith produces endurance (James 1:2–4). Let Your kingdom come and use every challenge to deepen my character. Let Your will be done as You shape me into someone strong, steadfast, and unmovable. Give me today my daily bread of perseverance, perspective, and hope. Forgive me for resenting trials, and I forgive those who contributed to difficulty in my life. Lead me not into the temptation of giving up, but deliver me into endurance rooted in faith (1 Peter 1:7). To You be the glory. Amen.

Reflection:
What recent challenge has revealed new strength in you?

_____

_____

Action:
Write one way you will persevere today with the strength God has built in you.

_____

_____

Scriptures Referenced Today:
James 1:2–4 (KJV) - "My brethren, count it all joy when ye fall into divers temptations;
Knowing this, that the trying of your faith worketh patience.
But let patience have her perfect work, that ye may be perfect and entire, wanting nothing."
1 Peter 1:7 (KJV) - "That the trial of your faith, being much more precious than of gold that perisheth, though it be tried with fire, might be found unto praise and honour and glory at the appearing of Jesus Christ:"

DAY 231 – God Calls You to Walk in Integrity and Truth

Prayer:
Father, thank You for calling me to live a life of integrity and truth.
Hallowed be Your name; remind me that You desire truth in my inward
parts (Psalm 51:6). Let Your kingdom come and purify my motives and
my actions. Let Your will be done as You shape me to reflect Christ in
honesty and consistency. Give me today my daily bread of purity,
strength, and unwavering integrity. Forgive me for any compromise, and
I forgive those who encouraged or excused dishonesty. Lead me not into
the temptation of cutting corners, but deliver me into a life that honors
You (Proverbs 12:22). To You be glory. Amen.

Reflection:
What area of your life needs a renewed commitment to integrity?

_____

_____

_____

Action:
Write one truthful or honest action you will take today.

_____

_____

_____

Scriptures Referenced Today:
Psalm 51:6 (KJV) - Behold, thou desirest truth in the inward parts: and in
the hidden part thou shalt make me to know wisdom."
Proverbs 12:22 (KJV) - "Lying lips are abomination to the Lord: but they
that deal truly are his delight."

DAY 232 – God Teaches You to Be Faithful in the Small Things

Prayer:
Father, thank You for teaching me to be faithful in the small things. Hallowed be Your name; remind me that faithfulness in little prepares me for much (Luke 16:10). Let Your kingdom come and help me honor You in the unseen and everyday moments. Let Your will be done as You build consistency, diligence, and devotion within me. Give me today my daily bread of discipline, focus, and steadfast faith. Forgive me for dismissing the small responsibilities, and I forgive those who overlooked my faithfulness. Lead me not into the temptation of neglect, but deliver me into excellence and consistency (Colossians 3:23). To You be the glory and honor forever. Amen.

Reflection:
Where is God asking you to be faithful in the small things today?

_____

_____

Action:
Write one small act of faithfulness you will commit to today.

_____

_____

Scriptures Referenced Today:
Luke 16:10 (KJV) - "He that is faithful in that which is least is faithful also in much: and he that is unjust in the least is unjust also in much."
Colossians 3:23 (KJV) - "And whatsoever ye do, do it heartily, as to the Lord, and not unto men;"

DAY 233 – God Forms Consistency in Your Walk

Prayer:
Father, thank You for forming consistency in my walk with You.
Hallowed be Your name; remind me that steady obedience matters more
than occasional intensity (1 Corinthians 15:58). Let Your kingdom come
and strengthen my daily rhythms of prayer, work, and devotion. Let Your
will be done as You build spiritual endurance within me. Give me today
my daily bread of discipline, focus, and faithful perseverance. Forgive me
for being inconsistent, and I forgive those who criticized my progress
instead of encouraging it. Lead me not into the temptation of
complacency, but deliver me into a life of steady, faithful obedience
(Galatians 6:9). To You be all glory and honor. Amen.

Reflection:
Where do you need greater consistency in this season?

_____

_____

_____

Action:
Write one small, consistent action you will commit to today.

_____

_____

_____

Scriptures Referenced Today:
1 Corinthians 15:58 (KJV) - "Therefore, my beloved brethren, be ye
steadfast, unmoveable, always abounding in the work of the Lord,
forasmuch as ye know that your labour is not in vain in the Lord."
Galatians 6:9 (KJV) - "And let us not be weary in well doing: for in due
season we shall reap, if we faint not."

DAY 234 – God Keeps You Grounded in Truth

Prayer:
Father, thank You for grounding me in Your truth as You shape my identity. Hallowed be Your name; remind me that Your Word is the anchor of my life (John 17:17). Let Your kingdom come and silence every lie that contradicts who You say I am. Let Your will be done as You root me deeply in Scripture. Give me today my daily bread of clarity, understanding, and discernment. Forgive me for believing lies, and I forgive those who spoke untruths over my life. Lead me not into the temptation of drifting from Your Word, but deliver me into truth that sets me free (Psalm 119:105). To You be all honor and glory forever. Amen.

Reflection:
What truth from God's Word do you need to stand on today?

_____

_____

_____

Action:
Write down one Scripture you will declare over your life today.

_____

_____

_____

Scriptures Referenced Today:
John 17:17 (KJV) - "Sanctify them through thy truth: thy word is truth."
Psalm 119:105 (KJV) - "Thy word is a lamp unto my feet, and a light unto my path."

DAY 235 – God Teaches You to Walk With Wisdom

Prayer:
Father, thank You for teaching me to walk with wisdom in every area of life. Hallowed be Your name; remind me that wisdom is a gift You generously give to those who ask (James 1:5). Let Your kingdom come and guide my decisions with clarity and sound judgment. Let Your will be done as You lead me away from foolish choices and toward wise paths. Give me today my daily bread of insight, understanding, and spiritual maturity. Forgive me for acting without wisdom, and I forgive those who influenced me poorly. Lead me not into the temptation of impulse or confusion, but deliver me into wisdom that honors You (Proverbs 4:7). To You be praise. Amen.

Reflection:
Where do you need wisdom most right now?

_____

_____

_____

Action:
Write one specific decision you will seek God's wisdom for today.

_____

_____

_____

Scriptures Referenced Today:
James 1:5 (KJV) - "If any of you lack wisdom, let him ask of God, that giveth to all men liberally, and upbraideth not; and it shall be given him."
Proverbs 4:7 (KJV) - "Wisdom is the principal thing; therefore get wisdom: and with all thy getting get understanding."

DAY 236 – God Strengthens Your Identity Through His Promises

Prayer:
Father, thank You for strengthening my identity through the promises in Your Word. Hallowed be Your name; remind me that every promise You make is sure and unchanging (2 Corinthians 1:20). Let Your kingdom come and anchor my identity in what You have spoken. Let Your will be done as You teach me to stand on Your promises instead of my feelings. Give me today my daily bread of assurance, hope, and confidence. Forgive me for doubting Your promises, and I forgive those who urged me to trust in myself instead of in You. Lead me not into the temptation of unbelief, but deliver me into the confidence of Your faithfulness (Hebrews 10:23). To You be all glory. Amen.

Reflection:
Which promise from God strengthens you most right now?

_____

_____

_____

Action:
Write one promise of God you will hold onto today.

_____

_____

_____

Scriptures Referenced Today:
2 Corinthians 1:20 (KJV) - "For all the promises of God in him are yea, and in him Amen, unto the glory of God by us."
Hebrews 10:23 (KJV) - "Let us hold fast the profession of our faith without wavering; (for he is faithful that promised;)"

DAY 237 – God Forms Patience for Your Calling

Prayer:
Father, thank You for forming patience in me as You unfold my calling.
Hallowed be Your name; remind me that patience is part of the fruit of
the Spirit and essential for my growth (Galatians 5:22). Let Your kingdom
come and help me wait with faith instead of frustration. Let Your will be
done as You teach me to trust Your timing in all things. Give me today
my daily bread of endurance, calmness, and steady hope. Forgive me for
growing impatient, and I forgive those who pushed me ahead of Your
timing. Lead me not into the temptation of rushing, but deliver me into
patient trust in Your plan (Romans 12:12). To You be all honor and
glory. Amen.

Reflection:
What area of your calling requires patience right now?

_____

_____

_____

Action:
Write one way you will practice patience today.

_____

_____

_____

Scriptures Referenced Today:
Galatians 5:22 (KJV) - "But the fruit of the Spirit is love, joy, peace,
longsuffering, gentleness, goodness, faith,"
Romans 12:12 (KJV) - "Rejoicing in hope; patient in tribulation;
continuing instant in prayer;"

DAY 238 – God Teaches You to Walk in Peace

Prayer:
Father, thank You for teaching me to walk in Your peace, not the world's chaos. Hallowed be Your name; remind me that You give a peace that surpasses all understanding (Philippians 4:7). Let Your kingdom come and calm every anxious place within me. Let Your will be done as You teach me to rest in Your presence. Give me today my daily bread of peace, stillness, and a steady heart. Forgive me for letting stress rule my decisions, and I forgive those who contributed to unrest in my life. Lead me not into the temptation of anxiety, but deliver me into Your perfect peace (Isaiah 26:3). To You be the honor and all glory forever and ever. Amen.

Reflection:
What situation in your life needs God's peace today?

_____

_____

_____

Action:
Write one way you will choose peace instead of anxiety today.

_____

_____

_____

Scriptures Referenced Today:
Philippians 4:7 (KJV) - "And the peace of God, which passeth all understanding, shall keep your hearts and minds through Christ Jesus."
Isaiah 26:3 (KJV) - "Thou wilt keep him in perfect peace, whose mind is stayed on thee: because he trusteth in thee."

DAY 239 – God Builds Confidence Through His Presence

Prayer:
Father, thank You for building confidence in me through Your presence. Hallowed be Your name; remind me that when You are with me, I lack nothing (Psalm 23:1). Let Your kingdom come and strengthen my heart with the assurance that You go before me. Let Your will be done as You teach me to walk boldly because I am never alone. Give me today my daily bread of assurance, courage, and holy confidence. Forgive me for relying on my own strength, and I forgive those who made me feel unsupported. Lead me not into the temptation of self-reliance, but deliver me into confidence rooted in You (Exodus 33:14). To You be all glory. Amen.

Reflection:
Where do you need the confidence that comes from God's presence?

_____

_____

_____

Action:
Write one situation where you will rely on God's presence instead of your own strength.

_____

_____

_____

Scriptures Referenced Today:
Psalm 23:1 (KJV) - "The Lord is my shepherd; I shall not want."
Exodus 33:14 (KJV) - "And he said, My presence shall go with thee, and I will give thee rest."

DAY 240 – God Teaches You to Let Your Light Shine

Prayer:
Father, thank You for calling me to shine Your light in the world around me. Hallowed be Your name; remind me that I am the light of the world because of Christ in me (Matthew 5:14). Let Your kingdom come and illuminate every place where fear or insecurity has dimmed my light. Let Your will be done as You teach me to reflect Your love, kindness, and truth. Give me today my daily bread of boldness, visibility, and divine opportunity. Forgive me for hiding my light, and I forgive those who discouraged my influence. Lead me not into the temptation of shrinking back, but deliver me into joyful, courageous shining (Philippians 2:15). To You be all honor. Amen.

Reflection:
Where is God asking you to shine your light more boldly?

_____

_____

_____

Action:
Write one way you can shine Christ's light to someone today.

_____

_____

_____

Scriptures Referenced Today:
Matthew 5:14 (KJV) - "Ye are the light of the world. A city that is set on an hill cannot be hid."
Philippians 2:15 (KJV) - "That ye may be blameless and harmless, the sons of God, without rebuke, in the midst of a crooked and perverse nation, among whom ye shine as lights in the world;"

DAY 241 – God Strengthens Your Resolve

Prayer:
Father, thank You for strengthening my resolve to walk out the calling You've placed on my life. Hallowed be Your name; remind me that You complete every good work You begin (Philippians 1:6). Let Your kingdom come and make my heart steadfast and unshakeable. Let Your will be done as You develop perseverance, commitment, and endurance within me. Give me today my daily bread of determination, focus, and spiritual grit. Forgive me for wavering, and I forgive those who doubted my perseverance. Lead me not into the temptation of giving up, but deliver me into steadfast faithfulness (Psalm 57:7). To You be the glory. Amen.

Reflection:
Where do you need God to strengthen your resolve today?

_____

_____

_____

Action:
Write one step you will take today that reflects renewed resolve.

_____

_____

_____

Scriptures Referenced Today:
Philippians 1:6 (KJV) - "Being confident of this very thing, that he which hath begun a good work in you will perform it until the day of Jesus Christ:"
Psalm 57:7 (KJV) - "My heart is fixed, O God, my heart is fixed: I will sing and give praise."

DAY 242 – God Helps You Overcome Self-Doubt

Prayer:
Father, thank You for helping me overcome self-doubt. Hallowed be
Your name; remind me that You are the One who qualifies me, equips
me, and strengthens me (2 Corinthians 3:5). Let Your kingdom come and
silence every voice of insecurity. Let Your will be done as You build
confidence rooted in Your Spirit rather than my abilities. Give me today
my daily bread of assurance, courage, and firm belief in who You say I
am. Forgive me for doubting myself, and I forgive those who planted
seeds of insecurity. Lead me not into the temptation of self-limitation,
but deliver me into God-given confidence (Jeremiah 1:8). To You be
glory and honor. Amen.

Reflection:
What area of your life is most affected by self-doubt?

_____

_____

_____

Action:
Write one confident step you will take today, trusting God's strength in
you.

_____

_____

_____

Scriptures Referenced Today:
2 Corinthians 3:5 (KJV) - "Not that we are sufficient of ourselves to
think any thing as of ourselves; but our sufficiency is of God;
Jeremiah 1:8 (KJV) - "Be not afraid of their faces: for I am with thee to
deliver thee, saith the Lord."

DAY 243 – God Teaches You to Steward Your Time Well

Prayer:
Father, thank You for teaching me to steward my time with wisdom. Hallowed be Your name; remind me that every day is a gift and every moment holds purpose (Psalm 90:12). Let Your kingdom come and remove distractions that waste the time You've entrusted to me. Let Your will be done as You align my schedule with Your priorities. Give me today my daily bread of focus, discipline, and intentionality. Forgive me for misusing time, and I forgive those who pressured me into giving my time away carelessly. Lead me not into the temptation of busyness without purpose, but deliver me into wise, meaningful stewardship (Ephesians 5:16). To You be the glory. Amen.

Reflection:
Where is your time being wasted or pulled away from God's purpose?

_____

_____

_____

Action:
Write one intentional change you will make today to steward your time wisely.

_____

_____

_____

Scriptures Referenced Today:
Psalm 90:12 (KJV) - "So teach us to number our days, that we may apply our hearts unto wisdom."
Ephesians 5:16 (KJV) - "Redeeming the time, because the days are evil."

DAY 244 – God Strengthens You to Steward Relationships Well

Prayer:
Father, thank You for teaching me to steward relationships with wisdom, patience, and grace. Hallowed be Your name; remind me that love, unity, and forgiveness reflect Your heart (Colossians 3:13–14). Let Your kingdom come and heal any relational strain in my life. Let Your will be done as You help me honor others and show Christlike love. Give me today my daily bread of compassion, gentleness, and humility. Forgive me for mishandling relationships, and I forgive those who have hurt mine. Lead me not into the temptation of resentment, but deliver me into harmony, grace, and healthy connection (Romans 12:18). To You be all glory and honor. Amen.

Reflection:
Which relationship needs intentional love, forgiveness, or effort today?

_____

_____

Action:
Write one relational action-encouragement, apology, prayer, or kindness-you will take today.

_____

_____

Scriptures Referenced Today:
Colossians 3:13–14 (KJV) - "Forbearing one another, and forgiving one another, if any man have a quarrel against any: even as Christ forgave you, so also do ye. And above all these things put on charity, which is the bond of perfectness."

Romans 12:18 (KJV) - "If it be possible, as much as lieth in you, live peaceably with all men."

MONTH 8 CLOSING REFLECTION: STEWARDSHIP, FAITHFULNESS & LIVING YOUR CALLING OUTWARDLY

Month 8 has been all about **taking ownership** of the life God entrusted to you. This month was practical, grounded, and deeply spiritual - because stewardship is worship. Stewardship is obedience. Stewardship is honor.

Through these weeks, God has been shaping you into someone who:

- manages time with intention
- invests relationships with love and grace
- guards influence with humility
- embraces responsibility in small things and large
- grows in discipline, diligence, and maturity
- examines motives and purifies priorities
- practices patience, endurance, and consistency
- honors God through habits, decisions, and daily choices
- pursues excellence without perfectionism
- carries calling with wisdom and accountability

Month 8 taught you that **calling is sustained through stewardship**, not emotion.

It taught you that:

- **Identity is who you are.**
- **Stewardship is what you do with who you are.**

You discovered that God cares not only about what you *feel* called to - but how you *live it out*:

- How you use your words
- How you manage your money
- How you treat people
- How you handle influence
- How you show up
- How you invest your days
- How you commit to growth

This month revealed something important:

Faithfulness is the bridge between identity and destiny.

As you close Month 8, reflect on these questions:

- What daily habit did God strengthen in you?
- Where did you become more disciplined?
- What waste or distraction did God uproot?
- What relationship became healthier?
- What area of stewardship grew deeper or wiser?
- Where did you see fruit because of small, faithful choices?

Month 8 doesn't end your stewardship - it launches you into the next season with **greater clarity, greater responsibility, and greater readiness** for what God is about to build in you.

Now, with the foundation of who you are and the structure of stewardship in place, you step into Month 9 - where God expands your capacity, enlarges your territory, and prepares you for greater impact.

MONTH 9 THEME: SPIRITUAL GROWTH, CAPACITY & EXPANDING YOUR TERRITORY

Month 7 established identity.

Month 8 shaped stewardship.

Now **Month 9 expands capacity.**

This month is about:

- spiritual growth
- stretching into deeper maturity
- strengthening your spiritual muscles
- expanding influence and responsibility
- preparing for new assignments
- deepening prayer, faith, and resilience
- enlarging your "territory" - internally and externally
- breaking limitations and building capacity
- growing roots *and* reach
- partnering with God in the next level of your calling

Month 9 is where God says: **"I've built your foundation. I've taught you stewardship.**

Now I will enlarge the place of your tent."

Spiritually, this month focuses on:

- deeper prayer life
- stronger faith
- greater endurance
- increased spiritual authority
- bolder obedience
- expanded spiritual awareness
- multiplied influence

Through the Lord's Prayer:

- **"Your kingdom come"** - becomes a request for greater territory.
- **"Give us this day"** - becomes the daily strength for increased assignments.
- **"Lead us not…"** - becomes protection as your influence grows.

Month 9 is about **growing in capacity so you can carry more of what God wants to entrust to you.**

DAY 245 – God Expands Your Capacity to Carry More

Prayer:
Father, thank You for expanding my capacity to carry what You are entrusting to me. Hallowed be Your name; remind me that You increase my strength as You increase my assignment (Isaiah 40:31). Let Your kingdom come and stretch my faith, my endurance, and my spiritual depth. Let Your will be done as You enlarge my heart for greater responsibility and greater impact. Give me today my daily bread of strength, resilience, and spiritual stamina. Forgive me for shrinking back from growth, and I forgive those who doubted my capacity. Lead me not into the temptation of relying on my own strength, but deliver me into the greater capacity that comes from Your Spirit (Philippians 4:13). To You be all honor and glory. Amen.

Reflection:
Where is God stretching your capacity in this season?

_____

_____

Action:
Write one area where you will embrace God's stretching instead of resisting it.

_____

_____

Scriptures Referenced Today:
Isaiah 40:31 (KJV) - "But they that wait upon the Lord shall renew their strength; they shall mount up with wings as eagles; they shall run, and not be weary; and they shall walk, and not faint."
Philippians 4:13 (KJV) - "I can do all things through Christ which strengtheneth me."

DAY 246 – God Enlarges the Territory of Your Life

Prayer:
Father, thank You for enlarging the territory of my life according to Your will. Hallowed be Your name; remind me that You are the One who opens doors, expands influence, and increases impact (1 Chronicles 4:10). Let Your kingdom come and stretch the borders of my gifting, my purpose, and my spiritual reach. Let Your will be done as You take me further than I have been before. Give me today my daily bread of courage, faith, and holy boldness. Forgive me for being afraid of expansion, and I forgive those who tried to limit my growth. Lead me not into the temptation of small thinking, but deliver me into the enlargement You have prepared (Isaiah 54:2). For Thine is the kingdom and the power and the glory forever and ever. Amen.

Reflection:
Where do you sense God enlarging your influence or reach?

_____

_____

_____

Action:
Write one step of faith you will take toward the territory God is opening.

_____

_____

_____

Scriptures Referenced Today:
1 Chronicles 4:10 (KJV) - "And Jabez called on the God of Israel, saying, Oh that thou wouldest bless me indeed, and enlarge my coast, and that thine hand might be with me, and that thou wouldest keep me from evil, that it may not grieve me! And God granted him that which he requested."
Isaiah 54:2 (KJV) - "Enlarge the place of thy tent, and let them stretch forth the curtains of thine habitations: spare not, lengthen thy cords, and strengthen thy stakes;"

DAY 247 – God Deepens Your Spiritual Strength for the Next Level

Prayer:
Father, thank You for deepening my spiritual strength for the next level You are calling me into. Hallowed be Your name; remind me that You strengthen my inner man by Your Spirit (Ephesians 3:16). Let Your kingdom come and build a foundation in me that can support greater responsibility. Let Your will be done as You develop courage, depth, endurance, and spiritual resilience within me. Give me today my daily bread of power, perseverance, and spiritual maturity. Forgive me for relying on surface-level strength, and I forgive those who underestimated my inner strength. Lead me not into the temptation of spiritual complacency, but deliver me into deeper growth and maturity (Colossians 1:11). For Thine is the kingdom and the power and the glory forever and ever Amen.

Reflection:
What area of your spiritual life needs deeper strength for what's ahead?

_____

_____

_____

Action:
Write one way you will intentionally strengthen your inner life today.

_____

_____

_____

Scriptures Referenced Today:
Ephesians 3:16 (KJV) - "That he would grant you, according to the riches of his glory, to be strengthened with might by his Spirit in the inner man;"
Colossians 1:11 (KJV) - "Strengthened with all might, according to his glorious power, unto all patience and longsuffering with joyfulness;"

DAY 248 – God Expands Your Faith to Believe for More

Prayer:
Father, thank You for expanding my faith to believe for more than I have before. Hallowed be Your name; remind me that with You nothing shall be impossible (Luke 1:37). Let Your kingdom come and stretch my faith beyond past limitations, disappointments, and small thinking. Let Your will be done as You teach me to trust You for bigger, deeper, and greater things. Give me today my daily bread of bold belief, expectancy, and confidence in Your power. Forgive me for limiting what I thought You could do, and I forgive those who taught me to expect little. Lead me not into the temptation of unbelief, but deliver me into a larger, stronger, growing faith (Mark 9:23). For Thine is the kingdom and the power and the glory forever and ever. Amen.

Reflection:
Where is God calling you to believe for something bigger?

_____

_____

_____

Action:
Write one bold prayer you will bring before God today.

_____

_____

_____

Scriptures Referenced Today:
Luke 1:37 (KJV) - "For with God nothing shall be impossible."
Mark 9:23 (KJV) - "Jesus said unto him, If thou canst believe, all things are possible to him that believeth."

DAY 249 – God Develops Spiritual Discernment for Greater Responsibility

Prayer:
Father, thank You for developing discernment in me as You prepare me for greater responsibility. Hallowed be Your name; teach me to distinguish between what is from You and what is not (Hebrews 5:14). Let Your kingdom come and sharpen my spiritual senses. Let Your will be done as You give me clarity, insight, and wisdom for decisions ahead. Give me today my daily bread of understanding, perception, and Spirit-led judgment. Forgive me for ignoring discernment in the past, and I forgive those who influenced me unwisely. Lead me not into the temptation of confusion or double-mindedness, but deliver me into clear, confident discernment (Proverbs 3:5–6). To You be all glory. Amen.

Reflection:
Where do you need sharpened discernment right now?

_____

_____

_____

Action:
Write one decision you will intentionally seek God's discernment for today.

_____

_____

_____

Scriptures Referenced Today:
Hebrews 5:14 (KJV) - "But strong meat belongeth to them that are of full age, even those who by reason of use have their senses exercised to discern both good and evil."
Proverbs 3:5–6 (KJV) - "Trust in the Lord with all thine heart; and lean not unto thine own understanding.
In all thy ways acknowledge him, and he shall direct thy paths."

DAY 250 – God Stretches You Into New Levels of Obedience

Prayer:
Father, thank You for stretching me into deeper levels of obedience. Hallowed be Your name; remind me that obedience brings blessing, growth, and alignment with Your will (Deuteronomy 28:1). Let Your kingdom come and teach me to say "yes" quickly, fully, and joyfully. Let Your will be done as You strip away hesitation and strengthen my desire to obey. Give me today my daily bread of courage, surrender, and decisiveness. Forgive me for delayed obedience, and I forgive those who discouraged my obedience in the past. Lead me not into the temptation of partial obedience, but deliver me into wholehearted surrender (John 14:23). To You be the glory and honor. Amen.

Reflection:
Where is God calling you to deeper obedience?

Action:
Write one act of obedience you will take today.

Scriptures Referenced Today:
Deuteronomy 28:1 (KJV) - "And it shall come to pass, if thou shalt hearken diligently unto the voice of the Lord thy God, to observe and to do all his commandments which I command thee this day, that the Lord thy God will set thee on high above all nations of the earth:"

John 14:23 (KJV) - "Jesus answered and said unto him, If a man love me, he will keep my words: and my Father will love him, and we will come unto him, and make our abode with him."

DAY 251 – God Strengthens You for Spiritual Battles at Higher Levels

Prayer:
Father, thank You for strengthening me for spiritual battles that come with higher levels of calling. Hallowed be Your name; remind me that the weapons of our warfare are mighty through You (2 Corinthians 10:4). Let Your kingdom come and prepare me for resistance, opposition, and warfare that arise as influence grows. Let Your will be done as You equip me with authority, clarity, and victory. Give me today my daily bread of courage, fortitude, and spiritual readiness. Forgive me for shrinking back when battles intensified, and I forgive those who added unnecessary conflict to my journey. Lead me not into the temptation of fear, but deliver me into confidence that You fight for me (Exodus 14:14). To You be the glory and power. Amen.

Reflection:
What spiritual battle are you facing that requires greater strength?

Action:
Write one way you will stand firm in God's strength today.

Scriptures Referenced Today:
2 Corinthians 10:4 (KJV) - "For the weapons of our warfare are not carnal, but mighty through God to the pulling down of strong holds;"
Exodus 14:14 (KJV) - "The Lord shall fight for you, and ye shall hold your peace."

DAY 252 – God Expands Your Vision for What's Possible

Prayer:
Father, thank You for expanding my vision for what is possible with You. Hallowed be Your name; open my eyes to see beyond the limits of my past and the constraints of my present (Ephesians 1:18). Let Your kingdom come and awaken fresh vision, fresh dreams, and fresh purpose within me. Let Your will be done as You broaden my perspective and enlarge my expectations. Give me today my daily bread of clarity, imagination, and Spirit-led insight. Forgive me for letting past disappointments shrink my vision, and I forgive those who discouraged what You placed in my heart. Lead me not into the temptation of small vision, but deliver me into the wide, expansive future You have prepared (Habakkuk 1:5). For Thine is the kingdom and the power and the glory forever and ever. Amen.

Reflection:
What vision is God expanding in your heart right now?

_____

_____

_____

Action:
Write one way you will honor the bigger vision God is giving you.

_____

_____

_____

Scriptures Referenced Today:
Ephesians 1:18 (KJV) - "The eyes of your understanding being enlightened; that ye may know what is the hope of his calling, and what the riches of the glory of his inheritance in the saints,"
Habakkuk 1:5 (KJV) - "Behold ye among the heathen, and regard, and wonder marvelously: for I will work a work in your days, which ye will not believe, though it be told you."

DAY 253 - Strength in the Waiting

Prayer:
Father, I come to You with a grateful and expectant heart. Hallowed be Your name; holy in every season and faithful in every need. Let Your kingdom come in the places where I have been discouraged, delayed, or uncertain. Let Your will be done, shaping my desires, decisions, and direction. Give me today my daily bread of patience and confidence. Lead me not into the temptation to give up too soon, complain, or doubt Your timing. Deliver me from every fear and every lie that whispers, "God has forgotten you." For Thine is the kingdom, and the power, and the glory forever and ever. Amen.

Reflection:
Where is God asking you to wait with courage instead of frustration?

_____

_____

_____

Action:
Write down one area where you will choose patience instead of pressure today.

_____

_____

_____

Scriptures Referenced Today:
Psalm 27:14 (KJV) - "Wait on the Lord: be of good courage, and he shall strengthen thine heart: wait, I say, on the Lord."
Isaiah 40:31 (KJV) - "But they that wait upon the Lord shall renew their strength; they shall mount up with wings as eagles; they shall run, and not be weary; and they shall walk, and not faint."
Lamentations 3:25 (KJV) - "The Lord is good unto them that wait for him, to the soul that seeketh him."

DAY 254 – God Expands Your Endurance for the Journey Ahead

Prayer:
Father, thank You for expanding my endurance for the journey You've set before me. Hallowed be Your name; remind me that the testing of my faith produces patience and maturity (James 1:3–4). Let Your kingdom come and strengthen me to keep going when the path becomes difficult. Let Your will be done as You grow my resilience, consistency, and staying power. Give me today my daily bread of perseverance, stability, and spiritual stamina. Forgive me for losing heart, and I forgive those who discouraged my endurance. Lead me not into the temptation of giving up, but deliver me into a steady, enduring faith (Hebrews 12:1). To You be the glory. Amen.

Reflection:
Where is God strengthening your endurance?

_____

_____

Action:
Write one step of perseverance you will take today.

_____

_____

Scriptures Referenced Today:
James 1:3–4 (KJV) - "Knowing this, that the trying of your faith worketh patience. But let patience have her perfect work, that ye may be perfect and entire, wanting nothing."
Hebrews 12:1 (KJV) - "Wherefore seeing we also are compassed about with so great a cloud of witnesses, let us lay aside every weight, and the sin which doth so easily beset us, and let us run with patience the race that is set before us,"

DAY 255 – God Expands Your Spiritual Authority

Prayer:
Father, thank You for expanding my spiritual authority as I grow in You. Hallowed be Your name; remind me that You have given me power over the enemy, not by my strength, but by the authority of Jesus Christ (Luke 10:19). Let Your kingdom come and teach me to walk confidently in the authority You provide. Let Your will be done as You deepen my understanding of spiritual truth. Give me today my daily bread of courage, boldness, and spiritual clarity. Forgive me for underestimating what You have given me, and I forgive those who taught me to walk in fear. Lead me not into the temptation of shrinking back, but deliver me into the full authority of Your Spirit (Ephesians 6:10). For Thine is the kingdom and the power and the glory forever and ever. Amen.

Reflection:
Where do you need to walk in greater spiritual authority?

Action:
Write one area where you will exercise Christ-given authority today.

Scriptures Referenced Today:
Luke 10:19 (KJV) - "Behold, I give unto you power to tread on serpents and scorpions, and over all the power of the enemy: and nothing shall by any means hurt you."
Ephesians 6:10 (KJV) - "Finally, my brethren, be strong in the Lord, and in the power of his might."

DAY 256 – God Expands Your Boldness to Step Into New Levels

Prayer:
Father, thank You for expanding my boldness as You call me into new levels of faith and obedience. Hallowed be Your name; remind me that the righteous are bold as a lion (Proverbs 28:1). Let Your kingdom come and remove every hesitation, insecurity, and fear that tries to limit me. Let Your will be done as You prepare me for greater opportunities and greater impact. Give me today my daily bread of courage, clarity, and holy boldness. Forgive me for drawing back, and I forgive those who minimized my voice or calling. Lead me not into the temptation of timidity, but deliver me into bold, Spirit-led obedience (Acts 4:31). For Thine is the kingdom and the power and the glory forever. Amen.

Reflection:
Where is God calling you to walk in boldness?

_____

_____

_____

Action:
Write one bold step you will take today.

_____

_____

_____

Scriptures Referenced Today:
Proverbs 28:1 (KJV) - "The wicked flee when no man pursueth: but the righteous are bold as a lion."
Acts 4:31 (KJV) - "And when they had prayed, the place was shaken where they were assembled together; and they were all filled with the Holy Ghost, and they spake the word of God with boldness."

DAY 257 – God Expands Your Spiritual Sensitivity and Awareness

Prayer:
Father, thank You for expanding my spiritual sensitivity so I can recognize Your voice more clearly. Hallowed be Your name; remind me that Your sheep hear Your voice, You know them, and they follow You (John 10:27). Let Your kingdom come and sharpen my awareness of Your presence and Your leading. Let Your will be done as You deepen my spiritual perception and quiet my heart to listen. Give me today my daily bread of clarity, stillness, and holy attentiveness. Forgive me for ignoring Your nudges, and I forgive those who discouraged my sensitivity to Your Spirit. Lead me not into the temptation of spiritual dullness, but deliver me into sharp, responsive awareness (1 Kings 19:12). To You be all glory. Amen.

Reflection:
Where do you sense God speaking or nudging you?

_____

_____

_____

Action:
Write one way you will intentionally tune your heart to God today.

_____

_____

_____

Scriptures Referenced Today:
John 10:27 (KJV) - "My sheep hear my voice, and I know them, and they follow me:"
1 Kings 19:12 (KJV) - "And after the earthquake a fire; but the Lord was not in the fire: and after the fire a still small voice."

DAY 258 – God Expands Your Ability to Hear and Obey Quickly

Prayer:
Father, thank You for expanding my ability to hear Your voice and obey without delay. Hallowed be Your name; remind me that blessing follows those who hear Your word and keep it (Luke 11:28). Let Your kingdom come and sharpen my responsiveness to Your prompting. Let Your will be done as You train my heart for quick, joyful obedience. Give me today my daily bread of attentiveness, willingness, and sensitivity. Forgive me for hesitating when You spoke, and I forgive those who taught me fear instead of obedience. Lead me not into the temptation of delayed obedience, but deliver me into instant, faith-filled action (Psalm 119:60). To You be the glory. Amen.

Reflection:
Where is God asking you to respond more quickly?

_____

_____

_____

Action:
Write one area where you will practice quick obedience today.

_____

_____

_____

Scriptures Referenced Today:
Luke 11:28 (KJV) - "But he said, Yea rather, blessed are they that hear the word of God, and keep it."
Psalm 119:60 (KJV) - "I made haste, and delayed not to keep thy commandments."

DAY 259 – God Expands Your Hope for the Future

Prayer:
Father, thank You for expanding my hope and renewing my expectation for the future. Hallowed be Your name; remind me that Your plans for me are thoughts of peace, and not of evil, to give me an expected end (Jeremiah 29:11). Let Your kingdom come and revive hope in areas that grew weary. Let Your will be done as You lift my eyes to what You are preparing. Give me today my daily bread of expectation, confidence, and renewed vision. Forgive me for letting disappointment steal my hope, and I forgive those who spoke hopelessness over me. Lead me not into the temptation of discouragement, but deliver me into confident, joyful anticipation (Romans 15:13). To You be the glory and honor. Amen.

Reflection:
Where is God restoring or expanding your hope right now?

_____

_____

Action:
Write one hope-filled prayer you will bring to God today.

_____

_____

Scriptures Referenced Today:
Jeremiah 29:11 (KJV) - "For I know the thoughts that I think toward you, saith the Lord, thoughts of peace, and not of evil, to give you an expected end."
Romans 15:13 (KJV) - "Now the God of hope fill you with all joy and peace in believing, that ye may abound in hope, through the power of the Holy Ghost."

DAY 260 – God Expands Your Courage to Face New Challenges

Prayer:
Father, thank You for expanding my courage to face new challenges without fear. Hallowed be Your name; remind me that You are with me wherever I go (Joshua 1:9). Let Your kingdom come and strengthen my heart for the unknown and the uncomfortable places You're calling me into. Let Your will be done as You build resilience, confidence, and trust. Give me today my daily bread of bravery, stability, and unwavering faith. Forgive me for letting fear block my steps, and I forgive those who planted fear in me. Lead me not into the temptation of retreat, but deliver me into bold, forward movement (Psalm 27:1). To You be all honor, glory and power. Amen.

Reflection:
What new challenge is God calling you to face with courage?

_____

_____

_____

Action:
Write one courageous step you will take today.

_____

_____

_____

Scriptures Referenced Today:
Joshua 1:9 (KJV) - "Have not I commanded thee? Be strong and of a good courage; be not afraid, neither be thou dismayed: for the Lord thy God is with thee whithersoever thou goest."
Psalm 27:1 (KJV) - "The Lord is my light and my salvation; whom shall I fear? the Lord is the strength of my life; of whom shall I be afraid?"

DAY 261 – God Expands Your Capacity to Love Difficult People

Prayer:
Father, thank You for expanding my capacity to love the people who are difficult to love. Hallowed be Your name; remind me that Your love is patient, kind, and long-suffering (1 Corinthians 13:4). Let Your kingdom come and fill my heart with supernatural grace. Let Your will be done as You teach me to love others the way You have loved me. Give me today my daily bread of compassion, patience, and emotional strength. Forgive me for withholding love, and I forgive those who made loving them difficult. Lead me not into the temptation of bitterness, but deliver me into love that reflects Christ (Colossians 3:14). For Thine is the kingdom and the power and the glory forever and ever. Amen.

Reflection:
Who is God asking you to love with a larger heart today?

_____

_____

Action:
Write one loving action you will take toward a difficult person today.

_____

_____

Scriptures Referenced Today:
1 Corinthians 13:4 (KJV) - "Charity suffereth long, and is kind; charity envieth not; charity vaunteth not itself, is not puffed up,"
Colossians 3:14 (KJV) - "And above all these things put on charity, which is the bond of perfectness."

DAY 262 – God Expands Your Strength Through Weakness

Prayer:
Father, thank You for expanding my strength in the very places where I feel weak. Hallowed be Your name; remind me that Your strength is made perfect in weakness (2 Corinthians 12:9). Let Your kingdom come and transform every weak place into a testimony of Your power. Let Your will be done as You teach me to rely not on myself, but on Your grace. Give me today my daily bread of humility, dependence, and courage. Forgive me for resenting my weaknesses, and I forgive those who used them against me. Lead me not into the temptation of self-reliance, but deliver me into strength that flows from Your presence (Isaiah 40:29). To You be all glory and honor. Amen.

Reflection:
What weakness is God transforming into strength?

_____

_____

_____

Action:
Write one way you will lean into God's strength today.

_____

_____

_____

Scriptures Referenced Today:
2 Corinthians 12:9 (KJV) - "And he said unto me, My grace is sufficient for thee: for my strength is made perfect in weakness: most gladly therefore will I rather glory in my infirmities, that the power of Christ may rest upon me."
Isaiah 40:29 (KJV) - "He giveth power to the faint; and to them that have no might he increaseth strength."

DAY 263 – God Expands Your Vision Beyond Your Current Limitations

Prayer:
Father, thank You for expanding my vision beyond the limits of what I see right now. Hallowed be Your name; remind me that You are able to do exceedingly abundantly above all I can ask or think (Ephesians 3:20). Let Your kingdom come and stretch my imagination, my faith, and my expectation. Let Your will be done as You help me see my life, calling, and future through Your eyes instead of my limitations. Give me today my daily bread of clarity, courage, and forward-looking faith. Forgive me for settling for small vision, and I forgive those who spoke limitation over my life. Lead me not into the temptation of disbelief, but deliver me into expanded vision that aligns with Your purpose (Psalm 119:18). For Thine is the kingdom and the power and the glory. Amen.

Reflection:
Where is God expanding your vision?

_____

_____

_____

Action:
Write one area where you will allow God to enlarge your perspective.

_____

_____

_____

Scriptures Referenced Today:
Ephesians 3:20 (KJV) - "Now unto him that is able to do exceeding abundantly above all that we ask or think, according to the power that worketh in us,"
Psalm 119:18 (KJV) - "Open thou mine eyes, that I may behold wondrous things out of thy law."

DAY 264 – God Expands Your Strength to Stand Firm

Prayer:
Father, thank You for expanding my strength to stand firm when pressure rises. Hallowed be Your name; remind me that You are my refuge and strength, a very present help in trouble (Psalm 46:1). Let Your kingdom come and make me unshakable in faith, hope, and confidence. Let Your will be done as You establish my steps and steady my heart. Give me today my daily bread of courage, endurance, and spiritual stability. Forgive me for wavering, and I forgive those who created instability in my life. Lead me not into the temptation of fear, but deliver me into steadfast strength grounded in Your presence (1 Corinthians 16:13). To You be all power and glory. Amen.

Reflection:
Where do you need God-given strength to stand firm?

_____

_____

_____

Action:
Write one step today that reflects spiritual stability and strength.

_____

_____

_____

Scriptures Referenced Today:
Psalm 46:1 (KJV) - "God is our refuge and strength, a very present help in trouble."
1 Corinthians 16:13 (KJV) - "Watch ye, stand fast in the faith, quit you like men, be strong."

DAY 265 – God Expands Your Influence for Kingdom Purpose

Prayer:
Father, thank You for expanding my influence for Your kingdom and Your purposes. Hallowed be Your name; remind me that a city set on a hill cannot be hidden (Matthew 5:14). Let Your kingdom come and increase my reach, my impact, and my ability to reflect Christ wherever I go. Let Your will be done as You align my influence with Your assignment. Give me today my daily bread of boldness, integrity, and Spirit-led opportunity. Forgive me for hiding my influence, and I forgive those who tried to silence my voice. Lead me not into the temptation of shrinking back, but deliver me into a life that shines brightly for You (Proverbs 4:18). To You be all power and glory. Amen.

Reflection:
Where is God expanding your influence?

_____

_____

_____

Action:
Write one way you will intentionally shine Christ's light today.

_____

_____

_____

Scriptures Referenced Today:
Matthew 5:14 (KJV) - "Ye are the light of the world. A city that is set on an hill cannot be hid."
Proverbs 4:18 (KJV) - "But the path of the just is as the shining light, that shineth more and more unto the perfect day."

DAY 266 – God Expands Your Capacity for Faithfulness in Difficulty

Prayer:
Father, thank You for expanding my capacity to remain faithful during difficulty. Hallowed be Your name; remind me that those who wait upon You shall renew their strength (Isaiah 40:31). Let Your kingdom come and deepen my trust when the road grows hard. Let Your will be done as You shape perseverance, patience, and steadfast faith. Give me today my daily bread of endurance, hope, and spiritual maturity. Forgive me for the moments I wanted to quit, and I forgive those who discouraged my walk. Lead me not into the temptation of giving up, but deliver me into steady, faithful endurance (Romans 5:3–4). To You be the glory. Amen.

Reflection:
What difficult place is God using to strengthen your faithfulness?

_____

_____

_____

Action:
Write one faithful step you can take today in the midst of difficulty.

_____

_____

_____

Scriptures Referenced Today:
Isaiah 40:31 (KJV) - "But they that wait upon the Lord shall renew their strength; they shall mount up with wings as eagles; they shall run, and not be weary; and they shall walk, and not faint."
Romans 5:3–4 (KJV) - "And not only so, but we glory in tribulations also: knowing that tribulation worketh patience; And patience, experience; and experience, hope:"

DAY 267 – God Expands Your Ability to Recognize Spiritual Opportunities

Prayer:
Father, thank You for expanding my ability to recognize the spiritual opportunities You place before me. Hallowed be Your name; remind me that the steps of a good man are ordered by the Lord (Psalm 37:23). Let Your kingdom come and open my eyes to divine appointments, open doors, and moments of purpose. Let Your will be done as You train me to see what You are doing around me. Give me today my daily bread of awareness, readiness, and Spirit-led boldness. Forgive me for missing opportunities in the past, and I forgive those who blinded or distracted me. Lead me not into the temptation of spiritual blindness, but deliver me into clear, intentional recognition of Your movement (Ephesians 5:15–16). For Thine is the kingdom and the power and the glory forever and ever. Amen.

Reflection:
What opportunity is God placing before you right now?

_____

_____

_____

Action:
Write one step you will take today to seize a God-given opportunity.

_____

_____

_____

Scriptures Referenced Today:
Psalm 37:23 (KJV) - "The steps of a good man are ordered by the Lord: and he delighteth in his way."
Ephesians 5:15–16 (KJV) - "See then that ye walk circumspectly, not as fools, but as wise, Redeeming the time, because the days are evil."

DAY 268 – God Expands Your Hunger for His Word

Prayer:
Father, thank You for expanding my hunger for Your Word as You grow my capacity in this season. Hallowed be Your name; remind me that man shall not live by bread alone, but by every word that comes from You (Matthew 4:4). Let Your kingdom come and ignite a fresh desire to know, study, and meditate on Scripture. Let Your will be done as You deepen my understanding and sharpen my discernment. Give me today my daily bread of revelation, insight, and illumination. Forgive me for neglecting time in Your Word, and I forgive those who minimized its importance. Lead me not into the temptation of spiritual apathy, but deliver me into a renewed hunger for truth (Psalm 119:103). To You be the glory. Amen.

Reflection:
Where is God calling you to dive deeper into His Word?

Action:
Write one passage you will meditate on today.

Scriptures Referenced Today:
Matthew 4:4 (KJV) - "But he answered and said, It is written, Man shall not live by bread alone, but by every word that proceedeth out of the mouth of God."
Psalm 119:103 (KJV) - "How sweet are thy words unto my taste! yea, sweeter than honey to my mouth!"

DAY 269 – God Expands Your Faith to Pray Bigger Prayers

Prayer:
Father, thank You for expanding my faith so I can pray bigger, bolder prayers. Hallowed be Your name; remind me that whatever I ask in prayer, believing, I shall receive (Matthew 21:22). Let Your kingdom come and grow my confidence to ask for what only You can do. Let Your will be done as You stretch my expectations and enlarge my spiritual vision. Give me today my daily bread of boldness, trust, and expectancy. Forgive me for praying small prayers, and I forgive those who discouraged my faith. Lead me not into the temptation of doubt, but deliver me into bold, faith-filled prayer (James 5:16). To You be all glory. Amen.

Reflection:
What big prayer is God leading you to pray today?

Action:
Write one bold prayer request you will lay before God.

Scriptures Referenced Today:
Matthew 21:22 (KJV) - "And all things, whatsoever ye shall ask in prayer, believing, ye shall receive."
James 5:16 (KJV) - "Confess your faults one to another, and pray one for another, that ye may be healed. The effectual fervent prayer of a righteous man availeth much."

DAY 270 – God Expands Your Strength to Push Through Resistance

Prayer:
Father, thank You for expanding my strength to press forward even when I face resistance. Hallowed be Your name; remind me that greater is He that is in me than he that is in the world (1 John 4:4). Let Your kingdom come and strengthen me through the battles, obstacles, and barriers that arise as my territory expands. Let Your will be done as You develop perseverance, resilience, and spiritual power within me. Give me today my daily bread of endurance, courage, and unwavering focus. Forgive me for slowing down when resistance increased, and I forgive those who created obstacles in my path. Lead me not into the temptation of discouragement, but deliver me into steadfast, Spirit-fueled perseverance (Philippians 3:14). To You be the glory. Amen.

Reflection:
Where are you experiencing resistance that God is using to strengthen you?

_____

_____

_____

Action:
Write one step you will take today to push through with God's strength.

_____

_____

_____

Scriptures Referenced Today:
1 John 4:4 (KJV) - "Ye are of God, little children, and have overcome them: because greater is he that is in you, than he that is in the world."
Philippians 3:14 (KJV) - "I press toward the mark for the prize of the high calling of God in Christ Jesus."

DAY 271 – God Expands Your Peace in Chaotic Situations

Prayer:
Father, thank You for expanding my peace even when situations around me feel chaotic. Hallowed be Your name; remind me that You will keep me in perfect peace when my mind is stayed on You (Isaiah 26:3). Let Your kingdom come and calm the storms inside me as well as the ones around me. Let Your will be done as You teach me to rest in Your presence and trust Your sovereignty. Give me today my daily bread of stillness, calmness, and unwavering inner peace. Forgive me for letting anxiety rule my heart, and I forgive those who contributed to stress in my life. Lead me not into the temptation of fear, but deliver me into steady, holy peace (John 14:27). To You be the glory. Amen.

Reflection:
Where do you need God's perfect peace today?

Action:
Write one way you will center your mind on God today.

Scriptures Referenced Today:
Isaiah 26:3 (KJV) - "Thou wilt keep him in perfect peace, whose mind is stayed on thee: because he trusteth in thee."
John 14:27 (KJV) - "Peace I leave with you, my peace I give unto you: not as the world giveth, give I unto you. Let not your heart be troubled, neither let it be afraid."

DAY 272 – God Expands Your Joy in Every Season

Prayer:
Father, thank You for expanding my joy and teaching me to remain
strong in every season. Hallowed be Your name; remind me that the joy
of the Lord is my strength (Nehemiah 8:10). Let Your kingdom come
and overflow my heart with joy that is not dependent on circumstances.
Let Your will be done as You renew my spirit and lighten my burdens.
Give me today my daily bread of gladness, gratitude, and holy joy.
Forgive me for letting discouragement steal my joy, and I forgive those
who drained my joy in the past. Lead me not into the temptation of
frustration or heaviness, but deliver me into joy that is full, lasting, and
rooted in You (Romans 15:13). To You be the glory. Amen.

Reflection:
Where is God restoring or increasing your joy?

_____

_____

_____

Action:
Write one joyful practice you will engage in today.

_____

_____

_____

Scriptures Referenced Today:
Nehemiah 8:10 (KJV) - "Then he said unto them, Go your way, eat the
fat, and drink the sweet, and send portions unto them for whom nothing
is prepared: for this day is holy unto our Lord: neither be ye sorry; for the
joy of the Lord is your strength."

Romans 15:13 (KJV) - "Now the God of hope fill you with all joy and
peace in believing, that ye may abound in hope, through the power of the
Holy Ghost."

DAY 273 – God Expands Your Confidence in His Promises

Prayer:
Father, thank You for expanding my confidence in every promise You've spoken. Hallowed be Your name; remind me that all Your promises in Christ are yes and amen (2 Corinthians 1:20). Let Your kingdom come and strengthen my faith to believe Your Word without hesitation. Let Your will be done as You build unshakable trust in Your character and faithfulness. Give me today my daily bread of assurance, certainty, and steadfast hope. Forgive me for doubting Your promises, and I forgive those who weakened my faith. Lead me not into the temptation of unbelief, but deliver me into bold confidence in what You have spoken (Psalm 119:140). To You be the glory. Amen.

Reflection:
Which promise of God do you need renewed confidence in today?

_____

_____

_____

Action:
Write one promise you will stand on today.

_____

_____

_____

Scriptures Referenced Today:
2 Corinthians 1:20 (KJV) - "For all the promises of God in him are yea, and in him Amen, unto the glory of God by us."
Psalm 119:140 (KJV) - "Thy word is very pure: therefore thy servant loveth it."

DAY 274 – God Expands Your Capacity to Trust His Timing

Prayer:
Father, thank You for expanding my capacity to trust Your perfect timing. Hallowed be Your name; remind me that to everything there is a season, and a time to every purpose under heaven (Ecclesiastes 3:1). Let Your kingdom come and settle my heart in the truth that You are never early and never late. Let Your will be done as You help me release my timelines and embrace Yours. Give me today my daily bread of patience, surrender, and rest. Forgive me for trying to rush Your process, and I forgive those who created pressure in my life. Lead me not into the temptation of anxiety, but deliver me into peaceful trust in Your timing (Psalm 37:7). For You reign in power and glory, both now and forever. Amen.

Reflection:
Where is God inviting you to trust His timing?

_____

_____

_____

Action:
Write one way you will release control of timing today.

_____

_____

_____

Scriptures Referenced Today:
Ecclesiastes 3:1 (KJV) - "To every thing there is a season, and a time to every purpose under the heaven:"
Psalm 37:7 (KJV) - "Rest in the Lord, and wait patiently for him: fret not thyself because of him who prospereth in his way, because of the man who bringeth wicked devices to pass."

DAY 275 – God Expands Your Courage to Walk Through Open Doors

Prayer:
Father, thank You for expanding my courage to walk through the doors You open. Hallowed be Your name; remind me that when You open a door, no man can shut it (Revelation 3:8). Let Your kingdom come and erase hesitation, fear, and insecurity. Let Your will be done as You empower me to step boldly into new places and new assignments. Give me today my daily bread of courage, readiness, and faith-filled action. Forgive me for ignoring open doors, and I forgive those who made me afraid to step forward. Lead me not into the temptation of shrinking back, but deliver me into bold obedience as You lead (1 Corinthians 16:9). To You be the glory. Amen.

Reflection:
What door has God opened that you need courage to step through?

_____

_____

_____

Action:
Write one step toward that open door you can take today.

_____

_____

_____

Scriptures Referenced Today:
Revelation 3:8 (KJV) - "I know thy works: behold, I have set before thee an open door, and no man can shut it: for thou hast a little strength, and hast kept my word, and hast not denied my name."
1 Corinthians 16:9 (KJV) - "For a great door and effectual is opened unto me, and there are many adversaries."

MONTH 9 CLOSING REFLECTION: SPIRITUAL GROWTH, CAPACITY & EXPANDING YOUR TERRITORY

Month 9 was a month of stretching. Of enlarging. Of becoming someone capable of carrying more than you carried before. God has been steadily increasing your capacity-spiritually, emotionally, mentally, and practically-preparing you for the seasons ahead.

This month you learned to:

- Embrace spiritual growth as an ongoing journey
- Develop endurance and resilience under pressure
- Pray bigger, bolder prayers
- Step through open doors with courage
- Recognize spiritual opportunities God brings
- Deepen your hunger for the Word
- Strengthen your ability to hear God clearly
- Walk in confidence grounded in His promises
- Trust His timing without anxiety
- Push through resistance with perseverance
- Carry joy, peace, and hope in every season

Month 9 showed you something essential:

When God expands your territory, He first expands you.

He strengthened your inner life so He can enlarge your outer assignments.

He grew your wisdom so He can entrust you with greater influence.

He increased your dependence on Him so He can increase your effectiveness for His kingdom.

As you close this month, reflect on these questions:

- Where did God stretch your faith?
- Where did He increase your capacity?
- What doors did He open?
- What areas of weakness became places of growth?
- What spiritual muscles are stronger now than they were 30 days ago?

Let Month 9 settle into your spirit with this truth:

You are being built, strengthened, and expanded for more than you realize.

And God wastes nothing in this process.

Now, you step into Month 10-where God shifts from expanding your capacity **within** to expanding your authority **through** Him.

MONTH 10 THEME: SPIRITUAL AUTHORITY, ANOINTING & WALKING IN YOUR GOD-GIVEN POWER

Month 10 marks a turning point. This is the month where you stop simply growing on the inside and begin walking in the authority God has already placed upon your life. Everything God has built in you over the last nine months - renewal, healing, courage, maturity, strength, capacity, identity - now becomes the foundation for a deeper truth: **you are called to walk in spiritual authority.**

Authority is not loud. It is not forceful. It is not prideful.

Authority is the quiet confidence of someone who knows who their Father is, knows what their Father has spoken, and walks forward in obedience and boldness.

This month is about stepping into the power of God's Spirit - not in arrogance, but in alignment.

There will be moments this month when God asks you to pray differently, speak differently, or stand differently. Not from your own strength, but from His. This is the month of learning what it means to carry the presence of God into every environment, and to recognize that you are not walking into situations alone - **you are walking in with the authority of heaven behind you.**

This month will help you:

- Recognize the authority Christ has already given you
- Pray with conviction, clarity, and spiritual boldness
- Discern spiritual resistance and stand firm without fear
- Speak words that carry weight because they are aligned with Scripture
- Walk confidently in the assignments God has prepared for you
- Move from hesitation to decisive obedience
- Stand firm in your identity when faced with spiritual pushback
- Carry God's peace and presence wherever you go
- Understand how anointing flows through obedience and humility
- Lead spiritually in your home, relationships, work, and community

Authority does not come from your personality - it comes from your position in Christ.

Anointing does not come from striving - it comes from surrender, purity, and intimacy with God.

And spiritual power is not something you "feel" - it is something you *walk in* by faith.

Let the Lord's Prayer guide your authority this month:

- **"Our Father in Heaven"** - Authority begins with identity. You speak and live as a child of the King.
- **"Hallowed be Your name"** - Holiness produces authority. Worship aligns you with God's character.
- **"Your kingdom come"** - Authority is released when you agree with God's agenda, not your own.
- **"Your will be done"** - Obedience is the doorway to anointing.
- **"Give us this day our daily bread"** - Authority requires daily dependence and fresh spiritual strength.
- **"Forgive us…"** - Unforgiveness weakens authority; humility strengthens it.
- **"Lead us not into temptation"** - Authority requires discernment and vigilance.
- **"Yours is the kingdom…"** - Spiritual power flows from recognizing God's reign, not your effort.

As you step into Month 10, remember this:

You are not becoming authoritative - you already carry authority in Christ.

This month teaches you how to walk in it.

Boldly.

Humbly.

Soberly.

Confidently.

And always in the power of the Holy Spirit.

This is your month of stepping into who you already are in Christ.

Not tentative.

Not unsure.

But empowered, equipped, and anointed to walk in the calling God has placed on your life.

DAY 276 – Walking in the Spiritual Authority God Has Given You

Prayer:
Father, thank You for the spiritual authority You have entrusted to me through Christ. Hallowed be Your name; remind me that You have given me power over all the power of the enemy (Luke 10:19). Let Your kingdom come as I walk boldly in the authority of Your Word. Let Your will be done as You strengthen my spirit and steady my confidence. Give me today my daily bread of courage, clarity, and spiritual boldness. Forgive me for shrinking back in fear, and I forgive those who tried to diminish my identity in You. Lead me not into the temptation of intimidation, but deliver me into fearless authority rooted in Your strength (Ephesians 6:10). To You be the glory. Amen.

Reflection:
Where do you need to walk in God-given authority today?

_____

_____

_____

Action:
Write one step of authority you will take today by faith.

_____

_____

_____

Scriptures Referenced Today:
Luke 10:19 (KJV) - "Behold, I give unto you power to tread on serpents and scorpions, and over all the power of the enemy: and nothing shall by any means hurt you."
Ephesians 6:10 (KJV) - "Finally, my brethren, be strong in the Lord, and in the power of his might."

DAY 277 – Praying With Boldness, Power, and Authority

Prayer:
Father, thank You for inviting me to Your throne with boldness.
Hallowed be Your name; remind me that I may come boldly unto the
throne of grace to obtain mercy and find grace to help in time of need
(Hebrews 4:16). Let Your kingdom come as You increase my confidence
in prayer. Let Your will be done as You teach me to pray with power and
conviction. Give me today my daily bread of boldness, assurance, and
Spirit-led faith. Forgive me for praying timidly, and I forgive those who
taught me to expect little. Lead me not into the temptation of small
prayers, but deliver me into bold intercession rooted in Your promises (1
John 5:14). For the kingdom is Yours, and the power is Yours, and the
glory is Yours, forever. Amen.

Reflection:
Where do you need to pray with bold authority today?

_____

_____

Action:
Write a bold, faith-filled prayer you will bring to God today.

_____

_____

Scriptures Referenced Today:
Hebrews 4:16 (KJV) - "Let us therefore come boldly unto the throne of
grace, that we may obtain mercy, and find grace to help in time of need."
1 John 5:14 (KJV) - "And this is the confidence that we have in him, that,
if we ask any thing according to his will, he heareth us."

DAY 278 – Standing Firm Against Spiritual Resistance

Prayer:
Father, thank You for giving me strength to stand firm against every form of spiritual resistance. Hallowed be Your name; remind me that no weapon formed against me shall prosper (Isaiah 54:17). Let Your kingdom come and anchor me in Your unshakeable truth. Let Your will be done as You teach me to resist the enemy with confidence, not fear. Give me today my daily bread of courage, stability, and holy determination. Forgive me for retreating in the past, and I forgive those who tried to weaken my faith. Lead me not into the temptation of discouragement, but deliver me into steadfast confidence in Your victory (James 4:7). For You reign in power and glory, both now and forever. Amen.

Reflection:
What form of resistance do you need to stand firm against?

Action:
Write one step of firm spiritual resistance you will take today.

Scriptures Referenced Today:
Isaiah 54:17 (KJV) - "No weapon that is formed against thee shall prosper; and every tongue that shall rise against thee in judgment thou shalt condemn. This is the heritage of the servants of the Lord, and their righteousness is of me, saith the Lord."
James 4:7 (KJV) - "Submit yourselves therefore to God. Resist the devil, and he will flee from you."

DAY 279 – Walking in the Power of the Holy Spirit

Prayer:
Father, thank You for the power of the Holy Spirit dwelling within me. Hallowed be Your name; remind me that I receive power when the Holy Ghost comes upon me (Acts 1:8). Let Your kingdom come as You activate spiritual power, boldness, and clarity within me. Let Your will be done as I walk in Spirit-led authority today. Give me today my daily bread of spiritual strength, guidance, and empowerment. Forgive me for relying on my own strength, and I forgive those who caused me to doubt the Spirit's work in my life. Lead me not into the temptation of self-reliance, but deliver me into the fullness of Your Spirit's power (Romans 8:14). For Yours is the kingdom and the power and the glory forever. Amen.

Reflection:
Where do you need to walk in Spirit-given power today?

_____

_____

_____

Action:
Write one way you will intentionally follow the Holy Spirit today.

_____

_____

_____

Scriptures Referenced Today:
Acts 1:8 (KJV) - "But ye shall receive power, after that the Holy Ghost is come upon you: and ye shall be witnesses unto me both in Jerusalem, and in all Judaea, and in Samaria, and unto the uttermost part of the earth."
Romans 8:14 (KJV) - "For as many as are led by the Spirit of God, they are the sons of God."

DAY 280 – Taking Authority Over Fear

Prayer:
Father, thank You for giving me authority over fear. Hallowed be Your name; remind me that You have not given me the spirit of fear, but of power, and of love, and of a sound mind (2 Timothy 1:7). Let Your kingdom come as You break fear's influence over my thoughts, emotions, and decisions. Let Your will be done as You fortify my spirit with courage and peace. Give me today my daily bread of confidence, strength, and fearless faith. Forgive me for letting fear direct my steps, and I forgive those who used fear against me. Lead me not into the temptation of anxiety, but deliver me into holy courage grounded in Your Word (Psalm 27:1). For You reign in power and glory, both now and forever. Amen.

Reflection:
What specific fear do you need to take authority over today?

_____

_____

_____

Action:
Write one action that reflects courage instead of fear.

_____

_____

_____

Scriptures Referenced Today:
2 Timothy 1:7 (KJV) - "For God hath not given us the spirit of fear; but of power, and of love, and of a sound mind."
Psalm 27:1 (KJV) - "The Lord is my light and my salvation; whom shall I fear? the Lord is the strength of my life; of whom shall I be afraid?"

DAY 281 – Declaring Victory Through the Authority of Christ

Prayer:
Father, thank You for giving me victory through the authority of Jesus Christ. Hallowed be Your name; remind me that thanks be to God, who gives us the victory through our Lord Jesus Christ (1 Corinthians 15:57). Let Your kingdom come as I stand on the finished work of Christ. Let Your will be done as You strengthen my confidence to declare victory over every battle I face. Give me today my daily bread of boldness, clarity, and unwavering faith. Forgive me for speaking defeat, and I forgive those who spoke fear into my life. Lead me not into the temptation of discouragement, but deliver me into victorious confidence rooted in Christ (Romans 8:37). To You be the glory. Amen.

Reflection:
Where do you need to declare the victory Christ has already given you?

_____

_____

_____

Action:
Write one victory declaration for your life today.

_____

_____

Scriptures Referenced Today:
1 Corinthians 15:57 (KJV) - "But thanks be to God, which giveth us the victory through our Lord Jesus Christ."
Romans 8:37 (KJV) - "Nay, in all these things we are more than conquerors through him that loved us."

DAY 282 – Taking Authority Over the Lies of the Enemy

Prayer:
Father, thank You for giving me authority over every lie of the enemy. Hallowed be Your name; remind me that the weapons of my warfare are not carnal, but mighty through God to the pulling down of strong holds (2 Corinthians 10:4). Let Your kingdom come and expose every lie that has tried to limit my life. Let Your will be done as You teach me to cast down imaginations and every high thing that exalts itself against Your truth. Give me today my daily bread of discernment, truth, and a sound mind. Forgive me for agreeing with lies, and I forgive those who spoke falsehood over me. Lead me not into the temptation of mental deception, but deliver me into truth, freedom, and clarity (John 8:32). For the kingdom is Yours, and the power is Yours, and the glory is Yours, forever. Amen.

Reflection:
What lie of the enemy do you need to confront today?

_____

_____

_____

Action:
Write the truth from Scripture that replaces that lie.

_____

_____

_____

Scriptures Referenced Today:
2 Corinthians 10:4–5 (KJV) - "(For the weapons of our warfare are not carnal, but mighty through God to the pulling down of strong holds;) Casting down imaginations, and every high thing that exalteth itself against the knowledge of God, and bringing into captivity every thought to the obedience of Christ;"
John 8:32 (KJV) - "And ye shall know the truth, and the truth shall make you free."

DAY 283 – Using Your Words With Spiritual Authority

Prayer:
Father, thank You for teaching me that my words carry spiritual weight.
Hallowed be Your name; remind me that life and death are in the power
of the tongue (Proverbs 18:21). Let Your kingdom come and purify my
speech so that what I declare aligns with Your truth. Let Your will be
done as You train me to speak blessing, victory, and faith. Give me today
my daily bread of wisdom, restraint, and Spirit-led speech. Forgive me for
careless or negative words, and I forgive those who spoke damaging
words over me. Lead me not into the temptation of speaking doubt, but
deliver me into declarations rooted in Your authority (Matthew 12:37).
To You be the glory. Amen.

Reflection:
What words do you need to speak differently today?

_____

_____

_____

Action:
Write one faith-filled declaration you will speak today.

_____

_____

_____

Scriptures Referenced Today:
Proverbs 18:21 (KJV) - "Death and life are in the power of the tongue:
and they that love it shall eat the fruit thereof."
Matthew 12:37 (KJV) - "For by thy words thou shalt be justified, and by
thy words thou shalt be condemned."

DAY 284 – Standing in the Authority of Your Identity in Christ

Prayer:
Father, thank You for anchoring my identity in who You say I am.
Hallowed be Your name; remind me that I am a chosen generation, a
royal priesthood, a holy nation, and a peculiar people (1 Peter 2:9). Let
Your kingdom come and reveal every part of my identity that reflects
Christ. Let Your will be done as You remove false labels and strengthen
my confidence in You. Give me today my daily bread of clarity,
confidence, and spiritual dignity. Forgive me for embracing false
identities, and I forgive those who misnamed or mislabeled me. Lead me
not into the temptation of insecurity, but deliver me into bold, Christ-
rooted identity (Galatians 2:20). For You reign in power and glory, both
now and forever. Amen.

Reflection:
What part of your identity in Christ do you need to embrace today?

_____

_____

_____

Action:
Write one truth about who you are in Christ that you will focus on today.

_____

_____

_____

Scriptures Referenced Today:
1 Peter 2:9 (KJV) - "But ye are a chosen generation, a royal priesthood,
an holy nation, a peculiar people; that ye should shew forth the praises of
him who hath called you out of darkness into his marvellous light:"
Galatians 2:20 (KJV) - "I am crucified with Christ: nevertheless I live; yet
not I, but Christ liveth in me: and the life which I now live in the flesh I
live by the faith of the Son of God, who loved me, and gave himself for
me."

DAY 285 – Exercising Authority Through the Armor of God

Prayer:
Father, thank You for equipping me with spiritual armor to stand strong. Hallowed be Your name; remind me to put on the whole armor of God so I may stand against the wiles of the devil (Ephesians 6:11). Let Your kingdom come as I walk protected, empowered, and confident in Your strength. Let Your will be done as You teach me to use each piece of armor with purpose. Give me today my daily bread of vigilance, strength, and spiritual readiness. Forgive me for neglecting the armor You have provided, and I forgive those who attacked me spiritually. Lead me not into the temptation of spiritual passivity, but deliver me into active, armored authority (Romans 13:12). For Thine alone is the kingdom, the power, and the glory, forever. Amen.

Reflection:
What piece of God's armor do you need most today?

_____

_____

_____

Action:
Write one intentional step you will take today to "put on" that armor.

_____

_____

_____

Scriptures Referenced Today:
Ephesians 6:11 (KJV) - "Put on the whole armour of God, that ye may be able to stand against the wiles of the devil."
Romans 13:12 (KJV) - "The night is far spent, the day is at hand: let us therefore cast off the works of darkness, and let us put on the armour of light."

DAY 286 – Exercising Authority Through Persistent Prayer

Prayer:
Father, thank You for giving me spiritual authority that grows stronger through persistent prayer. Hallowed be Your name; remind me that men ought always to pray and not to faint (Luke 18:1). Let Your kingdom come as You teach me to pray with perseverance, consistency, and confidence. Let Your will be done as You deepen my faith through persistence. Give me today my daily bread of endurance, focus, and unwavering devotion. Forgive me for giving up too quickly in prayer, and I forgive those who discouraged my persistence. Lead me not into the temptation of prayerlessness, but deliver me into faithful, powerful, persistent prayer (Colossians 4:2). For Yours is the kingdom and the power and the glory forever. Amen.

Reflection:
Where do you need to persist in prayer instead of giving up?

_____

_____

Action:
Write one prayer you will commit to praying persistently this week.

_____

_____

Scriptures Referenced Today:
Luke 18:1 (KJV) - "And he spake a parable unto them to this end, that men ought always to pray, and not to faint;"
Colossians 4:2 (KJV) - "Continue in prayer, and watch in the same with thanksgiving;"

DAY 287 – Taking Authority Over Spiritual Attacks

Prayer:
Father, thank You for giving me authority to stand firm in the face of spiritual attack. Hallowed be Your name; remind me that greater is He that is in me than he that is in the world (1 John 4:4). Let Your kingdom come as You strengthen my spirit against every scheme of the enemy. Let Your will be done as You teach me to fight from victory, not for victory. Give me today my daily bread of courage, discernment, and spiritual strength. Forgive me for feeling powerless in spiritual battles, and I forgive those who contributed to my fear. Lead me not into the temptation of intimidation, but deliver me into bold authority grounded in Your Word (Ephesians 6:13). For You alone are the King of glory, forever and ever. Amen.

Reflection:
What spiritual attack do you need to take authority over today?

_____

_____

_____

Action:
Write one way you will stand firm in God's strength today.

_____

_____

_____

Scriptures Referenced Today:
1 John 4:4 (KJV) - "Ye are of God, little children, and have overcome them: because greater is he that is in you, than he that is in the world."
Ephesians 6:13 (KJV) - "Wherefore take unto you the whole armour of God, that ye may be able to withstand in the evil day, and having done all, to stand."

DAY 288 – Walking in the Anointing God Has Placed on Your Life

Prayer:
Father, thank You for the anointing You have placed on my life. Hallowed be Your name; remind me that the anointing I have received from You abides in me (1 John 2:27). Let Your kingdom come as You activate, strengthen, and sustain the anointing within me. Let Your will be done as You increase my sensitivity to the Holy Spirit. Give me today my daily bread of wisdom, clarity, and Spirit-led obedience. Forgive me for ignoring or doubting the anointing You've given, and I forgive those who questioned my calling. Lead me not into the temptation of relying on my own ability, but deliver me into the power of the anointing You have placed upon me (Isaiah 61:1). For You reign in power and glory, both now and forever. Amen.

Reflection:
Where do you need to walk in the anointing God has given you?

_____

_____

_____

Action:
Write one anointed step of obedience you will take today.

_____

_____

Scriptures Referenced Today:
1 John 2:27 (KJV) - "But the anointing which ye have received of him abideth in you, and ye need not that any man teach you: but as the same anointing teacheth you of all things, and is truth, and is no lie, and even as it hath taught you, ye shall abide in him."

Isaiah 61:1 (KJV) - "The Spirit of the Lord God is upon me; because the Lord hath anointed me to preach good tidings unto the meek; he hath sent me to bind up the brokenhearted, to proclaim liberty to the captives, and the opening of the prison to them that are bound;"

DAY 289 – Exercising Authority Through Forgiveness

Prayer:
Father, thank You for the authority that comes through forgiveness. Hallowed be Your name; remind me that if I forgive others, You also forgive me (Matthew 6:14). Let Your kingdom come as You free my heart from bitterness, anger, and resentment. Let Your will be done as You strengthen me to release what I cannot carry. Give me today my daily bread of grace, compassion, and emotional strength. Forgive me for holding on to offense, and I forgive those who hurt me. Lead me not into the temptation of bitterness, but deliver me into freedom, healing, and spiritual authority (Ephesians 4:32). To You be the glory. Amen.

Reflection:
Who is God calling you to forgive so you can walk in freedom?

_____

_____

_____

Action:
Write one step of forgiveness you will take today.

_____

_____

_____

Scriptures Referenced Today:
Matthew 6:14 (KJV) - "For if ye forgive men their trespasses, your heavenly Father will also forgive you:"
Ephesians 4:32 (KJV) - "And be ye kind one to another, tenderhearted, forgiving one another, even as God for Christ's sake hath forgiven you."

DAY 290 – Using Your God-Given Authority to Speak Peace Over Your Life

Prayer:
Father, thank You for giving me authority to speak peace over my life, my home, and my circumstances. Hallowed be Your name; remind me that Jesus gives me peace not as the world gives (John 14:27). Let Your kingdom come as You fill my heart and mind with supernatural calm. Let Your will be done as You teach me to speak peace into chaos and confusion. Give me today my daily bread of rest, stability, and spiritual authority. Forgive me for agreeing with anxiety, and I forgive those who contributed to worry in my life. Lead me not into the temptation of fear, but deliver me into the peace that surpasses understanding (Philippians 4:7). For You alone are the King of glory, forever and ever. Amen.

Reflection:
Where do you need to speak God's peace today?

_____

_____

Action:
Write one declaration of peace you will speak over your life today.

_____

_____

Scriptures Referenced Today:
John 14:27 (KJV) - "Peace I leave with you, my peace I give unto you: not as the world giveth, give I unto you. Let not your heart be troubled, neither let it be afraid."
Philippians 4:7 (KJV) - "And the peace of God, which passeth all understanding, shall keep your hearts and minds through Christ Jesus."

DAY 291 – Taking Authority Over Your Thoughts

Prayer:
Father, thank You for giving me authority over my thoughts and mind.
Hallowed be Your name; remind me to bring every thought into captivity
to the obedience of Christ (2 Corinthians 10:5). Let Your kingdom come
and renew my mind with truth. Let Your will be done as You strengthen
me to think according to Your Word, not my fears. Give me today my
daily bread of clarity, peace, and mental strength. Forgive me for allowing
negative thoughts to rule me, and I forgive those who contributed to
unhealthy patterns. Lead me not into the temptation of mental defeat,
but deliver me into a disciplined, Christ-centered mind (Philippians 4:8).
For Thine alone is the kingdom, the power, and the glory, forever. Amen.

Reflection:
What thought do you need to take authority over today?

_____

_____

_____

Action:
Write the truth from Scripture that will replace that thought.

_____

_____

_____

Scriptures Referenced Today:
2 Corinthians 10:5 (KJV) - "Casting down imaginations, and every high
thing that exalteth itself against the knowledge of God, and bringing into
captivity every thought to the obedience of Christ;"

Philippians 4:8 (KJV) - "Finally, brethren, whatsoever things are true,
whatsoever things are honest, whatsoever things are just, whatsoever
things are pure, whatsoever things are lovely, whatsoever things are of
good report; if there be any virtue, and if there be any praise, think on
these things."

DAY 292 – Exercising Authority Through Spiritual Discernment

Prayer:
Father, thank You for sharpening my discernment as I walk in spiritual authority. Hallowed be Your name; remind me that strong meat belongs to those who have their senses exercised to discern both good and evil (Hebrews 5:14). Let Your kingdom come and heighten my awareness of what is from You and what is not. Let Your will be done as You help me make wise, Spirit-led decisions. Give me today my daily bread of wisdom, insight, and clear spiritual perception. Forgive me for leaning on my own understanding, and I forgive those who led me into confusion. Lead me not into the temptation of spiritual blindness, but deliver me into discernment that protects, directs, and empowers me (Proverbs 3:5–6). For You reign in power and glory, both now and forever. Amen.

Reflection:
Where do you need God's discernment today?

Action:
Write one decision where you will apply discernment today.

Scriptures Referenced Today:
Hebrews 5:14 (KJV) - "But strong meat belongeth to them that are of full age, even those who by reason of use have their senses exercised to discern both good and evil."
Proverbs 3:5–6 (KJV) - "Trust in the Lord with all thine heart; and lean not unto thine own understanding. In all thy ways acknowledge him, and he shall direct thy paths."

DAY 293 – Walking in Authority Through Your Identity as God's Child

Prayer:
Father, thank You that my authority comes from being Your child. Hallowed be Your name; remind me that You have given me power to become a child of God through faith in Your name (John 1:12). Let Your kingdom come as You strengthen my confidence in who I am in Christ. Let Your will be done as You free me from insecurity, doubt, and spiritual hesitation. Give me today my daily bread of confidence, identity, and holy boldness. Forgive me for forgetting who I am in You, and I forgive those who spoke against my identity. Lead me not into the temptation of insecurity, but deliver me into confident, grounded identity in Christ (Romans 8:16). To You be the glory. Amen.

Reflection:
What truth about your identity in Christ do you need to stand on today?

Action:
Write one declaration about who you are in Christ.

Scriptures Referenced Today:
John 1:12 (KJV) - "But as many as received him, to them gave he power to become the sons of God, even to them that believe on his name:"
Romans 8:16 (KJV) - "The Spirit itself beareth witness with our spirit, that we are the children of God:"

DAY 294 – Using Your Authority to Break Strongholds

Prayer:
Father, thank You for giving me the authority to break spiritual strongholds through Your power. Hallowed be Your name; remind me that the weapons of my warfare are mighty through God to pull down strongholds (2 Corinthians 10:4). Let Your kingdom come and dismantle every spiritual barrier that has stood against my growth. Let Your will be done as You teach me to speak truth, declare freedom, and stand in Your strength. Give me today my daily bread of courage, spiritual power, and clarity. Forgive me for tolerating strongholds, and I forgive those who contributed to them. Lead me not into the temptation of spiritual resignation, but deliver me into freedom and victory through Christ (Isaiah 10:27). For the kingdom is Yours, and the power is Yours, and the glory is Yours, forever. Amen.

Reflection:
What stronghold needs to be broken from your life?

_____

_____

_____

Action:
Write one step you will take today to confront that stronghold.

_____

_____

_____

Scriptures Referenced Today:
2 Corinthians 10:4 (KJV) - "For the weapons of our warfare are not carnal, but mighty through God to the pulling down of strong holds;"
Isaiah 10:27 (KJV) - "And it shall come to pass in that day, that his burden shall be taken away from off thy shoulder, and his yoke from off thy neck, and the yoke shall be destroyed because of the anointing."

DAY 295 – Walking in the Authority of Christ's Peace Over Your Mind

Prayer:
Father, thank You for giving me the authority to walk in Christ's peace. Hallowed be Your name; remind me that the peace of God guards my heart and mind through Christ Jesus (Philippians 4:7). Let Your kingdom come as You quiet every storm within me. Let Your will be done as You teach me to rule my thoughts and emotions through Your peace. Give me today my daily bread of calmness, stability, and holy rest. Forgive me for letting anxiety lead me, and I forgive those who contributed to my unrest. Lead me not into the temptation of fear, but deliver me into peace that establishes authority over my mind (Colossians 3:15). For Thine alone is the kingdom, the power, and the glory, forever. Amen.

Reflection:
Where do you need Christ's peace to rule today?

_____

_____

_____

Action:
Write a declaration of peace you will speak over your life.

_____

_____

_____

Scriptures Referenced Today:
Philippians 4:7 (KJV) - "And the peace of God, which passeth all understanding, shall keep your hearts and minds through Christ Jesus."
Colossians 3:15 (KJV) - "And let the peace of God rule in your hearts, to the which also ye are called in one body; and be ye thankful."

DAY 296 – Taking Authority Over the Atmosphere of Your Home

Prayer:
Father, thank You for giving me authority to set the spiritual atmosphere in my home. Hallowed be Your name; remind me that where Your Spirit is, there is liberty (2 Corinthians 3:17). Let Your kingdom come into every room, conversation, and relationship under my roof. Let Your will be done as You empower me to guard my home from fear, strife, and oppression. Give me today my daily bread of peace, protection, and spiritual covering. Forgive me for allowing negativity or darkness into my home, and I forgive those who brought unrest. Lead me not into the temptation of passivity, but deliver me into active spiritual leadership (Joshua 24:15). For You reign in power and glory, both now and forever. Amen.

Reflection:
What atmosphere do you need to establish in your home today?

_____

_____

_____

Action:
Write one declaration you will speak over your home.

_____

_____

_____

Scriptures Referenced Today:
2 Corinthians 3:17 (KJV) - "Now the Lord is that Spirit: and where the Spirit of the Lord is, there is liberty."
Joshua 24:15 (KJV) - "And if it seem evil unto you to serve the Lord, choose you this day whom ye will serve; whether the gods which your fathers served that were on the other side of the flood, or the gods of the Amorites, in whose land ye dwell: but as for me and my house, we will serve the Lord."

DAY 297 – Exercising Authority Through Faith-Filled Declarations

Prayer:
Father, thank You for teaching me to speak with faith and authority. Hallowed be Your name; remind me that I shall decree a thing, and it shall be established unto me (Job 22:28). Let Your kingdom come as You align my declarations with Your Word and Your will. Let Your will be done as You train me to speak life, truth, and victory. Give me today my daily bread of boldness, conviction, and Spirit-guided words. Forgive me for speaking defeat, and I forgive those who spoke negative words over my life. Lead me not into the temptation of careless speech, but deliver me into faith-filled declarations that shift spiritual reality (Mark 11:23). To You be the glory. Amen.

Reflection:
What truth from God's Word do you need to declare today?

_____

_____

_____

Action:
Write one declaration of faith you will speak out loud.

_____

_____

_____

Scriptures Referenced Today:
Job 22:28 (KJV) - "Thou shalt also decree a thing, and it shall be established unto thee: and the light shall shine upon thy ways."
Mark 11:23 (KJV) - "For verily I say unto you, That whosoever shall say unto this mountain, Be thou removed, and be thou cast into the sea; and shall not doubt in his heart, but shall believe that those things which he saith shall come to pass; he shall have whatsoever he saith."

DAY 298 – Walking in the Power of God's Word

Prayer:
Father, thank You for the power of Your Word working in my life. Hallowed be Your name; remind me that Your Word is quick, powerful, and sharper than any two-edged sword (Hebrews 4:12). Let Your kingdom come as Your Word strengthens, corrects, and directs me. Let Your will be done as You anchor my authority in the truth of Scripture. Give me today my daily bread of revelation, understanding, and spiritual insight. Forgive me for neglecting Your Word, and I forgive those who minimized its power. Lead me not into the temptation of ignorance, but deliver me into authority rooted in Scripture (Psalm 119:105). To You be the glory. Amen.

Reflection:
Where do you need God's Word to speak power into your life today?

_____

_____

_____

Action:
Write one Scripture you will meditate on today.

_____

_____

_____

Scriptures Referenced Today:
Hebrews 4:12 (KJV) - "For the word of God is quick, and powerful, and sharper than any two-edged sword, piercing even to the dividing asunder of soul and spirit, and of the joints and marrow, and is a discerner of the thoughts and intents of the heart."
Psalm 119:105 (KJV) - "Thy word is a lamp unto my feet, and a light unto my path."

DAY 299 – Taking Authority Over Every Form of Fear and Intimidation

Prayer:
Father, thank You for giving me authority over fear and intimidation. Hallowed be Your name; remind me that You are my light and salvation; whom shall I fear? (Psalm 27:1). Let Your kingdom come as You break every form of fear that tries to hold me back. Let Your will be done as You strengthen my spirit with courage and confidence. Give me today my daily bread of boldness, peace, and holy assurance. Forgive me for letting fear influence my decisions, and I forgive those who used fear against me. Lead me not into the temptation of retreat, but deliver me into fearless obedience (Isaiah 41:10). For Thine alone is the kingdom, the power, and the glory, forever. Amen.

Reflection:
What fear is trying to intimidate you today?

_____

_____

_____

Action:
Write one courageous step you will take in response.

_____

_____

Scriptures Referenced Today:
Psalm 27:1 (KJV) - "The Lord is my light and my salvation; whom shall I fear? the Lord is the strength of my life; of whom shall I be afraid?"
Isaiah 41:10 (KJV) - "Fear thou not; for I am with thee: be not dismayed; for I am thy God: I will strengthen thee; yea, I will help thee; yea, I will uphold thee with the right hand of my righteousness."

DAY 300 – Walking in Boldness Through the Power of the Holy Ghost

Prayer:
Father, thank You for filling me with boldness through the Holy Ghost. Hallowed be Your name; remind me that the early disciples prayed, and they were all filled with the Holy Ghost and spoke the Word of God with boldness (Acts 4:31). Let Your kingdom come as Your Spirit strengthens my voice, my witness, and my courage. Let Your will be done as You empower me to live boldly for Christ. Give me today my daily bread of Spirit-filled courage, clarity, and conviction. Forgive me for shrinking back, and I forgive those who silenced or diminished my boldness. Lead me not into the temptation of timidity, but deliver me into confident, Spirit-led boldness (2 Timothy 1:7). To You be the glory. Amen.

Reflection:
Where do you need Holy Spirit boldness today?

_____

_____

_____

Action:
Write one bold step you will take for Christ today.

_____

_____

_____

Scriptures Referenced Today:
Acts 4:31 (KJV) - "And when they had prayed, the place was shaken where they were assembled together; and they were all filled with the Holy Ghost, and they spake the word of God with boldness."
2 Timothy 1:7 (KJV) - "For God hath not given us the spirit of fear; but of power, and of love, and of a sound mind."

DAY 301 – Taking Authority Over Every Weapon Formed Against You

Prayer:
Father, thank You for giving me authority over every weapon formed against my life. Hallowed be Your name; remind me that no weapon formed against me shall prosper (Isaiah 54:17). Let Your kingdom come as You protect me from every attack, scheme, and assignment of the enemy. Let Your will be done as You strengthen my spirit to stand firm in faith. Give me today my daily bread of confidence, courage, and spiritual protection. Forgive me for fearing the threats of the enemy, and I forgive those who tried to harm me. Lead me not into the temptation of worry, but deliver me into assurance that You are my defender (Psalm 91:7). For You reign in power and glory, both now and forever. Amen.

Reflection:
What "weapon formed against you" do you need to reject today?

_____

_____

Action:
Write a declaration of protection you will stand on today.

_____

_____

Scriptures Referenced Today:
Isaiah 54:17 (KJV) - "No weapon that is formed against thee shall prosper; and every tongue that shall rise against thee in judgment thou shalt condemn. This is the heritage of the servants of the Lord, and their righteousness is of me, saith the Lord."

Psalm 91:7 (KJV) - "A thousand shall fall at thy side, and ten thousand at thy right hand; but it shall not come nigh thee."

DAY 302 – Walking in Authority Over Anxiety and Inner Turmoil

Prayer:
Father, thank You for giving me authority over anxiety, fear, and inner turmoil. Hallowed be Your name; remind me to cast all my care upon You, for You care for me (1 Peter 5:7). Let Your kingdom come as You calm the storms within my heart. Let Your will be done as I surrender my worries and embrace Your peace. Give me today my daily bread of rest, confidence, and spiritual quietness. Forgive me for holding onto anxiety, and I forgive those who added burdens to my life. Lead me not into the temptation of overthinking, but deliver me into the peace that guards my heart and mind (Philippians 4:6). For the kingdom is Yours, and the power is Yours, and the glory is Yours, forever. Amen.

Reflection:
What anxiety do you need to cast onto the Lord today?

_____

_____

Action:
Write a declaration of peace you will choose today.

_____

_____

Scriptures Referenced Today:
1 Peter 5:7 (KJV) - "Casting all your care upon him; for he careth for you."
Philippians 4:6 (KJV) - "Be careful for nothing; but in every thing by prayer and supplication with thanksgiving let your requests be made known unto God."

DAY 303 – Using Authority to Guard Your Heart and Spirit

Prayer:
Father, thank You for giving me authority to guard my heart and spirit. Hallowed be Your name; remind me to keep my heart with all diligence, for out of it are the issues of life (Proverbs 4:23). Let Your kingdom come as You protect me from influences that attempt to drain my spirit. Let Your will be done as You strengthen my discernment to know what to let in and what to shut out. Give me today my daily bread of vigilance, wisdom, and spiritual strength. Forgive me for letting harmful things shape my spirit, and I forgive those who wounded my heart. Lead me not into the temptation of complacency, but deliver me into intentional, Spirit-led guarding of my heart (Psalm 51:10). To You be the glory. Amen.

Reflection:
What do you need to guard your heart from today?

Action:
Write one boundary you will set to protect your heart.

Scriptures Referenced Today:
Proverbs 4:23 (KJV) - "Keep thy heart with all diligence; for out of it are the issues of life."
Psalm 51:10 (KJV) - "Create in me a clean heart, O God; and renew a right spirit within me."

DAY 304 – Standing in Your Authority When You Feel Weak

Prayer:
Father, thank You that Your strength is perfected in my weakness. Hallowed be Your name; remind me that when I am weak, then I am strong through Christ (2 Corinthians 12:10). Let Your kingdom come as You transform my weakness into God-given power. Let Your will be done as You strengthen me to stand with confidence even when I feel insufficient. Give me today my daily bread of courage, perseverance, and spiritual resilience. Forgive me for viewing weakness as failure, and I forgive those who shamed me for struggling. Lead me not into the temptation of self-pity, but deliver me into Your supernatural strength (Isaiah 40:31). To You be the glory. Amen.

Reflection:
Where do you feel weak and need God's strength today?

_____

_____

_____

Action:
Write one step you will take in faith even if you feel weak.

_____

_____

_____

Scriptures Referenced Today:
2 Corinthians 12:10 (KJV) - "Therefore I take pleasure in infirmities, in reproaches, in necessities, in persecutions, in distresses for Christ's sake: for when I am weak, then am I strong."
Isaiah 40:31 (KJV) - "But they that wait upon the Lord shall renew their strength; they shall mount up with wings as eagles; they shall run, and not be weary; and they shall walk, and not faint."

DAY 305 – Taking Authority Over the Enemy's Accusations

Prayer:
Father, thank You for giving me authority over every accusation of the enemy. Hallowed be Your name; remind me that the accuser of the brethren is cast down because of the blood of the Lamb (Revelation 12:10–11). Let Your kingdom come as You silence every voice of condemnation, shame, or fear. Let Your will be done as You strengthen me to stand in the righteousness of Christ. Give me today my daily bread of confidence, assurance, and spiritual clarity. Forgive me for agreeing with condemnation, and I forgive those who judged or accused me. Lead me not into the temptation of self-condemnation, but deliver me into freedom through Christ's victory (Romans 8:1). For Yours is the kingdom and the power and the glory forever. Amen.

Reflection:
What accusation-spoken or internal-do you need to silence today?

_____

_____

_____

Action:
Write one truth that breaks the power of that accusation.

_____

_____

_____

Scriptures Referenced Today:
Revelation 12:10–11 (KJV) -
"And I heard a loud voice saying in heaven, Now is come salvation, and strength, and the kingdom of our God, and the power of his Christ: **for the accuser of our brethren is cast down, which accused them before our God day and night.**
And they overcame him by the blood of the Lamb, and by the word of their testimony; and they loved not their lives unto the death."
Romans 8:1 (KJV) -
"There is therefore now no condemnation to them which are in Christ Jesus, who walk not after the flesh, but after the Spirit."

MONTH 10 CLOSING REFLECTION: AUTHORITY, ANOINTING, & WALKING IN GOD-GIVEN POWER

Month 10 has invited you into the reality of the spiritual authority God has placed on your life-authority rooted not in your strength, but in Christ's. Through these days, you've learned that authority is not something you earn; it is something you receive. It is a mantle given by your Father, carried through obedience, activated by the Holy Spirit, and strengthened through prayer.

This month you stepped into deeper truths:

- You carry the authority of Christ because you belong to Him.
- You have power over the lies, accusations, and intimidation of the enemy.
- You can guard your heart, your home, your mind, and your atmosphere.
- You are anointed to live boldly-not quietly or timidly-in the purposes of God.
- You can declare God's Word with confidence, knowing that heaven backs what He has spoken.
- Your weaknesses do not disqualify you; they position you to display His strength.
- Persistence in prayer strengthens your authority.
- Discernment is a weapon.
- Peace is a form of power.
- Identity is a shield.

You discovered that authority is not loud-it is steady.

It is not proud-it is surrendered.

It is not self-created-it is Spirit-given.

Through every prayer, you stepped deeper into the reality that:

You are not walking into battles alone; you are walking into them appointed, anointed, and backed by heaven.

As you close Month 10, take time to reflect:

- Where did God strengthen your courage?
- What lies did He silence?
- What fears did He break?
- What decisions did He clarify?

- What part of your identity grew stronger?
- What attacks lost their grip because you stood in truth?
- What areas of your life now operate from confidence instead of hesitation?

Carry this forward:

The authority Christ has given you is not seasonal. It is not temporary. It is not fragile. It is built on the unchanging victory of Jesus.

Month 10 has prepared you for the next stretch of this journey-one that goes deeper into the heart of the Father, deeper into spiritual transformation, and deeper into becoming who God designed you to be.

MONTH 11 INTRODUCTION: TRANSFORMATION, RENEWAL, & THE MAKING OF A NEW HEART

Month 11 invites you into the sacred work God does *within* you-renewing, reshaping, and transforming the deepest parts of your heart. Where Month 10 focused on spiritual authority, Month 11 focuses on spiritual formation-what God does in the inner life so that you can carry His presence with strength, humility, and purity.

This is the month of spiritual renewal.

- This month, through the rhythm of the Lord's Prayer, God will lead you into:
- The renewing of your mind by His Word
- The softening of hard places in your heart
- The healing of wounds that have shaped your decisions
- The restoration of joy, peace, and spiritual passion
- The cleansing of thoughts, motives, and desires
- The rebuilding of identity in areas where it was shaken
- The reordering of priorities to reflect God's will
- The transformation that only the Holy Spirit can produce

This is not surface-level change. This is deep, tender, Spirit-led renewal.

As you pray through this month, let these themes guide your heart:

"Our Father in heaven" - He is the One who restores and renews.

"Hallowed be Your name" - Worship rebuilds what life has worn down.

"Your kingdom come" - His rule brings transformation to every broken place.

"Your will be done" - Surrender becomes the soil where healing grows.

"Give us this day…" - God supplies daily strength for the renewing work.

"Forgive us…" - Repentance clears away what blocks transformation.

"Lead us not…" - God protects the new work He is forming in you.

"Yours is the kingdom…" - Renewal turns into worship that lasts.

Month 11 is an invitation:

Come and let God make your heart new.

Come and let Him transform what you've carried for too long.

Come and let the Holy Spirit restore strength, hope, joy, and purpose within you.

This month will take you into deeper surrender, deeper healing, and deeper spiritual renewal-preparing you for the final stretch of the year with a heart strengthened and reshaped by the hands of God.

DAY 306 – Inviting God to Renew Your Heart

Prayer:
Father, I come asking You to renew my heart from the inside out. Hallowed be Your name; remind me that You create in me a clean heart and renew a right spirit within me (Psalm 51:10). Let Your kingdom come as You search my heart and reveal anything that does not honor You (Psalm 139:23). Let Your will be done as You soften every hardened place and restore every discouraged part of me. Give me today my daily bread of tenderness, humility, and spiritual renewal. Forgive me for resisting Your transforming work, and I forgive those who contributed to the wounds in my heart. Lead me not into the temptation of returning to old patterns, but deliver me into the new heart You are shaping. For Yours is the kingdom and the power and the glory forever. Amen.

Reflection:
What part of your heart needs God's renewing touch?

_____

_____

_____

Action:
Write one area where you are asking God to renew you.

_____

_____

_____

Scriptures Referenced Today:
Psalm 51:10 (KJV) - "Create in me a clean heart, O God; and renew a right spirit within me."
Psalm 139:23 (KJV) - "Search me, O God, and know my heart: try me, and know my thoughts:"

DAY 307 – Allowing God to Transform Your Mind

Prayer:
Father, thank You for transforming me through the renewing of my mind. Hallowed be Your name; remind me not to be conformed to this world, but to be transformed by the renewing of my mind (Romans 12:2). Let Your kingdom come as You remove thoughts that do not align with Your truth and replace them with wisdom from above (James 3:17). Let Your will be done as You cleanse my thinking and purify my perspective. Give me today my daily bread of clarity, discernment, and mental renewal. Forgive me for letting old thought patterns shape me, and I forgive those who planted lies in my mind. Lead me not into the temptation of negative thinking, but deliver me into the freedom of a renewed mind. For Thine is the kingdom, the power, and the glory, forever and ever. Amen.

Reflection:
What thought patterns need to be replaced with God's truth?

_____

_____

_____

Action:
Write one truth you will meditate on today to renew your mind.

_____

_____

_____

Scriptures Referenced Today:
Romans 12:2 (KJV) - "And be not conformed to this world: but be ye transformed by the renewing of your mind, **that ye may prove what is that good, and acceptable, and perfect, will of God.**"
James 3:17 (KJV) - "But the wisdom that is from above is first pure, then peaceable, gentle, and easy to be intreated, **full of mercy and good fruits, without partiality, and without hypocrisy.**"

DAY 308 – Letting God Heal Deep Wounds

Prayer:
Father, thank You for being near to the brokenhearted. Hallowed be
Your name; remind me that You heal the broken in heart and bind up
their wounds (Psalm 147:3). Let Your kingdom come as You comfort me
in all my afflictions (2 Corinthians 1:3–4). Let Your will be done as You
replace pain with peace, sorrow with joy, and heaviness with hope. Give
me today my daily bread of courage, openness, and deep inner healing.
Forgive me for hiding my wounds from You, and I forgive those who
caused them. Lead me not into the temptation of shutting down
emotionally, but deliver me into the healing work of Your Spirit. For
Yours is the eternal kingdom, the eternal power, and the eternal glory.
Amen.

Reflection:
What wound are you inviting God to heal today?

_____

_____

_____

Action:
Write one step of openness you will take toward healing.

_____

_____

_____

Scriptures Referenced Today:
Psalm 147:3 (KJV) - "He healeth the broken in heart, and bindeth up
their wounds."
2 Corinthians 1:3–4 (KJV) - "Blessed be God, even the Father of our
Lord Jesus Christ, the Father of mercies, and the God of all comfort;
Who comforteth us in all our tribulation, that we may be able to comfort
them which are in any trouble, by the comfort wherewith we ourselves are
comforted of God."

DAY 309 – Asking God to Restore Your Joy

Prayer:
Father, thank You for restoring joy where it has been lost. Hallowed be Your name; remind me that in Your presence is fullness of joy; at Your right hand there are pleasures forevermore (Psalm 16:11). Let Your kingdom come as You breathe joy into the weary places of my heart. Let Your will be done as You revive what discouragement tried to silence. Give me today my daily bread of joy, hope, and renewed strength. Forgive me for settling for a joyless life, and I forgive those who drained joy from me. Lead me not into the temptation of discouragement, but deliver me into the joy of Your salvation. For Thine alone is the kingdom, the power, and the glory, forever. Amen.

Reflection:
Where do you need God to restore joy in your life?

Action:
Write one joy-building step you will take today.

Scriptures Referenced Today:
Psalm 16:11 (KJV) - "Thou wilt shew me the path of life: in thy presence is fulness of joy; **at thy right hand there are pleasures for evermore**."
Psalm 30:5 (KJV) - "For his anger endureth but a moment; in his favour is life: weeping may endure for a night, but joy cometh in the morning."

DAY 310 – Inviting God to Renew Your Strength

Prayer:
Father, thank You for renewing my strength when I am weary. Hallowed be Your name; remind me that those who wait upon the Lord shall renew their strength; they shall mount up with wings as eagles; they shall run and not be weary; and they shall walk and not faint (Isaiah 40:31). Let Your kingdom come and infuse my spirit with fresh endurance and hope. Let Your will be done as You strengthen what has grown tired or worn down. Give me today my daily bread of perseverance, rest, and spiritual power. Forgive me for striving in my own strength, and I forgive those who drained my energy. Lead me not into the temptation of burnout, but deliver me into renewed strength in Your presence. For You reign in power and glory, both now and forever. Amen.

Reflection:
What part of your life needs God's renewing strength today?

Action:
Write one restorative step you will take today.

Scriptures Referenced Today:
Isaiah 40:31 (KJV) - "But they that wait upon the Lord shall renew their strength; they shall mount up with wings as eagles; they shall run, and not be weary; and they shall walk, and not faint."
Psalm 73:26 (KJV) - "My flesh and my heart faileth: but God is the strength of my heart, and my portion for ever."

DAY 311 – Asking God to Renew Your Spirit

Prayer:
Father, thank You for renewing my spirit when I feel depleted. Hallowed be Your name; remind me that You revive the spirit of the humble and the heart of the contrite ones (Isaiah 57:15). Let Your kingdom come as You breathe new life into the places within me that have grown weary. Let Your will be done as You strengthen my inner man with might by Your Spirit (Ephesians 3:16). Give me today my daily bread of rest, refreshing, and spiritual vitality. Forgive me for trying to live in my own strength, and I forgive those who discouraged my spirit. Lead me not into the temptation of spiritual dryness, but deliver me into Your renewing presence. For Yours is the kingdom and the power and the glory forever. Amen.

Reflection:
Where do you need God to revive your spirit today?

Action:
Write one way you will make room for God's refreshing presence today.

Scriptures Referenced Today:
Isaiah 57:15 (KJV) - "For thus saith the high and lofty One that inhabiteth eternity, whose name is Holy; I dwell in the high and holy place, with him also that is of a contrite and humble spirit, to revive the spirit of the humble, and to revive the heart of the contrite ones."
Ephesians 3:16 (KJV) - "That he would grant you, according to the riches of his glory, to be strengthened with might by his Spirit in the inner man;"

DAY 312 – Inviting God to Transform Your Desires

Prayer:
Father, thank You for shaping my desires to align with Yours. Hallowed be Your name; remind me that if I delight myself in You, You will give me the desires of my heart (Psalm 37:4). Let Your kingdom come as You purify my motives and redirect my longings. Let Your will be done as You work in me both to will and to do of Your good pleasure (Philippians 2:13). Give me today my daily bread of holy desire, godly focus, and renewed affections. Forgive me for chasing desires that led me away from You, and I forgive those who influenced my desires wrongly. Lead me not into the temptation of misplaced desires, but deliver me into Your perfect will. For Thine is the kingdom, and Thine is the power, and Thine is the glory, forever. Amen.

Reflection:
What desire does God want to reshape in you?

_____

_____

_____

Action:
Write one desire you are surrendering to God today.

_____

_____

_____

Scriptures Referenced Today:
Psalm 37:4 (KJV) - "Delight thyself also in the Lord: and he shall give thee the desires of thine heart."
Philippians 2:13 (KJV) - "For it is God which worketh in you both to will and to do of his good pleasure."

DAY 313 – Allowing God to Renew Your Hope

Prayer:
Father, thank You for renewing my hope when it feels weak. Hallowed be Your name; remind me that You are the God of hope who fills me with all joy and peace in believing (Romans 15:13). Let Your kingdom come as You restore expectation where disappointment has lived. Let Your will be done as You strengthen me to wait on You with confidence (Lamentations 3:25–26). Give me today my daily bread of hope, patience, and enduring faith. Forgive me for letting discouragement overshadow Your promises, and I forgive those who damaged my hope. Lead me not into the temptation of hopeless thinking, but deliver me into confident expectation in You. For Yours is the kingdom, the power, and the glory without end. Amen.

Reflection:
Where do you need God to renew your hope?

_____

_____

_____

Action:
Write one promise from God you will hope in today.

_____

_____

_____

Scriptures Referenced Today:
Romans 15:13 (KJV) - "Now the God of hope fill you with all joy and peace in believing, that ye may abound in hope, through the power of the Holy Ghost."
Lamentations 3:25–26 (KJV) - "The Lord is good unto them that wait for him, to the soul that seeketh him. It is good that a man should both hope and quietly wait for the salvation of the Lord."

DAY 314 – Asking God to Cleanse Your Thoughts

Prayer:
Father, thank You for cleansing my thoughts and renewing my mind. Hallowed be Your name; remind me to set my affection on things above, not on things on the earth (Colossians 3:2). Let Your kingdom come as You purify my thinking and remove anything that is not pleasing to You. Let Your will be done as You teach me to take every thought captive to the obedience of Christ (2 Corinthians 10:5). Give me today my daily bread of clarity, purity, and sound thinking. Forgive me for letting unclean or negative thoughts linger, and I forgive those who influenced my thinking wrongly. Lead me not into the temptation of mental distraction, but deliver me into a mind anchored in Your truth. For the kingdom is Yours, and the power is Yours, and the glory is Yours, forever. Amen.

Reflection:
What thoughts do you need God to cleanse today?

_____

_____

_____

Action:
Write one thought pattern you are surrendering to God.

_____

_____

_____

Scriptures Referenced Today:
Colossians 3:2 (KJV) - "Set your affection on things above, not on things on the earth."
2 Corinthians 10:5 (KJV) - "Casting down imaginations, and every high thing that exalteth itself against the knowledge of God, and bringing into captivity every thought to the obedience of Christ;"

DAY 315 – Inviting God to Restore Your Peace

Prayer:
Father, thank You for restoring peace to my mind and soul. Hallowed be Your name; remind me that You will keep him in perfect peace whose mind is stayed on You because he trusts in You (Isaiah 26:3). Let Your kingdom come as You calm fear, anxiety, and unrest within me. Let Your will be done as You fill me with the peace of God that passes all understanding (Philippians 4:7). Give me today my daily bread of rest, quietness, and spiritual stability. Forgive me for letting anxiety reign, and I forgive those who contributed to my unrest. Lead me not into the temptation of fear, but deliver me into Your peace.
For Thine is the everlasting kingdom, and the power, and the glory. Amen.

Reflection:
Where do you need God's peace to rule today?

_____

_____

_____

Action:
Write one step you will take today to center your mind on the Lord.

_____

_____

_____

Scriptures Referenced Today:
Isaiah 26:3 (KJV) - "Thou wilt keep him in perfect peace, whose mind is stayed on thee: because he trusteth in thee."
Philippians 4:7 (KJV) - "And the peace of God, which passeth all understanding, shall keep your hearts and minds through Christ Jesus."

DAY 316 – Asking God to Purify Your Motives

Prayer:
Father, thank You for refining the hidden places of my heart. Hallowed be Your name; remind me that man looks on the outward appearance, but You look on the heart (1 Samuel 16:7). Let Your kingdom come as You test my thoughts and motives (Jeremiah 17:10). Let Your will be done as You cleanse the intentions behind my words, actions, and desires. Give me today my daily bread of sincerity, purity, and godly intentions. Forgive me for any motive that was rooted in pride, fear, or self-gain, and I forgive those whose motives harmed me. Lead me not into the temptation of selfish ambition, but deliver me into motives shaped by Your love. For Yours is the kingdom and the power and the glory forever. Amen.

Reflection:
What motive is God asking you to surrender?

Action:
Write one motive you are asking God to purify today.

Scriptures Referenced Today:
1 Samuel 16:7 (KJV) - "But the Lord said unto Samuel, Look not on his countenance, or on the height of his stature; because I have refused him: for the Lord seeth not as man seeth; for man looketh on the outward appearance, but the Lord looketh on the heart."
Jeremiah 17:10 (KJV) - "I the Lord search the heart, I try the reins, even to give every man according to his ways, and according to the fruit of his doings."

DAY 317 – Letting God Renew Your Perspective

Prayer:

Father, thank You for renewing my perspective and lifting my eyes above what I see. Hallowed be Your name; remind me to set my affection on things above, not on things on the earth (Colossians 3:2). Let Your kingdom come as You help me see life through the lens of Your truth, not my emotions. Let Your will be done as You teach me that Your ways are higher than my ways and Your thoughts higher than my thoughts (Isaiah 55:8–9). Give me today my daily bread of clarity, wisdom, and renewed perspective. Forgive me for viewing my circumstances through fear or frustration, and I forgive those who clouded my perspective. Lead me not into the temptation of tunnel vision, but deliver me into a renewed, heaven-focused mindset.

For Thine is the kingdom, the power, and the glory, forever and ever. Amen.

Reflection:

Where does your perspective need renewing?

_____

_____

_____

Action:

Write one viewpoint or assumption you will surrender to God today.

_____

_____

_____

Scriptures Referenced Today:

Colossians 3:2 (KJV) - "Set your affection on things above, not on things on the earth."

Isaiah 55:8–9 (KJV) - "For my thoughts are not your thoughts, neither are your ways my ways, saith the Lord. For as the heavens are higher than the earth, so are my ways higher than your ways, and my thoughts than your thoughts."

DAY 318 – Inviting God to Renew Your Purpose

Prayer:
Father, thank You for renewing the purpose You have placed on my life. Hallowed be Your name; remind me that You know the thoughts You think toward me, thoughts of peace and not of evil, to give me an expected end (Jeremiah 29:11). Let Your kingdom come as You reveal the works You prepared beforehand that I should walk in them (Ephesians 2:10). Let Your will be done as You restore passion, direction, and confidence in the path You've called me to. Give me today my daily bread of purpose, vision, and clarity. Forgive me for losing sight of my calling, and I forgive those who discouraged my purpose. Lead me not into the temptation of drifting, but deliver me into renewed purpose in You.
For Yours is the kingdom, and the power, and the glory, for all ages. Amen.

Reflection:
Where has your sense of purpose grown dim and needs renewing?

_____

_____

_____

Action:
Write one step you will take today toward God's purpose for your life.

_____

_____

_____

Scriptures Referenced Today:
Jeremiah 29:11 (KJV) - "For I know the thoughts that I think toward you, saith the Lord, thoughts of peace, and not of evil, to give you an expected end."
Ephesians 2:10 (KJV) - "For we are his workmanship, created in Christ Jesus unto good works, which God hath before ordained that we should walk in them."

DAY 319 – Asking God to Create a Willing Spirit

Prayer:
Father, thank You for working in me both to will and to do of Your good pleasure. Hallowed be Your name; remind me that the spirit indeed is willing, but the flesh is weak (Matthew 26:41). Let Your kingdom come as You create in me a willing, responsive, and obedient heart. Let Your will be done as You strengthen me to obey quickly, joyfully, and fully. Give me today my daily bread of willingness, surrender, and spiritual readiness. Forgive me for resisting Your nudges, and I forgive those who pressured me into the wrong things. Lead me not into the temptation of procrastination or reluctance, but deliver me into joyful obedience. For Thine alone is the kingdom, the power, and the glory, forever. Amen.

Reflection:
Where is God calling you to say "yes" with a willing heart?

_____

_____

_____

Action:
Write one act of obedience you will say yes to today.

_____

_____

_____

Scriptures Referenced Today:
Matthew 26:41 (KJV) - "Watch and pray, that ye enter not into temptation: the spirit indeed is willing, but the flesh is weak."
Philippians 2:13 (KJV) - "For it is God which worketh in you both to will and to do of his good pleasure."

DAY 320 – Asking God to Renew Your Compassion

Prayer:
Father, thank You for renewing compassion within me. Hallowed be
Your name; remind me that Your mercies are new every morning and
great is Your faithfulness (Lamentations 3:22–23). Let Your kingdom
come as You fill my heart with kindness, empathy, and gentleness toward
others. Let Your will be done as You help me put on bowels of mercies,
kindness, humbleness of mind, meekness, and longsuffering (Colossians
3:12). Give me today my daily bread of patience, tenderness, and
Christlike compassion. Forgive me for withholding compassion when it
was needed, and I forgive those who were harsh with me. Lead me not
into the temptation of becoming calloused, but deliver me into a heart
that reflects Your mercy.
For Thine is the everlasting kingdom, and the power, and the glory.
Amen.

Reflection:
Where do you need God to renew compassion in your heart?

Action:
Write one compassionate action you will take today.

Scriptures Referenced Today:
Lamentations 3:22–23 (KJV) - "It is of the Lord's mercies that we are
not consumed, because his compassions fail not. They are new every
morning: great is thy faithfulness."
Colossians 3:12 (KJV) - "Put on therefore, as the elect of God, holy and
beloved, bowels of mercies, kindness, humbleness of mind, meekness,
longsuffering;"

DAY 321 – Asking God to Renew Your Emotional Strength

Prayer:
Father, thank You for renewing my emotional strength when I feel overwhelmed. Hallowed be Your name; remind me that You are my refuge and strength, a very present help in trouble (Psalm 46:1). Let Your kingdom come as You heal emotional burdens I have carried for too long. Let Your will be done as You calm my anxious thoughts and steady my heart (Psalm 94:19). Give me today my daily bread of emotional stability, comfort, and peace. Forgive me for letting my emotions lead me instead of Your Spirit, and I forgive those who contributed to emotional heaviness. Lead me not into the temptation of emotional exhaustion, but deliver me into renewed strength in You. For Thine is the kingdom, the power, and the glory, forever and ever. Amen.

Reflection:
Where do your emotions need God's renewing touch today?

_____

_____

_____

Action:
Write one step you will take to invite God into your emotional life today.

_____

_____

_____

Scriptures Referenced Today:
Psalm 46:1 (KJV) - "God is our refuge and strength, a very present help in trouble."
Psalm 94:19 (KJV) - "In the multitude of my thoughts within me thy comforts delight my soul."

DAY 322 – Inviting God to Restore Your Sense of Identity

Prayer:
Father, thank You for restoring my identity according to Your truth.
Hallowed be Your name; remind me that I am fearfully and wonderfully
made (Psalm 139:14). Let Your kingdom come as You reveal the identity
You wrote over my life before I was formed (Jeremiah 1:5). Let Your will
be done as You pull down every false identity spoken over me. Give me
today my daily bread of confidence, truth, and a renewed sense of who I
am in You. Forgive me for believing lies about myself, and I forgive
those who spoke damaging words over my identity. Lead me not into the
temptation of insecurity, but deliver me into the identity You designed for
me. For Yours is the kingdom and the power and the glory forever.
Amen.

Reflection:
What false identity or label is God asking you to release?

_____

_____

_____

Action:
Write one truth about your God-given identity.

_____

_____

_____

Scriptures Referenced Today:
Psalm 139:14 (KJV) - "I will praise thee; for I am fearfully and
wonderfully made: marvellous are thy works; and that my soul knoweth
right well."
Jeremiah 1:5 (KJV) - "Before I formed thee in the belly I knew thee; and
before thou camest forth out of the womb I sanctified thee, and I
ordained thee a prophet unto the nations."

DAY 323 – Asking God to Renew Your Willingness to Change

Prayer:
Father, thank You for giving me a willing heart to embrace Your transformation. Hallowed be Your name; remind me that You give a new heart and put a new spirit within me (Ezekiel 36:26). Let Your kingdom come as You teach me to walk in newness of life (Romans 6:4). Let Your will be done as You remove resistance, hesitation, and fear of change. Give me today my daily bread of willingness, surrender, and courage. Forgive me for clinging to what You're trying to change, and I forgive those who discouraged my growth. Lead me not into the temptation of staying the same, but deliver me into the transformation You have prepared. For the kingdom is Yours, and the power is Yours, and the glory is Yours, forever. Amen.

Reflection:
Where do you sense God calling you to greater willingness?

_____

_____

_____

Action:
Write one change you are ready to embrace with God's help.

_____

_____

_____

Scriptures Referenced Today:
Ezekiel 36:26 (KJV) - "A new heart also will I give you, and a new spirit will I put within you: and I will take away the stony heart out of your flesh, and I will give you an heart of flesh."
Romans 6:4 (KJV) - "Therefore we are buried with him by baptism into death: that like as Christ was raised up from the dead by the glory of the Father, even so we also should walk in newness of life."

DAY 324 – Allowing God to Renew Your Ability to Love

Prayer:
Father, thank You for renewing my capacity to love others with purity and sincerity. Hallowed be Your name; remind me that love is of God, and everyone who loves is born of God and knows God (1 John 4:7). Let Your kingdom come as You help me love others fervently with a pure heart (1 Peter 1:22). Let Your will be done as You heal the wounds that have limited my ability to love freely. Give me today my daily bread of kindness, grace, and renewed love. Forgive me for withholding love where it was needed, and I forgive those who withheld love from me. Lead me not into the temptation of bitterness, but deliver me into a heart that loves like Christ. For Thine is the kingdom, Thine is the power, and Thine is the glory, now and always. Amen.

Reflection:
Where do you need God to renew your ability to love?

_____

_____

_____

Action:
Write one act of love you will intentionally show today.

_____

_____

_____

Scriptures Referenced Today:
1 John 4:7 (KJV) - "Beloved, let us love one another: for love is of God; and every one that loveth is born of God, and knoweth God."
1 Peter 1:22 (KJV) - "Seeing ye have purified your souls in obeying the truth through the Spirit unto unfeigned love of the brethren, see that ye love one another with a pure heart fervently."

DAY 325 – Inviting God to Renew Your Inner Peace

Prayer:
Father, thank You for renewing the peace within me. Hallowed be Your name; remind me that the Lord will bless His people with peace (Psalm 29:11). Let Your kingdom come as You quiet the storms within my mind and heart. Let Your will be done as You help me dwell in safety and rest securely in You (Psalm 4:8). Give me today my daily bread of calm, stillness, and steady trust. Forgive me for allowing worry to steal my peace, and I forgive those who contributed to chaos in my life. Lead me not into the temptation of fear, but deliver me into perfect peace through You. For You alone are the King of glory, forever and ever. Amen.

Reflection:
Where do you need God to restore inner peace?

_____

_____

_____

Action:
Write one practical step you will take today to rest in God's peace.

_____

_____

_____

Scriptures Referenced Today:
Psalm 29:11 (KJV) - "The Lord will give strength unto his people; the Lord will bless his people with peace."
Psalm 4:8 (KJV) - "I will both lay me down in peace, and sleep: for thou, Lord, only makest me dwell in safety."

DAY 326 – Asking God to Renew Your Inner Strength

Prayer:
Father, thank You for renewing my inner strength. Hallowed be Your name; remind me that though my outward man perishes, the inward man is renewed day by day (2 Corinthians 4:16). Let Your kingdom come as You become the strength of my heart and my portion forever (Psalm 73:26). Let Your will be done as You refresh what has grown tired, weary, or overwhelmed. Give me today my daily bread of endurance, spiritual power, and revived hope. Forgive me for relying on my own strength, and I forgive those who have drained my strength. Lead me not into the temptation of fainting, but deliver me into renewed inner strength through You. For Yours is the kingdom and the power and the glory forever. Amen.

Reflection:
Where do you feel weak and need God's renewing strength?

_____

_____

Action:
Write one area where you will rely on God's strength today.

_____

_____

Scriptures Referenced Today:
2 Corinthians 4:16 (KJV) - "For which cause we faint not; but though our outward man perish, yet the inward man is renewed day by day."
Psalm 73:26 (KJV) - "My flesh and my heart faileth: but God is the strength of my heart, and my portion for ever."

DAY 327 – Asking God to Renew Your Gratitude

Prayer:

Father, thank You for renewing gratitude within me. Hallowed be Your name; remind me to give thanks always for all things unto God and the Father in the name of our Lord Jesus Christ (Ephesians 5:20). Let Your kingdom come as You fill my heart with thanksgiving instead of frustration. Let Your will be done as You teach me to be content in all circumstances (Philippians 4:11). Give me today my daily bread of thankfulness, perspective, and joy. Forgive me for complaining or forgetting Your blessings, and I forgive those who have taken me for granted. Lead me not into the temptation of grumbling, but deliver me into a renewed spirit of gratitude. For Thine is the kingdom, the power, and the glory, forever and ever. Amen.

Reflection:

What blessing have you forgotten to thank God for?

Action:

Write down three things you will thank God for today.

Scriptures Referenced Today:

Ephesians 5:20 (KJV) - "Giving thanks always for all things unto God and the Father in the name of our Lord Jesus Christ."

Philippians 4:11 (KJV) - "Not that I speak in respect of want: for I have learned, in whatsoever state I am, therewith to be content."

DAY 328 – Inviting God to Renew Your Patience

Prayer:
Father, thank You for renewing patience in my heart. Hallowed be Your name; remind me that they that wait upon You shall renew their strength; they shall mount up with wings as eagles (Isaiah 40:31). Let Your kingdom come as You produce patience in me through Your Spirit (Galatians 5:22). Let Your will be done as You develop endurance and quiet trust within me. Give me today my daily bread of patience, calmness, and long-suffering. Forgive me for rushing Your timing, and I forgive those who have tested my patience. Lead me not into the temptation of haste, but deliver me into patience rooted in trust. For Yours is the kingdom, and the power, and the glory, for all ages. Amen.

Reflection:
Where is God calling you to wait with patience?

_____

_____

_____

Action:
Write one area where you will slow down and wait on God today.

_____

_____

_____

Scriptures Referenced Today:
Isaiah 40:31 (KJV) - "But they that wait upon the Lord shall renew their strength; they shall mount up with wings as eagles; they shall run, and not be weary; and they shall walk, and not faint."
Galatians 5:22 (KJV) - "But the fruit of the Spirit is love, joy, peace, longsuffering, gentleness, goodness, faith."

DAY 329 – Asking God to Renew Your Courage

Prayer:

Father, thank You for renewing courage within me. Hallowed be Your name; remind me to be strong and of a good courage, not afraid or discouraged, for You are with me wherever I go (Joshua 1:9). Let Your kingdom come as You strengthen my heart to trust in You (Psalm 27:14). Let Your will be done as You replace fear with boldness and anxiety with confidence. Give me today my daily bread of courage, determination, and brave obedience. Forgive me for shrinking back when You asked me to step forward, and I forgive those who discouraged my courage. Lead me not into the temptation of fear, but deliver me into bold faith. For Thine alone is the kingdom, the power, and the glory, forever. Amen.

Reflection:

Where do you need God to renew your courage?

_____

_____

_____

Action:

Write one step of courage you will take today.

_____

_____

_____

Scriptures Referenced Today:

Joshua 1:9 (KJV) - "Have not I commanded thee? Be strong and of a good courage; be not afraid, neither be thou dismayed: for the Lord thy God is with thee whithersoever thou goest."

Psalm 27:14 (KJV) - "Wait on the Lord: be of good courage, and he shall strengthen thine heart: wait, I say, on the Lord."

DAY 330 – Asking God to Renew Your Ability to Forgive

Prayer:
Father, thank You for renewing my ability to forgive. Hallowed be Your name; remind me that I must forgive others as You have forgiven me (Colossians 3:13). Let Your kingdom come as You soften places hardened by hurt. Let Your will be done as You help me be kind, tenderhearted, and forgiving (Ephesians 4:32). Give me today my daily bread of compassion, humility, and grace. Forgive me for withholding forgiveness, and I forgive those who have wronged me. Lead me not into the temptation of bitterness, but deliver me into the freedom of forgiveness. For Thine is the everlasting kingdom, and the power, and the glory. Amen.

Reflection:
Who is God calling you to forgive today?

_____

_____

_____

Action:
Write one step you will take toward forgiveness.

_____

_____

_____

Scriptures Referenced Today:
Colossians 3:13 (KJV) - "Forbearing one another, and forgiving one another, if any man have a quarrel against any: even as Christ forgave you, so also do ye."
Ephesians 4:32 (KJV) - "And be ye kind one to another, tenderhearted, forgiving one another, even as God for Christ's sake hath forgiven you."

DAY 331 – Asking God to Renew Your Desire for His Word

Prayer:
Father, thank You for renewing my hunger for Your Word. Hallowed be Your name; remind me that Your Word is a lamp unto my feet and a light unto my path (Psalm 119:105). Let Your kingdom come as You open my eyes to behold wondrous things out of Your law (Psalm 119:18). Let Your will be done as You grow my desire to read, meditate, and obey Your Word. Give me today my daily bread of understanding, revelation, and spiritual appetite. Forgive me for neglecting Scripture, and I forgive those who discouraged my pursuit of truth. Lead me not into the temptation of spiritual laziness, but deliver me into renewed passion for Your Word. For You reign in power and glory, both now and forever. Amen.

Reflection:
Where do you sense God calling you back to His Word?

_____

_____

_____

Action:
Write one passage of Scripture you will meditate on today.

_____

_____

_____

Scriptures Referenced Today:
Psalm 119:105 (KJV) - "Thy word is a lamp unto my feet, and a light unto my path."
Psalm 119:18 (KJV) - "Open thou mine eyes, that I may behold wondrous things out of thy law."

DAY 332 – Asking God to Renew Your Boldness in Prayer

Prayer:
Father, thank You for renewing boldness in my prayers. Hallowed be Your name; remind me that I can come boldly unto the throne of grace to obtain mercy and find grace to help in time of need (Hebrews 4:16). Let Your kingdom come as You teach me to pray with confidence, not fear. Let Your will be done as You fill my mouth with faith-filled prayer aligned with Your Word (1 John 5:14). Give me today my daily bread of holy boldness, confidence, and expectancy. Forgive me for praying timid prayers, and I forgive those who weakened my confidence in prayer. Lead me not into the temptation of doubt, but deliver me into bold, faith-filled prayer. For Thine is the kingdom, Thine is the power, and Thine is the glory, now and always. Amen.

Reflection:
Where do you need greater boldness in prayer?

Action:
Write one bold prayer request you will bring before God today.

Scriptures Referenced Today:
Hebrews 4:16 (KJV) - "Let us therefore come boldly unto the throne of grace, that we may obtain mercy, and find grace to help in time of need."
1 John 5:14 (KJV) - "And this is the confidence that we have in him, that, if we ask any thing according to his will, he heareth us."

DAY 333 – Inviting God to Renew Your Ability to Encourage Others

Prayer:
Father, thank You for renewing my ability to build others up. Hallowed be Your name; remind me to exhort one another daily (Hebrews 3:13). Let Your kingdom come as You teach me to use my words to minister grace to those who hear (Ephesians 4:29). Let Your will be done as You soften my heart toward those who are discouraged. Give me today my daily bread of kindness, encouragement, and Spirit-led words. Forgive me for staying silent when I could have encouraged, and I forgive those who failed to encourage me. Lead me not into the temptation of negativity, but deliver me into uplifting speech that reflects Your heart. For Yours is the kingdom, the power, and the glory without end. Amen.

Reflection:
Who needs encouragement from you today?

_____

_____

_____

Action:
Write one person you will intentionally encourage today.

_____

_____

Scriptures Referenced Today:
Hebrews 3:13 (KJV) - "But exhort one another daily, while it is called To day; lest any of you be hardened through the deceitfulness of sin."
Ephesians 4:29 (KJV) - "Let no corrupt communication proceed out of your mouth, but that which is good to the use of edifying, that it may minister grace unto the hearers."

DAY 334 – Allowing God to Renew Your Focus

Prayer:
Father, thank You for renewing my focus on what truly matters. Hallowed be Your name; remind me to lay aside every weight and the sin which doth so easily beset me, and run with patience the race set before me (Hebrews 12:1). Let Your kingdom come as You teach me to number my days, that I may apply my heart unto wisdom (Psalm 90:12). Let Your will be done as You remove distractions and sharpen my focus on Your calling. Give me today my daily bread of clarity, intentionality, and wisdom. Forgive me for allowing distractions to rule my attention, and I forgive those who have pulled me off course. Lead me not into the temptation of drifting, but deliver me into focused obedience. For Thine is the kingdom, and the power, and the glory, for all ages. Amen.

Reflection:
What distractions is God asking you to lay aside?

Action:
Write one practical step to improve your focus today.

Scriptures Referenced Today:
Hebrews 12:1 (KJV) - "Wherefore seeing we also are compassed about with so great a cloud of witnesses, let us lay aside every weight, and the sin which doth so easily beset us, and let us run with patience the race that is set before us."
Psalm 90:12 (KJV) - "So teach us to number our days, that we may apply our hearts unto wisdom."

DAY 335 – Asking God to Renew Your Ability to Listen

Prayer:
Father, thank You for renewing my ability to listen-both to You and to others. Hallowed be Your name; remind me to be swift to hear, slow to speak, and slow to wrath (James 1:19). Let Your kingdom come as You open my ears to hear what the Spirit is saying (Revelation 2:7). Let Your will be done as You help me listen with grace, patience, and understanding. Give me today my daily bread of attentiveness, humility, and spiritual sensitivity. Forgive me for speaking too quickly or listening too little, and I forgive those who did not listen to me. Lead me not into the temptation of impatience, but deliver me into a renewed ability to listen well. For You alone are the King of glory, forever and ever. Amen.

Reflection:
Where do you need to listen more intentionally?

_____

_____

_____

Action:
Write one person or one area where you will practice attentive listening today.

_____

_____

_____

Scriptures Referenced Today:
James 1:19 (KJV) - "Wherefore, my beloved brethren, let every man be swift to hear, slow to speak, slow to wrath."
Revelation 2:7 (KJV) - "He that hath an ear, let him hear what the Spirit saith unto the churches; To him that overcometh will I give to eat of the tree of life, which is in the midst of the paradise of God."

MONTH 11 CLOSING REFLECTION: TRANSFORMATION, RENEWAL, & THE MAKING OF A NEW HEART

Month 11 has taken you into the deep inner work of God - the quiet, steady, holy transformation that happens beneath the surface. You didn't just pray for change this month; you stepped into the kind of renewal that rewrites the inside of a person. God touched your heart, your motives, your mind, your emotions, your identity, your habits, and your desires.
This wasn't shallow change - it was spiritual renovation.
You learned that transformation is not instant.
It is a daily yielding.
A daily softening.
A daily returning.
A daily renewing.
And God was faithful in every part of it.
This month, the Spirit led you to:

- Invite God to renew your heart
- Ask Him to renew your mind and thought patterns
- Allow Him to heal deep wounds and restore joy
- Receive renewed strength, peace, and stability
- Embrace new desires shaped by God
- Rediscover purpose and identity
- Release old patterns that no longer fit
- Rebuild emotional, mental, and spiritual resilience
- Walk in forgiveness, compassion, and willingness
- Return to God's Word with fresh hunger
- Pray with renewed boldness and confidence
- Love people with a purified, sincere heart

Month 11 revealed a powerful truth:
Transformation is not about becoming a better version of yourself - it's about becoming who you were created to be.
God didn't patch the old - He began making things new.
He didn't strengthen your old patterns - He invited you to new ones.
He didn't simply encourage you - He renewed you.
As you step forward, reflect on what God has done:

- Where did He soften your heart?
- What lies did He remove from your identity?
- What wounds did He begin healing?
- What inner strength did He rebuild?
- What new desires did He awaken?
- What old habits did He break?
- What peace did He restore?

God has been shaping you from the inside out - preparing you for the final stretch of this year with a renewed heart, renewed mind, renewed strength, and renewed purpose.

And now you are ready for the final chapter of this journey.

MONTH 12 INTRODUCTION: COMPLETION, BLESSING, & A YEAR OF TRANSFORMATION

You've walked through nearly a full year of praying the way Jesus taught us to pray. Month 12 is the culmination of everything God has done - the month of completion, blessing, reflection, and holy gratitude. This final month is not just about finishing the book; it's about recognizing **what God has formed in you this year**.

Month 12 invites you into:

- Deep gratitude for all God has done
- Reflection on answered prayers and spiritual growth
- Recognition of God's faithfulness throughout the journey
- Commitment to carry these practices forward
- Celebration of spiritual victories and breakthroughs
- Strengthening the foundation God built in you
- Releasing the old year and entering the new with expectancy
- Declaring God's promises over your future
- Blessing your family, your work, your home, and your walk
- Closing this year in worship, trust, and surrender

Month 12 is the month of *amen* - the month where you look back and say, "God did it." The month where you stand in awe of His hand. The month where you seal everything He taught you, healed in you, and awakened in you.

As you pray through this final stretch, the Lord's Prayer will guide you with special significance:

"Our Father in heaven" - You've known Him more deeply this year.

"Hallowed be Your name" - You've learned to worship in every season.

"Your kingdom come" - You've seen His rule reshape your life.

"Your will be done" - You've surrendered, grown, and trusted.

"Give us this day…" - You've depended on Him daily.

"Forgive us…" - You've been cleansed and freed.

"Lead us not…" - You've been protected and strengthened.

"Yours is the kingdom…" - You've seen His glory in your journey.

Month 12 is a month of blessing.

A month of testimony. A month of reflection and renewal. A month of gratitude for everything God has formed in you. A month that completes a year spent walking closely with Him.

God brought you this far - and He is not done yet.

DAY 336 – Thanking God for His Faithfulness This Year

Prayer:
Father, thank You for Your steady faithfulness throughout this entire year. Hallowed be Your name; remind me that Your compassions fail not; they are new every morning, great is Your faithfulness (Lamentations 3:22–23). Let Your kingdom come as I reflect on Your goodness, mercy, and provision. Let Your will be done as I remember that You have been faithful in every season of this journey (Psalm 36:5). Give me today my daily bread of gratitude, remembrance, and joyful praise. Forgive me for the moments I overlooked Your faithfulness, and I forgive those who doubted what You were doing in my life. Lead me not into the temptation of forgetfulness, but deliver me into a grateful heart that sees Your hand clearly. For Thine is the kingdom, and the power, and the glory, for all ages. Amen.

Reflection:
Where have you seen God's faithfulness most clearly this year?

_____

_____

_____

Action:
Write down at least three ways God has been faithful to you this year.

_____

_____

_____

Scriptures Referenced Today:
Lamentations 3:22–23 (KJV) - "It is of the Lord's mercies that we are not consumed, because his compassions fail not. They are new every morning: great is thy faithfulness."
Psalm 36:5 (KJV) - "Thy mercy, O Lord, is in the heavens; and thy faithfulness reacheth unto the clouds."

DAY 337 – Remembering God's Answered Prayers

Prayer:
Father, thank You for all the prayers You have answered this year-big and small. Hallowed be Your name; remind me that before I call, You answer, and while I am yet speaking, You hear (Isaiah 65:24). Let Your kingdom come as You help me recall the moments where You moved on my behalf (Psalm 116:1). Let Your will be done as You strengthen my faith through remembrance. Give me today my daily bread of gratitude, reflection, and renewed trust. Forgive me for forgetting Your answers, and I forgive those who doubted that You would respond. Lead me not into the temptation of overlooking Your work, but deliver me into joyful remembrance of Your faithfulness. For Yours is the kingdom and the power and the glory forever. Amen.

Reflection:
What prayers has God answered for you this year?

_____

_____

_____

Action:
Write one answered prayer from each season of the year-winter, spring, summer, fall.

_____

_____

_____

Scriptures Referenced Today:
Isaiah 65:24 (KJV) - "And it shall come to pass, that before they call, I will answer; and while they are yet speaking, I will hear."
Psalm 116:1 (KJV) - "I love the Lord, because he hath heard my voice and my supplications."

DAY 338 – Thanking God for the Growth He Produced in You

Prayer:
Father, thank You for the spiritual growth You have produced in me this year. Hallowed be Your name; remind me that You are the One who works in me both to will and to do of Your good pleasure (Philippians 2:13). Let Your kingdom come as You continue to shape me into the image of Christ (Romans 8:29). Let Your will be done as I acknowledge that this year's growth was Your doing, not mine. Give me today my daily bread of humility, gratitude, and renewed surrender. Forgive me for resisting Your shaping hand, and I forgive those who hindered my growth. Lead me not into the temptation of pride or self-reliance, but deliver me into gratitude for the person You are forming me to be. For You reign in power and glory, both now and forever. Amen.

Reflection:
How has God grown or changed you this year?

Action:
Write one way you are spiritually different today than you were on January 1.

Scriptures Referenced Today:
Philippians 2:13 (KJV) - "For it is God which worketh in you both to will and to do of his good pleasure."
Romans 8:29 (KJV) - "For whom he did foreknow, he also did predestinate to be conformed to the image of his Son, that he might be the firstborn among many brethren."

DAY 339 – Thanking God for His Protection This Year

Prayer:
Father, thank You for the protection You have given me this year-seen and unseen. Hallowed be Your name; remind me that You give Your angels charge over me, to keep me in all my ways (Psalm 91:11). Let Your kingdom come as You help me recognize the battles You fought on my behalf. Let Your will be done as I acknowledge that You are my refuge and fortress, my God in whom I trust (Psalm 91:2). Give me today my daily bread of peace, assurance, and deep gratitude. Forgive me for underestimating the protection You provide, and I forgive those who contributed to fear. Lead me not into the temptation of anxiety, but deliver me into peace rooted in Your faithfulness. For Thine is the kingdom, Thine is the power, and Thine is the glory, now and always. Amen.

Reflection:
Where have you seen God's protection in your life this year?

_____

_____

_____

Action:
Write one situation this year where God clearly protected you.

_____

_____

_____

Scriptures Referenced Today:
Psalm 91:11 (KJV) - "For he shall give his angels charge over thee, to keep thee in all thy ways."
Psalm 91:2 (KJV) - "I will say of the Lord, He is my refuge and my fortress: my God; in him will I trust."

DAY 340 – Thanking God for His Provision This Year

Prayer:
Father, thank You for providing for me this year in every way. Hallowed be Your name; remind me that You supply all my need according to Your riches in glory by Christ Jesus (Philippians 4:19). Let Your kingdom come as You open my eyes to the ways You provided-spiritually, emotionally, financially, and relationally. Let Your will be done as I trust that You are my Shepherd and I shall not want (Psalm 23:1). Give me today my daily bread of gratitude, trust, and acknowledgement of Your hand in my life. Forgive me for worrying instead of trusting, and I forgive those who caused financial or emotional strain. Lead me not into the temptation of self-reliance, but deliver me into confidence in Your provision. For Yours is the eternal kingdom, the eternal power, and the eternal glory. Amen.

Reflection:
How did God provide for you this year?

Action:
Write down the most unexpected provision God gave you this year.

Scriptures Referenced Today:
Philippians 4:19 (KJV) - "But my God shall supply all your need according to his riches in glory by Christ Jesus."
Psalm 23:1 (KJV) - "The Lord is my shepherd; I shall not want."

DAY 341 – Thanking God for the Strength He Gave You This Year

Prayer:
Father, thank You for the strength You have given me throughout this year. Hallowed be Your name; remind me that You are the God who strengthens me with strength in my soul (Psalm 138:3). Let Your kingdom come as I remember how You upheld me with Your right hand (Isaiah 41:10). Let Your will be done as I acknowledge that Your strength carried me through every high and low. Give me today my daily bread of gratitude, reflection, and renewed confidence in You. Forgive me for relying too much on my own strength, and I forgive those who added to my burdens. Lead me not into the temptation of fear or exhaustion, but deliver me into the strength that comes only from You. For Thine is the kingdom and the power and the glory forever. Amen.

Reflection:
Where did God strengthen you this year in ways you couldn't have strengthened yourself?

_____

_____

_____

Action:
Write down one moment this year where God clearly strengthened you.

_____

_____

_____

Scriptures Referenced Today:
Psalm 138:3 (KJV) - "In the day when I cried thou answeredst me, and strengthenedst me with strength in my soul."
Isaiah 41:10 (KJV) - "Fear thou not; for I am with thee: be not dismayed; for I am thy God: I will strengthen thee; yea, I will help thee; yea, I will uphold thee with the right hand of my righteousness."

DAY 342 – Thanking God for the People He Placed in Your Life This Year

Prayer:
Father, thank You for the people You have placed in my life this year. Hallowed be Your name; remind me that iron sharpeneth iron; so a man sharpeneth the countenance of his friend (Proverbs 27:17). Let Your kingdom come as I recognize the friendships, mentors, and relationships You used to bless, guide, and strengthen me. Let Your will be done as I acknowledge that every good and perfect gift comes from You (James 1:17). Give me today my daily bread of gratitude, appreciation, and love for the people around me. Forgive me for overlooking the blessing of others, and I forgive those who hurt or disappointed me. Lead me not into the temptation of isolation, but deliver me into community, connection, and gratitude. For Thine alone is the kingdom, the power, and the glory, forever. Amen.

Reflection:
Who did God use in your life this year to encourage, sharpen, or bless you?

_____

_____

_____

Action:
Write the names of two people you will intentionally thank or bless today.

_____

_____

Scriptures Referenced Today:
Proverbs 27:17 (KJV) - "Iron sharpeneth iron; so a man sharpeneth the countenance of his friend."
James 1:17 (KJV) - "Every good gift and every perfect gift is from above, and cometh down from the Father of lights, with whom is no variableness, neither shadow of turning."

DAY 343 – Thanking God for the Lessons He Taught You

Prayer:
Father, thank You for the lessons You taught me this year-through blessings, trials, victories, and challenges. Hallowed be Your name; remind me that all things work together for good to them that love You (Romans 8:28). Let Your kingdom come as You help me see how every lesson shaped me. Let Your will be done as I treasure wisdom and understanding (Proverbs 4:7). Give me today my daily bread of gratitude for the lessons learned and the growth gained. Forgive me for resisting Your teaching moments, and I forgive those whose actions became part of my lessons. Lead me not into the temptation of repeating old mistakes, but deliver me into wisdom and maturity. For the kingdom is Yours, and the power is Yours, and the glory is Yours, forever. Amen.

Reflection:
What is one major lesson God taught you this year?

Action:
Write down a lesson you want to carry into next year.

Scriptures Referenced Today:
Romans 8:28 (KJV) - "And we know that all things work together for good to them that love God, to them who are the called according to his purpose."
Proverbs 4:7 (KJV) - "Wisdom is the principal thing; therefore get wisdom: and with all thy getting get understanding."

DAY 344 – Thanking God for His Mercy This Year

Prayer:
Father, thank You for the mercy that covered me this year. Hallowed be Your name; remind me that Your mercy endureth forever (Psalm 136:1). Let Your kingdom come as You help me see all the ways Your mercy sustained me, protected me, and forgave me. Let Your will be done as You remind me that You delight in mercy (Micah 7:18). Give me today my daily bread of gratitude, humility, and awareness of Your mercy. Forgive me for taking Your mercy for granted, and I forgive those who withheld mercy from me. Lead me not into the temptation of harshness, but deliver me into a heart softened by mercy. For Yours is the kingdom, the power, and the glory forever. Amen.

Reflection:
Where did you experience God's mercy this year?

_____

_____

_____

Action:
Write one place where God's mercy gave you another chance.

_____

_____

_____

Scriptures Referenced Today:
Psalm 136:1 (KJV) - "O give thanks unto the Lord; for he is good: for his mercy endureth for ever."
Micah 7:18 (KJV) - "Who is a God like unto thee, that pardoneth iniquity, and passeth by the transgression of the remnant of his heritage? he retaineth not his anger for ever, because he delighteth in mercy."

DAY 345 – Thanking God for Never Leaving You This Year

Prayer:
Father, thank You for never leaving me or forsaking me this year. Hallowed be Your name; remind me that You are with me always, even unto the end of the world (Matthew 28:20). Let Your kingdom come as I reflect on the moments when Your presence sustained me. Let Your will be done as You strengthen my faith through the assurance that You never abandoned me (Hebrews 13:5). Give me today my daily bread of confidence, peace, and deep gratitude for Your nearness. Forgive me for doubting Your presence, and I forgive those who left me when I needed them. Lead me not into the temptation of loneliness, but deliver me into the assurance that You are always with me. For Yours is the eternal kingdom, the eternal power, and the eternal glory. Amen.

Reflection:
Where did you sense God's presence carrying you this year?

_____

_____

_____

Action:
Write down one moment this year when God's presence was especially real to you.

_____

_____

_____

Scriptures Referenced Today:
Matthew 28:20 (KJV) - "Teaching them to observe all things whatsoever I have commanded you: and, lo, I am with you always, even unto the end of the world. Amen."
Hebrews 13:5 (KJV) - "Let your conversation be without covetousness; and be content with such things as ye have: for he hath said, I will never leave thee, nor forsake thee."

DAY 346 – Thanking God for His Guidance This Year

Prayer:
Father, thank You for guiding me faithfully this year. Hallowed be Your name; remind me that You will instruct me and teach me in the way which I should go; You will guide me with Your eye (Psalm 32:8). Let Your kingdom come as You show me that the steps of a good man are ordered by the Lord (Psalm 37:23). Let Your will be done as I recognize the paths You corrected, the doors You opened, and the directions You adjusted. Give me today my daily bread of clarity, gratitude, and trust. Forgive me for ignoring Your leading at times, and I forgive those who misled or confused me. Lead me not into the temptation of trying to guide myself, but deliver me into full confidence in Your leadership. For Yours is the kingdom and the power and the glory forever. Amen.

Reflection:
Where did God guide your steps this year?

_____

_____

_____

Action:
Write one way God redirected your path for your good this year.

_____

_____

_____

Scriptures Referenced Today:
Psalm 32:8 (KJV) - "I will instruct thee and teach thee in the way which thou shalt go: I will guide thee with mine eye."
Psalm 37:23 (KJV) - "The steps of a good man are ordered by the Lord: and he delighteth in his way."

DAY 347 – Thanking God for the Joy He Gave You This Year

Prayer:
Father, thank You for the joy You placed in my heart throughout this year. Hallowed be Your name; remind me that in Your presence is fullness of joy; at Your right hand there are pleasures forevermore (Psalm 16:11). Let Your kingdom come as You renew joy where hardship tried to take it. Let Your will be done as You remind me that the joy of the Lord is my strength (Nehemiah 8:10). Give me today my daily bread of joy, gladness, and renewed praise. Forgive me for letting circumstances steal my joy, and I forgive those who contributed to discouragement. Lead me not into the temptation of gloom, but deliver me into joy rooted in You. For Thine is the kingdom, the power, and the glory, forever and ever. Amen.

Reflection:
Where did God restore joy in your life this year?

_____

_____

_____

Action:
Write down one joyful moment from this year that you want to remember.

_____

_____

_____

Scriptures Referenced Today:
Psalm 16:11 (KJV) - "Thou wilt shew me the path of life: in thy presence is fulness of joy; at thy right hand there are pleasures for evermore."
Nehemiah 8:10 (KJV) - "Then he said unto them, Go your way, eat the fat, and drink the sweet, and send portions unto them for whom nothing is prepared: for this day is holy unto our Lord: neither be ye sorry; for the joy of the Lord is your strength."

DAY 348 – Thanking God for Carrying You Through Hard Times

Prayer:
Father, thank You for carrying me through the hardest moments of this year. Hallowed be Your name; remind me that when my soul was overwhelmed, You led me to the Rock that is higher than I (Psalm 61:2). Let Your kingdom come as I remember that You are a refuge and a strength, a very present help in trouble (Psalm 46:1). Let Your will be done as You show me how You sustained me when I had nothing left. Give me today my daily bread of gratitude, remembrance, and deep trust. Forgive me for doubting You in moments of weakness, and I forgive those who added to my burdens. Lead me not into the temptation of discouragement, but deliver me into the confidence that You carried me every step. For Thine alone is the kingdom, the power, and the glory, forever. Amen.

Reflection:
What difficult moment did God carry you through this year?

_____

_____

Action:
Write one testimony from a hard season that you want to remember.

_____

_____

Scriptures Referenced Today:
Psalm 61:2 (KJV) - "From the end of the earth will I cry unto thee, when my heart is overwhelmed: lead me to the rock that is higher than I."
Psalm 46:1 (KJV) - "God is our refuge and strength, a very present help in trouble."

DAY 349 – Thanking God for Growing Your Faith

Prayer:
Father, thank You for the faith You built in me this year. Hallowed be Your name; remind me that faith comes by hearing, and hearing by the word of God (Romans 10:17). Let Your kingdom come as You strengthen the shield of faith that quenches all the fiery darts of the wicked (Ephesians 6:16). Let Your will be done as I acknowledge how my faith has grown through trials, prayers, and Your faithfulness. Give me today my daily bread of belief, endurance, and confident trust. Forgive me for unbelief or doubt, and I forgive those who weakened my faith. Lead me not into the temptation of wavering, but deliver me into steady, anchored faith. For Thine is the everlasting kingdom, and the power, and the glory. Amen.

Reflection:
Where did God grow your faith this year?

_____

_____

_____

Action:
Write one moment when your faith grew stronger than before.

_____

_____

_____

Scriptures Referenced Today:
Romans 10:17 (KJV) - "So then faith cometh by hearing, and hearing by the word of God."
Ephesians 6:16 (KJV) - "Above all, taking the shield of faith, wherewith ye shall be able to quench all the fiery darts of the wicked."

DAY 350 – Thanking God for the Peace He Gave You This Year

Prayer:
Father, thank You for the peace that has covered me this year. Hallowed be Your name; remind me that You will keep him in perfect peace whose mind is stayed on You (Isaiah 26:3). Let Your kingdom come as You rule my heart with the peace of Christ (Colossians 3:15). Let Your will be done as I recognize how You calmed storms within me and around me. Give me today my daily bread of rest, calmness, and steady trust in You. Forgive me for letting anxiety overtake me, and I forgive those who contributed to unrest. Lead me not into the temptation of fear, but deliver me into Your perfect peace. For You alone are the King of glory, forever and ever. Amen.

Reflection:
Where did God bring peace to your life this year?

Action:
Write one situation where God replaced chaos with peace.

Scriptures Referenced Today:
Isaiah 26:3 (KJV) - "Thou wilt keep him in perfect peace, whose mind is stayed on thee: because he trusteth in thee."
Colossians 3:15 (KJV) - "And let the peace of God rule in your hearts, to the which also ye are called in one body; and be ye thankful."

DAY 351 – Thanking God for His Wisdom This Year

Prayer:
Father, thank You for the wisdom You have given me this year.
Hallowed be Your name; remind me that if any of us lacks wisdom, we
can ask of God, who gives to all men liberally and upbraids not (James
1:5). Let Your kingdom come as You show me how often You guided
my decisions with Your wisdom. Let Your will be done as I remember
that the fear of the Lord is the beginning of wisdom (Proverbs 9:10).
Give me today my daily bread of insight, clarity, and understanding.
Forgive me for leaning on my own understanding, and I forgive those
who influenced me unwisely. Lead me not into the temptation of foolish
decisions, but deliver me into Your wisdom that has carried me all year.
For Yours is the kingdom, and the power, and the glory, for all ages.
Amen.

Reflection:
Where did God give you wisdom this year that you did not naturally
possess?

_____

_____

_____

Action:
Write one wise decision God helped you make this year.

_____

_____

_____

Scriptures Referenced Today:
James 1:5 (KJV) - "If any of you lack wisdom, let him ask of God, that
giveth to all men liberally, and upbraideth not; and it shall be given him."
Proverbs 9:10 (KJV) - "The fear of the Lord is the beginning of wisdom:
and the knowledge of the holy is understanding."

DAY 352 – Thanking God for His Correction This Year

Prayer:
Father, thank You for the correction You lovingly gave me this year.
Hallowed be Your name; remind me that whom the Lord loves He
corrects, even as a father the son in whom he delights (Proverbs 3:12).
Let Your kingdom come as You continue to shape my character through
loving discipline. Let Your will be done as I remember that no chastening
is joyous for the moment, but afterward it yields the peaceable fruit of
righteousness (Hebrews 12:11). Give me today my daily bread of
humility, gratitude, and teachability. Forgive me for resisting Your
correction, and I forgive those who corrected me imperfectly. Lead me
not into the temptation of pride, but deliver me into growth through Your
loving discipline. For Thine is the kingdom, the power, and the glory,
forever and ever. Amen.

Reflection:
Where did God's correction help you grow this year?

_____

_____

_____

Action:
Write one correction from God this year that you are grateful for.

_____

_____

_____

Scriptures Referenced Today:
Proverbs 3:12 (KJV) - "For whom the Lord loveth he correcteth; even as
a father the son in whom he delighteth."
Hebrews 12:11 (KJV) - "Now no chastening for the present seemeth to
be joyous, but grievous: nevertheless afterward it yieldeth the peaceable
fruit of righteousness unto them which are exercised thereby."

DAY 353 – Thanking God for His Presence in Every Season

Prayer:
Father, thank You for Your presence in every season of this year. Hallowed be Your name; remind me that in Your presence is fullness of joy (Psalm 16:11). Let Your kingdom come as I reflect on the moments when Your nearness carried me. Let Your will be done as You remind me that You go with me, You will not fail me nor forsake me (Deuteronomy 31:6). Give me today my daily bread of assurance, gratitude, and renewed awareness of Your presence. Forgive me for overlooking Your nearness, and I forgive those who were absent when I needed support. Lead me not into the temptation of feeling abandoned, but deliver me into the truth that You have been with me in every moment. For Yours is the kingdom and the power and the glory forever. Amen.

Reflection:
When did you most clearly sense God's presence this year?

_____

_____

Action:
Write one memory of God's presence that you want to carry into next year.

_____

_____

Scriptures Referenced Today:
Psalm 16:11 (KJV) - "Thou wilt shew me the path of life: in thy presence is fulness of joy; at thy right hand there are pleasures for evermore."
Deuteronomy 31:6 (KJV) - "Be strong and of a good courage, fear not, nor be afraid of them: for the Lord thy God, he it is that doth go with thee; he will not fail thee, nor forsake thee."

DAY 354 – Thanking God for His Unseen Work

Prayer:
Father, thank You for all the unseen work You did in my life this year.
Hallowed be Your name; remind me that You are working in ways I
cannot see, for we walk by faith, not by sight (2 Corinthians 5:7). Let
Your kingdom come as You reveal glimpses of how You have been
moving behind the scenes. Let Your will be done as You help me trust
that all things are working together for my good (Romans 8:28). Give me
today my daily bread of faith, peace, and trust in Your unseen hand.
Forgive me for doubting when I could not see, and I forgive those who
misjudged my journey. Lead me not into the temptation of needing all
the answers, but deliver me into faith that rests in You. For Thine is the
kingdom, Thine is the power, and Thine is the glory, now and always.
Amen.

Reflection:
Where do you now see evidence of God's unseen work in your life?

Action:
Write one area of your life where God was working even when you didn't
see it.

Scriptures Referenced Today:
2 Corinthians 5:7 (KJV) - "For we walk by faith, not by sight."
Romans 8:28 (KJV) - "And we know that all things work together for
good to them that love God, to them who are the called according to his
purpose."

DAY 355 – Thanking God for the Hope He Has Given You for the Future

Prayer:
Father, thank You for the hope You have placed in my heart for the days ahead. Hallowed be Your name; remind me that You know the thoughts You think toward me, thoughts of peace and not of evil, to give me an expected end (Jeremiah 29:11). Let Your kingdom come as You fill me with hope and joyful expectation for the future. Let Your will be done as You help me abound in hope through the power of the Holy Ghost (Romans 15:13). Give me today my daily bread of encouragement, expectation, and renewed hope. Forgive me for any fear of the future, and I forgive those who discouraged my hope. Lead me not into the temptation of doubt, but deliver me into confident, Spirit-filled hope for the days to come. For You reign in power and glory, both now and forever. Amen.

Reflection:
What hope has God restored or strengthened in you this year?

Action:
Write one hope or promise you are carrying into next year.

Scriptures Referenced Today:
Jeremiah 29:11 (KJV) - "For I know the thoughts that I think toward you, saith the Lord, thoughts of peace, and not of evil, to give you an expected end."
Romans 15:13 (KJV) - "Now the God of hope fill you with all joy and peace in believing, that ye may abound in hope, through the power of the Holy Ghost."

DAY 356 – Thanking God for His Patience With You This Year

Prayer:
Father, thank You for Your patience toward me throughout this year. Hallowed be Your name; remind me that You are merciful and gracious, slow to anger, and plenteous in mercy (Psalm 103:8). Let Your kingdom come as You shape me to reflect Your patience toward others. Let Your will be done as You teach me that You are not willing that any should perish, but that all should come to repentance (2 Peter 3:9). Give me today my daily bread of humility, gratitude, and gentleness. Forgive me for testing Your patience, and I forgive those whose actions tested mine. Lead me not into the temptation of irritation, but deliver me into a patient spirit formed by You. For Thine is the kingdom, and the power, and the glory, forever and ever. Amen.

Reflection:
Where did God show you extra patience this year?

_____

_____

_____

Action:
Write one way you will show patience to someone today.

_____

_____

_____

Scriptures Referenced Today:
Psalm 103:8 (KJV) - "The Lord is merciful and gracious, slow to anger, and plenteous in mercy."
2 Peter 3:9 (KJV) - "The Lord is not slack concerning his promise, as some men count slackness; but is longsuffering to us-ward, not willing that any should perish, but that all should come to repentance."

DAY 357 – Thanking God for Every Spiritual Victory This Year

Prayer:
Father, thank You for the spiritual victories You gave me this year-seen and unseen. Hallowed be Your name; remind me that thanks be to God, which giveth us the victory through our Lord Jesus Christ (1 Corinthians 15:57). Let Your kingdom come as You show me how You fought battles on my behalf. Let Your will be done as I walk in the freedom You purchased for me, remembering that the weapons of our warfare are mighty through God (2 Corinthians 10:4). Give me today my daily bread of remembrance, gratitude, and renewed strength. Forgive me for forgetting the victories You won for me, and I forgive those who opposed my progress. Lead me not into the temptation of discouragement, but deliver me into confidence in the victories You secured. For the kingdom is Yours, and the power is Yours, and the glory is Yours, forever. Amen.

Reflection:
What victory-big or small-did God give you this year?

_____

_____

_____

Action:
Write one spiritual victory you want to remember going into next year.

_____

_____

_____

Scriptures Referenced Today:
1 Corinthians 15:57 (KJV) - "But thanks be to God, which giveth us the victory through our Lord Jesus Christ."
2 Corinthians 10:4 (KJV) - "(For the weapons of our warfare are not carnal, but mighty through God to the pulling down of strong holds;)"

DAY 358 – Thanking God for His Forgiveness All Year Long

Prayer:
Father, thank You for the forgiveness You have extended to me all year. Hallowed be Your name; remind me that if we confess our sins, You are faithful and just to forgive us our sins and to cleanse us from all unrighteousness (1 John 1:9). Let Your kingdom come as You deepen my understanding of Your mercy. Let Your will be done as You teach me to forgive others as freely as You forgive me (Mark 11:25). Give me today my daily bread of cleansing, renewal, and gratitude. Forgive me for every sin, and I forgive those who sinned against me. Lead me not into the temptation of bitterness, but deliver me into the freedom of full forgiveness. For Thine is the kingdom, Thine is the power, and Thine is the glory, now and always. Amen.

Reflection:
Where did God's forgiveness meet you this year?

_____

_____

_____

Action:
Write one area where you are choosing to extend forgiveness like Christ.

_____

_____

_____

Scriptures Referenced Today:
1 John 1:9 (KJV) - "If we confess our sins, he is faithful and just to forgive us our sins, and to cleanse us from all unrighteousness."
Mark 11:25 (KJV) - "And when ye stand praying, forgive, if ye have ought against any: that your Father also which is in heaven may forgive you your trespasses."

DAY 359 – Thanking God for His Unchanging Character

Prayer:
Father, thank You that You have never changed-not once-throughout this entire year. Hallowed be Your name; remind me that Jesus Christ is the same yesterday, and today, and forever (Hebrews 13:8). Let Your kingdom come as You teach me to anchor my life in Your unchanging nature. Let Your will be done as I remember that every good and perfect gift comes from the Father of lights, with whom is no variableness, neither shadow of turning (James 1:17). Give me today my daily bread of stability, assurance, and trust. Forgive me for doubting Your consistency, and I forgive those who were inconsistent toward me. Lead me not into the temptation of insecurity, but deliver me into the peace that comes from Your unchanging character. For You alone are the King of glory, forever and ever. Amen.

Reflection:
How has God's unchanging character given you stability this year?

_____

_____

_____

Action:
Write one attribute of God you've come to trust more deeply this year.

_____

_____

_____

Scriptures Referenced Today:
Hebrews 13:8 (KJV) - "Jesus Christ the same yesterday, and to day, and for ever."
James 1:17 (KJV) - "Every good gift and every perfect gift is from above, and cometh down from the Father of lights, with whom is no variableness, neither shadow of turning."

DAY 360 – Thanking God for His Blessings This Year

Prayer:
Father, thank You for the blessings You have poured into my life this year-those I saw and those I overlooked. Hallowed be Your name; remind me that the blessing of the Lord, it maketh rich, and He addeth no sorrow with it (Proverbs 10:22). Let Your kingdom come as You open my eyes to the abundance You've given. Let Your will be done as I acknowledge You have loaded me daily with benefits (Psalm 68:19). Give me today my daily bread of gratitude, joy, and remembrance. Forgive me for taking blessings for granted, and I forgive those who minimized the blessings You gave. Lead me not into the temptation of entitlement, but deliver me into gratefulness that honors You. For Thine is the everlasting kingdom, and the power, and the glory. Amen.

Reflection:
What blessing from this year stands out the most?

_____

_____

_____

Action:
List five blessings you experienced this year-large or small.

_____

_____

_____

Scriptures Referenced Today:
Proverbs 10:22 (KJV) - "The blessing of the Lord, it maketh rich, and he addeth no sorrow with it."
Psalm 68:19 (KJV) - "Blessed be the Lord, who daily loadeth us with benefits, even the God of our salvation. Selah."

DAY 361 – Thanking God for His Provision of Community This Year

Prayer:
Father, thank You for the community, fellowship, and connections You provided this year. Hallowed be Your name; remind me that we are called to consider one another and provoke one another unto love and good works (Hebrews 10:24). Let Your kingdom come as You show me the value of the people You placed in my life. Let Your will be done as I remember that two are better than one, because they have a good reward for their labor (Ecclesiastes 4:9). Give me today my daily bread of gratitude, connection, and awareness of the people who strengthened me. Forgive me for isolating myself at times, and I forgive those who failed to be there when I needed them. Lead me not into the temptation of withdrawing, but deliver me into the blessing of godly community. For Yours is the kingdom and the power and the glory forever. Amen.

Reflection:
Who strengthened or supported your walk with God this year?

_____

_____

_____

Action:
Write down one person you will thank or pray for today.

_____

_____

_____

Scriptures Referenced Today:
Hebrews 10:24 (KJV) - "And let us consider one another to provoke unto love and to good works."
Ecclesiastes 4:9 (KJV) - "Two are better than one; because they have a good reward for their labour."

DAY 362 – Thanking God for His Faithfulness in Your Family

Prayer:
Father, thank You for Your faithfulness to my family this year. Hallowed be Your name; remind me that the righteous walk in integrity and their children are blessed after them (Proverbs 20:7). Let Your kingdom come as You continue the good work You began in those I love. Let Your will be done as You show me that You are faithful to a thousand generations of those who love You and keep Your commandments (Deuteronomy 7:9). Give me today my daily bread of gratitude, peace, and renewed trust for my family's future. Forgive me for worrying over what is in Your hands, and I forgive those who created tension or division this year. Lead me not into the temptation of fear for my family, but deliver me into confidence in Your faithfulness. For Thine alone is the kingdom, the power, and the glory, forever. Amen.

Reflection:
Where did you see God move in your family this year?

_____

_____

Action:
Write a prayer of blessing for your family today.

_____

_____

Scriptures Referenced Today:
Proverbs 20:7 (KJV) - "The just man walketh in his integrity: his children are blessed after him."
Deuteronomy 7:9 (KJV) - "Know therefore that the Lord thy God, he is God, the faithful God, which keepeth covenant and mercy with them that love him and keep his commandments to a thousand generations."

DAY 363 – Thanking God for His Faithfulness in Your Work and Calling

Prayer:
Father, thank You for Your faithfulness in my work, my calling, and the purpose You gave me this year. Hallowed be Your name; remind me that whatever I do, I should do it heartily, as to the Lord, and not unto men (Colossians 3:23). Let Your kingdom come as You show me the fruit You produced through my labor. Let Your will be done as You strengthen my hands for the work You assign (Psalm 90:17). Give me today my daily bread of diligence, gratitude, and renewed purpose. Forgive me for the times I worked in my own strength, and I forgive those who opposed or misunderstood my calling. Lead me not into the temptation of discouragement, but deliver me into confidence that You will establish the work of my hands. For Yours is the kingdom, the power, and the glory without end. Amen.

Reflection:
How did God bless your work, ministry, or calling this year?

_____

_____

Action:
Write one way God confirmed or strengthened your calling this year.

_____

_____

Scriptures Referenced Today:
Colossians 3:23 (KJV) - "And whatsoever ye do, do it heartily, as to the Lord, and not unto men."
Psalm 90:17 (KJV) - "And let the beauty of the Lord our God be upon us: and establish thou the work of our hands upon us; yea, the work of our hands establish thou it."

DAY 364 – Thanking God for Carrying You Through the Entire Year

Prayer:
Father, thank You for carrying me through this entire year, from the first day to this very moment. Hallowed be Your name; remind me that You have borne me from birth and carried me from the womb; and even to old age You will carry me (Isaiah 46:3–4). Let Your kingdom come as You bring to remembrance all the ways You sustained me. Let Your will be done as You show me that surely goodness and mercy have followed me all the days of my life (Psalm 23:6). Give me today my daily bread of remembrance, gratitude, and praise for Your sustaining grace. Forgive me for moments when I doubted Your care, and I forgive those who made my journey harder than it needed to be. Lead me not into the temptation of forgetfulness, but deliver me into worship for Your faithfulness across all 12 months. For Yours is the kingdom and the power and the glory forever. Amen.

Reflection:
What is one moment from this year where you know God carried you?

_____

_____

_____

Action:
Write a short prayer of gratitude summarizing your entire year with God.

_____

_____

_____

Scriptures Referenced Today:
Isaiah 46:3–4 (KJV) - "Hearken unto me, O house of Jacob, and all the remnant of the house of Israel, which are borne by me from the belly, which are carried from the womb: And even to your old age I am he; and even to hoar hairs will I carry you: I have made, and I will bear; even I will carry, and will deliver you."
Psalm 23:6 (KJV) - "Surely goodness and mercy shall follow me all the days of my life: and I will dwell in the house of the Lord for ever."

DAY 365 – A Prayer of Completion, Victory, and Worship

Prayer:

Father, You have brought me through an entire year of seeking You, knowing You, and praying the way Jesus taught. Hallowed be Your name; You are the Alpha and the Omega, the beginning and the ending (Revelation 1:8). Let Your kingdom come as I stand in awe of all You have done in me, around me, and through me. Let Your will be done as I step into a new year rooted in Your faithfulness, strengthened by Your Spirit, and anchored in Your Word.

Today I lift a triumphant shout of thanksgiving: You have been my Shepherd and I have lacked nothing (Psalm 23:1). You have been my refuge, my fortress, my deliverer, and my song (Psalm 18:2). You have been my help, my strength, and the lifter of my head (Psalm 3:3). You have restored me, taught me, corrected me, protected me, and led me. Give me today my daily bread of worship, gratitude, and holy celebration. Forgive me for every moment I fell short, doubted, or wandered-yet You remained faithful. And I forgive every person who wounded, hindered, or misunderstood me. Lead me not into the temptation of forgetting what You have done this year, but deliver me into a life that continually remembers, continually worships, continually trusts, and continually walks with You. I lift this final prayer of the year in triumph, declaring: For Yours is the kingdom and the power and the glory, from everlasting to everlasting. Amen.

Reflection:

What is the single greatest thing God did in you-or for you-this year?

Action:

Write a personal prayer of dedication for the coming year, sealing everything God has done and surrendering everything that is ahead.

Scriptures Referenced Today:

Revelation 1:8 (KJV) - "I am Alpha and Omega, the beginning and the ending, saith the Lord, which is, and which was, and which is to come, the Almighty."

Psalm 23:1 (KJV) - "The Lord is my shepherd; I shall not want."

Psalm 18:2 (KJV) - "The Lord is my rock, and my fortress, and my deliverer; my God, my strength, in whom I will trust; my buckler, and the horn of my salvation, and my high tower."

Psalm 3:3 (KJV) - "But thou, O Lord, art a shield for me; my glory, and the lifter up of mine head."

MONTH 12 CLOSING REFLECTION: COMPLETION, GRATITUDE, & A HEART FULL OF PRAISE

Month 12 brought you into a season of holy reflection-where every prayer, every breakthrough, every tear, every victory, every moment of growth became evidence of a faithful God who carried you all year long. This month was not simply a conclusion; it was a celebration of the God who never left your side.

As you walked through these final days, your heart was invited to:

- Remember His faithfulness
- Reflect on His protection
- Celebrate His provision
- Recall answered prayers
- Notice spiritual victories
- Honor His presence
- See His wisdom in the journey
- Acknowledge His correction
- Cherish His peace
- Rejoice in His goodness

This month reminded you that gratitude is not an event-it is a posture. And worship is not a moment-it is a lifestyle.

You discovered that:

- You were never alone.
- God carried you through every season.
- His blessings far exceeded what you saw in the moment.
- His grace met you every single day.
- His mercy covered your weaknesses.
- His strength filled your empty places.
- His wisdom guided your decisions.

His peace protected your heart.

Month 12 closes with one great truth:

Everything you have is from Him, sustained by Him, and for Him.

You did not reach the end of this year by accident.

You reached it by grace.

By mercy.

By His unshakable faithfulness.

And now, as you step toward the very last page of this year-long journey, your heart is prepared-for closure, for worship, and for a new beginning.

YEAR-END CLOSING: A FINAL WORD OF COMPLETION & CONSECRATION

You have reached the end of a year spent praying the prayer Jesus gave-365 days of walking with God, listening to God, trusting God, surrendering to God, and growing in God.

This is not simply the end of a book.

This is the culmination of a transformation.

Over the course of this year:

- You prayed through joy and sorrow.
- You prayed through clarity and confusion.
- You prayed through triumphs and battles.
- You prayed through healing and rebuilding.
- You prayed through seasons of abundance and seasons of need.
- You prayed through victories and wounds.

And in every day, God met you.

You discovered:

- A deeper relationship with your Father
- A clearer understanding of His kingdom
- A surrendered heart to His will
- Daily dependence on His provision
- Cleansing through His forgiveness
- Freedom through forgiving others
- Protection from the schemes of the enemy
- Strength through every trial
- Hope for every tomorrow
- Confidence in His eternal glory

This year, you learned that the Lord's Prayer is not a recitation-it is a foundation, a pattern, a lifeline, a roadmap, a weapon, a conversation with the God who loves you.

And now, standing at the threshold of a new year, pause and take in these truths:

You are not who you were when you began. Your faith is stronger. Your heart is softer. Your mind is renewed. Your spirit is anchored. Your trust is deeper. Your worship is fuller. Your identity is firmer. Your future is steadier.

You have completed the journey- and God has completed a work within you.

As you step into the year ahead:

- Go with confidence.
- Go with gratitude.
- Go with expectation.
- Go with humility.
- Go with joy.
- Go with strength.
- Go with worship.
- Go with the Father's blessing over you.
- And above all, go with this truth sealed upon your spirit: **"For Thine is the kingdom, and the power, and the glory, forever and ever."**

This year is complete.

Your heart is full.

Your steps are ordered.

Your future is held.

Your God is faithful.

Amen. And amen.

A Final Prayer from the Author Over You

Our Father in heaven,
I lift every reader of this book before You-Your sons and daughters
whom You love with an everlasting love. May they know You not as a
distant God, but as their Father, Provider, Protector, Shepherd, and
Friend.

Hallowed be Your name.
May Your name be honored in their homes, in their work, in their
families, and in the deepest parts of their hearts. Let Your holiness shape
their desires, their decisions, their values, and their worship. May Your
presence fill their days with awe and their nights with peace.

Your kingdom come.
Establish Your rule and reign in their thoughts, their conversations, their
priorities, and their identity. Let Your kingdom advance in their hearts
and expand through their lives. May Your Spirit empower them to walk
in purpose, authority, and boldness as citizens of heaven.

Your will be done on earth as it is in heaven.
May Your perfect will unfold in their lives-Your plans, not theirs; Your
timing, not their own. Close every door that is not from You. Open
every door that *is* from You. Lead them into their calling with clarity,
courage, and confidence. Align their desires with Your desires, their
dreams with Your dreams, and their future with Your purpose.

Give us this day our daily bread.
Father, meet their every need-spiritual, emotional, physical, relational, and
financial. Give them wisdom for their decisions, strength for their
challenges, peace for their anxiety, and provision for their journey. May
they never lack what Your love supplies.

Forgive us our debts, as we forgive our debtors.
Wash them clean from every sin, every failure, every regret. May they
walk in the freedom of forgiveness, both received and extended. Heal
every wound that others caused, and soften every place where bitterness
tried to live. Restore their hearts with Your grace.

Lead us not into temptation, but deliver us from evil.
Protect them from deception, distraction, fear, and every scheme of the
enemy. Surround them with Your angels. Strengthen them in their spirit.
Guard their minds with truth, their hearts with purity, and their steps with
righteousness. Deliver them into victory in every battle ahead.

For Thine is the kingdom, and the power, and the glory forever. Amen.

Father, seal this year of prayer with Your blessing. Let their lives declare Your glory. Let their homes reflect Your kingdom. Let their future display Your power. And may they continue walking with You day by day, prayer by prayer, step by step-until the day they see You face to face. Amen.

Final Author's Note

When I began writing these prayers, I had no idea how deeply God would use them to shape, stretch, strengthen, and steady me. What started as a simple desire to help people pray the Lord's Prayer became a year-long journey the Lord used to teach me just as much as anyone who would eventually read these pages.

If you made it to the end of this book, I want you to know something:

I am proud of you.

And God is pleased with you.

You showed up.

You prayed through the hard days and the hopeful days.

You wrestled with Scripture.

You softened your heart.

You grew in ways you may not even fully see yet.

My prayer is that this year of prayer becomes a foundation-something you don't leave behind, but something you build your life upon. I pray that the rhythm of "Our Father" becomes your anchor. I pray that Scripture becomes your language. I pray that worship becomes your posture. And above all, I pray that God becomes more real, more present, and more personal to you than ever before.

Thank you for letting me walk this year with you.

Thank you for trusting me with your prayer life.

Thank you for letting these words guide your steps.

It has been an honor. A calling. A gift from His hands that I now pass on to yours.

May this not be the end of a journey, but the beginning of a deeper one. God is not done with you. And He never will be.

With gratitude and faith,

- Brandon Davis

Acknowledgments

I give all glory to God, who placed this calling in my heart during one of the darkest seasons of my life and gave me the Lord's Prayer as a path forward. This book exists because He spoke, He led, and He sustained me every step of the way.

To my family - thank you for your patience, support, and encouragement as I walked out an assignment that required time, focus, and faith. You carried this with me more than you know, and I am grateful beyond words.

To my church family and the pastors, leaders, and teachers who helped shape my spiritual foundation - thank you for pointing me toward Jesus, for feeding my faith, and for modeling what it means to walk closely with God.

To the thousands who have prayed with me in The Lord's Prayer Across America community - thank you for showing up day after day, for sharing your testimonies and prayers, and for confirming the purpose behind this book. Your hunger for prayer, unity, and spiritual growth helped bring this vision to life.

To every friend, encourager, and prayer partner along the way - your messages and support strengthened my hands in moments when I needed it most.

And to you, the reader - thank you for stepping into this journey with me. My prayer is that these pages draw you closer to the Father, deepen your faith, and strengthen your daily walk with Him.

In Loving Gratitude to Reverend Elvin L. Ervin

I want to give special thanks to Reverend Elvin L. Ervin, who went home to be with the Lord in 2008, yet continues to shape lives long after his passing. He was the first person who taught me and so many others at Southern Illinois Worship Center how to pray using the Lord's Prayer as a guide. What he passed on wasn't just instruction; it was a way of life, a way of walking with God with purpose, humility, and confidence.

Reverend Ervin planted seeds in us that kept growing. His voice still echoes in my memory, steadying my faith and reminding me that prayer is not complicated-it is surrendered, honest, and anchored in the words Jesus Himself gave us. The foundation he laid in my life became part of the calling that ultimately produced this book.

Though he is no longer with us, his impact remains. His teaching continues to multiply through every person who learned to pray because he took the time to disciple us. And now, through these pages, his influence reaches even farther.

Reverend Ervin-thank you for your faithfulness, your obedience, and your willingness to teach ordinary people how to touch the heart of God. Your legacy lives on.

www.ingramcontent.com/pod-product-compliance
Lightning Source LLC
Chambersburg PA
CBHW030905120626
46554CB00001B/17